SmartStart

Your Maryland Business

THE OASIS PRESS®
GRANTS PASS, OREGON

1.0—01/98

SmartStart Your Maryland Business
Published by The Oasis Press®

Please direct any comments, questions, or suggestions regarding this book to:

PSI Research
The Oasis Press®
300 North Valley Drive
Grants Pass, Oregon 97526

(541) 479-9464 *phone*
(541) 476-1479 *fax*
psi2@magick.net *email*

SmartStart Editorial Team
Managing Editor: Camille Akin
Contributing Editors: Mary Lee Arthur, Laura Guevin, Mike Houghton, Sheryl Adams Siebenborn
Graphic Design: Steven Burns
Typography: Dan Benson

The Oasis Press is a registered trademark of Publishing Services, Inc., an Oregon company doing business as PSI Research.

SmartStart your Maryland business. -- 1st ed.
p. cm.
Includes index.
ISBN 1-55571-424-2 (pbk.)
1. New business enterprises--Maryland. 2. Small business--Law and legislation--Maryland. 3. Small business--Maryland--Management. 4. Economic indicators--Maryland. 5. Social indicators--Maryland. I. Oasis Press/PSI Research.
HD62.5.S62374 1998
658.1'1'09752 -- dc21 97-52646
CIP

Printed and bound in the United States of America
First edition 10 9 8 7 6 5 4 3 2 1 0
♻ Printed on recycled paper when available.

Contents

Preface

Everybody loves a success story. Virtually every person in today's society strives for success. Lately, a growing number of Americans are attempting to start their own small businesses. However, for the last decade we have been bombarded with stories about business failures. So, where is a fledgling entrepreneur like yourself to start? What is the smartest move you can make toward achieving success in the burgeoning world of small business? We believe the answer lies in understanding the bigger picture — in understanding what your future holds and using your past and present experiences and knowledge to strengthen your quest for small business success.

Our story is remarkably similar to many other small business owners. We began as a two-person operation working out of a garage. We knew our business goals and thought we understood the bigger picture until we began to register our business with the regulating state and federal agencies. Frustrated by the mounds of business start-up paperwork, we saw only one solution — the need for an all-inclusive, yet friendly guide to lead new business owners through the start-up process.

That was 23 years ago, and now, with a solid grasp of the bigger picture we are operating a healthy and profitable small business. Operating under the name PSI Research, we have published more than 200 titles for small business owners and prospective business owners under the imprint The Oasis Press®. Ranging from topics like tax savings to creating a business plan, one or more of our Successful Business Library titles have filled the bookshelves of numerous entrepreneurs throughout the nation. In addition, we have received accolades from some of the top business magazines, including *Inc.*, and *Forbes.*

Everyday we talk to people who are either in the process of starting their own business or part of an existing operation. We have found a common thread among these people. They seek easy-to-use, step-by-step instructions on how to conquer one or more major aspects of their businesses. That is why our books are designed to be easy to read and understand as well as helpful for making the decisions that most businesses must face.

We want to help you become aware of the legal and social changes that may affect your business in coming years. We welcome your comments either through the questionnaire at the back of this book or through our Internet Web site, *http://www.psi-research.com.* If you find errors, or if changes to existing laws are not reflected in this book, let us know so we can better help others who will be using this information in the future.

The PSI Research Editorial Staff
August, 1997

Introduction

There has never been a better time than now to start a business. Today's economic and social climate is opening doors for millions of entrepreneurs throughout the nation. In fact, a recent survey by the Entrepreneurial Research Consortium found that some 37 percent of U.S. households have someone who has tried to start or has helped fund a small business. That means that more than 35 million U.S. households have had an involvement with a new or small business. The amateur entrepreneur of the 1950s and 1960s has been reinvented: Enter the professional entrepreneur.

Several factors have helped pave the way for the evolution of the entrepreneur. The flow of information, trade, capital, and ideas is nearing its peak. Never before have people been able to communicate so rapidly and so effectively than now. With the use of the Internet, the number of new ventures will continue to grow at exponential rates.

Also, the number of small business startups is increasing as the downsizing of large, established corporations continues. The assurance of being part of the corporate world is a thing of the past — and many see entrepreneurship as the smarter alternative to making a living. Finally, over the last 20 years, an awareness among bankers, accountants, and real estate agents as well as state, federal, and local agencies has surfaced. People are beginning to understand the need to support small business as a vital part of America's livelihood and economic future.

In fact, today's Americans support and encourage the growth of new and existing small businesses as part of the renewal of the

American Dream. The truth is plain and simple: Small business creates jobs and financial independence. Take a look at some of the facts compiled by the U.S. Small Business Administration and decide for yourself.

- Fifty-three percent of the private workforce in the United States is employed by small businesses.
- In 1994, 3.3 million jobs were created with an estimated 62 percent from small business-dominated industries.
- 800,000 new businesses were incorporated in 1995.
- The earnings of sole proprietors and partners increased eight percent from 1994 to 1995 — from $415.9 billion to $449.2 billion.

These facts are dizzying, yet exciting. It's enough to motivate at least one person in every U.S. household to get involved with a small business. But before you get caught up in the excitement, make sure you understand the ins and outs of small business ownership — what it takes to smartstart your venture, how to manage your daily operation, how to make a profit, find and retain customers, and stay above water during lean times.

This is where PSI Research comes in. Known as the Number One Small Business Resource, PSI Research under the imprint of Oasis Press Books and Software, has put together a series of start-up books for entrepreneurs in each state. Based on its experience of more than 23 years of book publishing for small business owners, the editorial staff has compiled a comprehensive resource of the tools needed for building a successful business. This critical information is presented throughout the book in an easy-to-understand and helpful way. You will find a wealth of business start-up and operating knowledge, including:

- State and federal information on the specifics for starting your business — from choosing a legal form to filing taxes, the first few chapters of the book lay the foundation for becoming a business owner in the state of your choice.
- Tips for operating your business once you have officially conquered the start-up phase — helpful hints regarding proper accounting methods, how

to market your product or service, and how to choose and keep top-quality employees.

- Guidelines for developing a business plan — possibly the most important step in forming and operating a profitable business — and a sample business plan to help you draft a smart business plan.

- Statistical information about your state that will help you anticipate trends and give you the ability to compare economic and social factors that will affect your business.

- An appendix section filled with addresses, phone numbers, and Web site and email addresses for the agencies and resources you need to contact — from financing alternatives to business registration, from licenses and permits to workers' compensation and unemployment taxes.

It's all here. In one helpful, easy-to-use volume, you can learn the fundamentals of starting a business and get to know the essential resources to help you achieve your goals. Once you are up and running, use the PSI Research Web site (*psi-research.com*) to keep you informed of the latest business issues.

CHAPTER 1

Initial Business Considerations

smart (smärt) *adj.* 1) characterized by sharp, quick thought: intelligent; 2) shrewd in dealings: canny

start (stärt) *v.* 1) to begin an activity or movement: set out; 2) to have a beginning: commence; 3) to move suddenly or involuntarily; 4) to come quickly into view, life, or activity: spring forth

---

A smart start — this phrase certainly has a ring to it. In fact, it sounds like what all burgeoning small business owners and entrepreneurs strive to achieve. And, yet, the statistics show that only one out of 20 new ventures will survive to celebrate its fifth anniversary. So what is it that will give you the edge on starting your new venture? The answer involves knowledge and preplanning.

Look back at the definitions of smart and start. These two words imply action — action on your part. You have a dream — starting your own business. You are the one responsible for making that dream come true. You won't be working for a boss; you will be the boss. You won't have a set nine to five schedule; you will work whatever hours are necessary to stay on course.

Of course, with any dream comes inherent challenges. A 1996 study published by Dun & Bradstreet lends some insight into the common challenges faced by today's small business owners. The top ten challenges include:

Knowing your business. This aspect entails in-depth industry knowledge, market savvy, and a certain practical knowledge.

Knowing the basics of business management. The basics include accounting and bookkeeping principles, production scheduling, personnel management, financial management, marketing, and planning for the future.

Having the proper attitude. Realistic expectations coupled with a strong personal commitment will carry you through.

Having adequate capital. From establishing a good relationship with a bank to maintaining a business credit report, sufficient capital is vital to surviving the first year.

Managing finances effectively. In a phrase ... cash flow. Cash flow entails ongoing capital, inventory management, extending credit to customers, and managing accounts receivable.

Managing time efficiently. A combination of discipline, delegation, and planning (your business plan has already set the priorities) is essential for effective time management.

Managing people. Finding and keeping qualified personnel is critical to building a successful business.

Satisfying customers by providing high quality. You will establish and maintain credibility with your customers when you constantly deliver the best possible product or service.

Knowing how to compete. New ways of selling, knowing the marketplace, a clear understanding of your niche, and sticking to your original plan all qualify as must-do's for the stiff competition that may lie ahead.

Coping with regulations and paperwork. Welcome to red tape central — where you may be required to file anything from quarterly tax payments to withholding taxes, from employee manuals to profit-sharing and pension plans, from sales tax records to industry-related reports.

You have heard the phrase "work smarter, not harder." Working smarter means overcoming these ten challenges by knowing what lies ahead of you. A smart start for your business means understanding the course, possessing the skills to overcome the obstacles, and knowing the right way to clear the hurdles. Whether you've competed in athletics, academics, or in a simple game of cards, if you are starting a small business then you're in for the race of a lifetime. Before you run out and buy a pair of the best and fanciest running shoes, take a moment to consider what it takes to be an effective and profitable small business owner.

THE ENTREPRENEURIAL ARCHETYPE

entrepreneur (än'tre pre nʉr') *n.:* One who organizes, operates, and assumes the risk in a business in expectation of gaining the profit.

Today more than ever entrepreneurs are playing a vital role in America's diverse economic structure. According to the John F. Baugh Center for Entrepreneurship at Baylor University, as the year 2000 approaches the number one course of new jobs in the United States will continue to be entrepreneurial ventures and emerging firms. Even large corporations are beginning to recognize the value and importance of the "entrepreneurial spirit." Numerous books have been written on this so-called entrepreneurial spirit and the subject is the focus of many research groups at business colleges throughout the world. A cursory look at what many believe to be the entrepreneurial archetype may help you discover if owning your own small business is right for you.

SOME SERIOUS SELF-EVALUATION

What lies within you? Today's researchers believe some of the necessary traits for successful entrepreneuring are drive, commitment, passion, energy, leadership, and pride of ownership. As a fledgling entrepreneur, it is important to understand your strongest talents and skills and realize your areas of weakness. Successful business owners choose a business that allows them to do the things they love to do. Ask yourself questions like:

- What kinds of things do I most enjoy doing?
- What do I like to do on my day off?
- What have I always wanted to do but have never had time to do it?
- What do other people compliment me on?
- Do I enjoy interacting with others?
- What types of things do I not enjoy?

These types of questions and many others are listed in self-assessment worksheets in the small business development centers (SBDCs) throughout the nation. SBDC counselors are located in various communities of all 50 states and the District of Columbia to help you plan your business startup. (See Chapter 5 for more details on how SBDCs can assist you.) As you identify your strengths and weaknesses you become more aware of what business type will compliment your personality. Once you have done some self-assessment, you will need to ask yourself some more practical questions related to four major areas of concern:

- Your experience and motivation
- Your product or service
- Your customer
- Your competition

YOUR EXPERIENCE AND MOTIVATION

You may have all the drive and ambition in the world. But without some experience or way to gain experience in the type of business you plan to start, you may be facing some major hurdles. If you don't have direct experience in the business you want to start, don't be discouraged. Start now by plugging in to the right resources for your industry or trade. For instance, you can join one or more of the trade associations that represent your industry. By joining an association you will get information about legal and other issues of interest to your industry. Membership or affiliation with these associations will also help you support lobbying efforts to represent your interest in the state legislatures and Congress.

Other types of assistance and support you will receive from membership in an association include:

- Periodic newsletters or magazines that keep you abreast of important changes occurring in your industry;
- Seminars and meetings that you can attend to get information from other business owners and experts; and

- A network of small business owners like yourself to help you stay in touch with what others are doing in their communities.

Your local library should have association directories. If you prefer, you can access information and oftentimes direct links to the associations via the Internet. For more information, contact:

The Oasis Press®
http://www.psi-research.com

YOUR PRODUCT OR SERVICE

Nearly all businesses fall into one of two categories: selling products or selling services. If you have an innovative product and the know-how to produce it cost-effectively and know a distinct market for it exists, then you have the basis for a successful venture. In addition, if you want to start a service business you may be looking at quicker startup and lower start-up costs due to reduced or no inventory.

Have you clearly identified what you will be selling? In attempting to answer this question, make sure you know how your product or service is different from that of your competitors. Determine what is unique about your product — is it less expensive or of better quality than your competitor's? Maybe it is the same price as your competitor's but you offer guarantees and place warranties. Does it have more options at the same price? You will need to know (not to mention be able to convince) your customers that your product or service is better than the competition's. Further, you will need to know how to measure the demand for your product or service.

Your challenge, among many, will be to establish your product or service upfront — that is, before you open your doors for business. The true test of whether you have clearly identified what you will sell will be sitting down to write your business plan. Your business plan will guide your business to achieve its purpose, its product's or service's purpose, and its long and short-term goals. You will learn more on this critical aspect of business planning in Chapter 7. A sample business plan for a service-type business is at the end of Chapter 7 to help you create your own plan.

YOUR CUSTOMERS

Part of knowing your product or service is knowing who will buy it. To smartstart your business you must have a clear idea of who your customers are and where they are located. You should understand the demographic and psychographic makeup of your customer base. Make sure you know the answers to questions like:

- Which age group, income range, and gender will my product or service target?
- Will my product or service appeal to a specific ethnic group?
- Do I know the marital status, education level, and family size of the people I will be selling to?
- Do I know the lifestyles and buying preferences of my target market?

Further, you will need to determine things like the number of potential customers that exist in your geographic market area and how you will attract and retain buyers. You will want to understand the purchasing patterns and buying sensitivity of your potential customers. In addition, make sure you understand the current size of your market and its growth rate. Things like social values and concerns may influence your customers' buying habits.

As a prospective business owner, your top priority goals should be establishing a strong sales and marketing plan and a smart business plan. As you gain a thorough understanding of your target market you will begin to reap the benefits of repeat business from loyal and satisfied customers. Customer loyalty is a challenge for all businesses; but with the right sales and marketing plan and quality control measures, you can establish a solid customer base.

YOUR COMPETITION

As important as knowing your customers, you will be one step ahead of the game if you have clearly identified your competitors. Make sure your start-up efforts involve researching your competitors. Who are your major competitors? What advantages and disadvantages do you have compared with the existing competition? Does your business face any barriers for entry? How do customers perceive your competitors. For instance, do their customers remain loyal because of perceived quality, image, or value? Further, determine how you will gain a sufficient share of the market. For the most part, unless you are part of a new industry, your market is probably already served by one of your competitors. You goal is to carefully plan how you will snatch some of this market share and show that you will continue to reach new markets.

You can be confident about one thing as you start your business — the competition will be fierce. To gain the business street smarts to beat the competition you must know your industry and the number of businesses in your field that have succeeded and failed. Knowing why these businesses survived or died quick deaths will help you in your planning efforts. In addition to understanding where you fit in the entrepreneurial world, you will need to carefully consider how you want to get into business.

METHODS OF GETTING INTO BUSINESS

As a potential business owner, you have three primary choices for staring your business. You can:

- Start a business from the ground up — either from your home or other office/warehouse space;
- Buy an existing business; or
- Buy a franchise.

Each method has its pros and cons and it is up to you to decide which is the best alternative for your situation.

STARTING A SMALL BUSINESS

Starting a new venture allows you to let your imagination and efforts take you to wherever your imagination and efforts may lead. You may be able to start your business on a shoestring in your home or small office with little capital. If so, you can design all the business identification signage, logos, letterhead, and business name. If you are very successful, you may even be able to franchise your idea.

The main factor in starting the business is you. As previously discussed, you will need to have the drive, energy, passion, and determination to make the business work — no matter how many hours, days, or weeks it takes. If the business succeeds, you will reap the financial rewards, pride of ownership, and sense of accomplishment that a new venture can bring. But, if the business fails, you will have no one to blame but yourself.

The reality of starting a new venture — not buying an existing business nor buying into a franchise — is shouldering the responsibility for each and every detail of business operation. You will have to build the business from the ground up and attract customers based on your own efforts and reputation. You and, if applicable, you partner are the individuals solely responsible for anticipating problems, defining marketing, finding the proper location, and achieving your business plan goals.

For a helpful guide to point you in the right direction, consider getting a copy of *Start Your Business: A Beginner's Guide.* This award-winning book will help you develop a plan of action for your new business and contains numerous checklists for keeping you on track in terms of your start-up efforts. For more information, see the Useful Resources section located at the end of this chapter.

BUYING AN EXISTING BUSINESS

When you purchase a business, you buy many unknowns. For instance, what is the true reputation of the previous owner and did the business truly make a profit or do the books give a false impression of the business' true profitability? How current and usable is the inventory and equipment? Will you inherit employees that you don't want to retain? These and numerous other concerns face the would-be buyer. Research and investigation are critical to buying an existing business.

As the buyer of an existing business you will need to have your attorney or other qualified professional look at all accounting records for the last three to five years minimum. In addition, you need to arrange for a thorough inspection of the inventory and all contracts. Your goal in doing this research is to protect yourself from future liabilities. For instance, make sure your attorney checks for any judgment liens or other recorded security interests. Usually, the secretary of state will have this information. Further, if you will be purchasing real property, get a title search done to make sure the seller has good title and that there are no recorded claims or deeds against the property.

Today's business owners are faced with many environmental responsibilities for their businesses including proper handling of hazardous materials, maintaining proper water or air quality standards, proper waste disposal methods, or removal or monitoring of underground storage tanks.

Also, although not necessary, you may want to have a licensed professional conduct an environmental audit of the property. The last thing you want to deal with are federal or state liabilities for environmental hazards. (For more information on business environmental issues, see chapters 3 and 4.)

Recent Legislation

The method of amortizing the amount paid for a business changed as a result of federal legislation. As a buyer of an existing business, you may now amortize intangible items such as goodwill, customer lists, patents, copyrights, and permits and licenses. The old law only allowed amortization of tangible items. The new law requires amortization to occur over a 15-year period. Ask your tax accountant about the best tax treatment for your situation before buying a business.

Many states have repealed their bulk sale laws that required sellers and buyers of certain types of businesses to notify creditors of the impending sale of the business. When purchasing a business be aware of the current status of the bulk sale law in your state. You can obtain information from your secretary of state's office or consult your attorney.

The IRS now requires the buyer and seller to file *Form 8594, Asset Acquisition Statement.* Whether you are the buyer or seller, the business' taxable situation will be affected. A copy of *Form 8594* is available via the Internet at *http://www.irs.ustreas.gov.* If you prefer, contact an IRS field office near you. See Appendix B for address and phone number information.

Purchase Agreement

Another important factor of buying an existing business is that both parties agree to a purchase price, terms of payment, and the items involved in the sale. These matters are all addressed in a purchase agreement. Consult your attorney for more information on drafting a purchase agreement.

A great source of information on buying an existing business is the comprehensive guide *The Secrets to Buying and Selling a Business* by Ira K. Nottonson. To learn more about this book, see the Useful Resources section at the end of this chapter.

BUYING A FRANCHISE

Approximately 850,000 franchised outlets exist nationwide and it is estimated that a new franchisee opens for business approximately every ten minutes. With figures like these, it's no wonder that people across the nation are buying into the more than 3,000 U.S. franchise operations. Even the U.S. Small Business Administration (SBA) has found that your chances of business success are higher with a franchise than with a typical startup. And, Department of Commerce figures show that 92% of all franchise companies formed during the last decade are still in business. But before you jump the gun and decide a franchise is your best bet, consider the advantages and disadvantages of franchising.

The biggest advantage is that the franchisor has done most of the work for you. For instance, the franchisor will have already developed the product(s) or service(s), a positive name recognition, eye-catching signage and interior and exterior store layout, training methods, and effective ways of operating the business. The franchisor should assist you in finding a location for the business as well. Since the franchisor wants you to succeed, the franchisor often provides help for developing your business. Much of the trial-and-error that all business must experience has been learned by the franchisor or by other franchisees and this knowledge is passed on to new franchisees. Overall, you may have a lower risk when you buy a franchise than when you start a business from scratch.

In looking at the downsides of franchising, the first concern is cost. Some franchises cost $500,000 in total capital investment and may even require ongoing payments of up to 20 percent of gross sales for rent, marketing, royalties, and advertising. Also, when you buy a franchise you give up quite a bit of freedom. Since the franchise has its own protocol, you will have very specific limits on what you can and cannot do.

The Federal Trade Commission (FTC) regulates the franchise industry. The FTC has a hotline that will give information on:

- Federal disclosure for franchises,

- Getting a copy of a disclosure statement for a specific franchise, and
- How to file a complaint against a particular franchisor.

An attorney is available to answer your questions regarding franchises. For more information, contact the Bureau of Consumer Protection of the Federal Trade Commission.

State governments also have shown their interest in franchising by publishing guidelines like those issued by the FTC. Thirteen states keep franchise disclosure statements available to individual investors for their review before they purchase. These thirteen states include California, Hawaii, Illinois, Indiana, Maryland, Minnesota, New York, North Dakota, Rhode Island, South Dakota, Virginia, Washington, and Wisconsin. Two other states — Michigan and Oregon — have franchise disclosure laws that don't require a filing, but do give important legal rights. Refer to Appendix B for the addresses and phone numbers for the FTC and the state government franchising sources.

Although legal guidelines exist, this is not to say that the legislation has prevented bad business practices. If you are considering purchasing a franchise you are encouraged to look at all FTC disclosure documents before signing any agreements. Also, review the franchisor's financial statements and Securities and Exchange Commission (SEC) quarterly and yearly filings to determine its financial strength. You can also contact other franchisees to determine if they are satisfied with the franchisor. In addition, know how to read and understand the prospectus offered by the franchisor. To learn more about the many facets of franchising, consider obtaining a copy of *The Franchise Bible: How to Buy a Franchise or Franchise Your Own Business* by Erwin Keup. For more information on this book, refer to the Useful Resources section at the end of this chapter.

RESEARCH, RESEARCH, RESEARCH

Research is to small business what location is to real estate. With so many businesses, so many personalities, so many approaches, it is easy to get overwhelmed. Although numerous variables exist, the reality of starting a business is actually more tangible now than ever before. But where do you start? One of the most important things you can do for your startup is to research all matters related to your business. You can conduct preliminary research via numerous routes, including:

- Local public and college libraries;
- Federal, state, and community business organizations and assistance programs; and
- The World Wide Web, or the Internet.

After reading through this book, you will have a jump start on your research. In fact, your research time may be cut in half.

CHAPTER WRAP-UP

This chapter has helped you consider many of the initial factors of starting your small business. Despite what the experts may tell you, there is no "right" way to start your business. You cannot follow ten easy steps to ensure success of your venture. What you can do, however, is know the various tasks that lie ahead and approach each task with a can-do attitude. Use the following worksheet as a primer for the many business decisions you will need to make. For your convenience, use the chapter reference column of the worksheet to learn more about the various tasks you must complete.

USEFUL RESOURCES

Start Your Business: A Beginner's Guide. Published by the editors at The Oasis Press®, this all-in-one start-up guide lists the major requirements and issues that every new business owner needs to know, including start-up financing, creating a business plan, marketing strategies, environmental laws, and more!

The Secrets to Buying and Selling a Business by Ira K. Nottonson. This comprehensive workbook will prepare a business buyer or seller for negotiations that will achieve win-win results. Outlines how to determine the real worth of a business — also known as business valuation — and deals with issues like putting a value on "goodwill." More than 36 checklists and worksheets to guide the prospective buyer or seller are included.

The Franchise Bible: How to Buy a Franchise or Franchise Your Own Business by Erwin Keup. This up-to-date guide will help prospective franchisees or those who want to franchise their businesses. Contains the latest FTC-approved offering circular plus dozens of worksheets for evaluating franchise companies, locations, and organizing information before seeing an attorney.

Which Business? Help in Selecting Your New Venture by Nancy Drescher. This fun, yet informative book profiles the success stories of 24 different business areas. Each profile shows how the business owners got their start and the problems they have since overcome. Helps defines a prospective business owner's skills and interest.

http://www.psi-research.com. This Web site will help you clear the myriad of business hurdles you will encounter as a small business owner. The site includes detailed information on start-up issues, money matters, marketing, employment, producing and delivering your product or service, and environmental issues. It also lists the numerous state and federal agencies you will need to contact to get your business up and running and prepared to stay in the race!

Planning Primer for New Entrepreneurs	Yes	No	N/A	Find it in Chapter...
YOUR PRODUCT OR SERVICE				
Have you clearly defined your business?				1 and 7
What distinguishes your product or service from your competitors? ______ ______				6 and 7
Do you plan to manufacture or purchase parts?				7
Do you know the turnaround time for ordering parts and are they guaranteed?				6
Is there a discount for purchasing a larger quantity?				6
Do you know how your product or service will reach its market?				6

YOUR PERSONAL NEEDS	Yes	No	N/A	Find it in Chapter...
How long can you survive financially without drawing your assigned salary or wage? ______ ______ ______				1
Are your family members prepared to withstand the time constraints placed on you as a new business owner?				1
If yours will be a home-based business, how will your home office space accommodate both your customers, vendors, and family members? ______ ______ ______				12

YOUR PERSONAL NEEDS (CONTINUED)	Yes	No	N/A	Find it in Chapter...
Are you ready to work long hours and weekends?				1
If you will have partners or co-owners, have you clearly identified what each member will bring to the overall operation? (Think in terms of time, money, equipment, and commitment)				2
If yours is a partnership, do all partners have similar goals and can you work with them?				2
Are you a self starter and can you maintain a disciplined approach to making your business succeed?				1

YOUR BUSINESS' INDUSTRY	Yes	No	N/A	Find it in Chapter...
Have you explored the risks associated with selling or manufacturing your product or service?				7
Do you know the seasonal or cyclical nature of your industry and how these changes can affect your ability to sell?				7
Have you researched the credit terms that your suppliers offer and can these terms accommodate your business' needs?				6
How much control do you want or are you willing to give up based on your choice of legal structure?				2

MARKETING ISSUES	Yes	No	N/A	Find it in Chapter...
Are there sufficient willing buyers who will be attracted to your current price, quality, and convenience levels?				6
What is the demographic makeup of your customer base? ____________________				1 and 6

MARKETING ISSUES (CONTINUED)	Yes	No	N/A	Find it in Chapter...
Do you know your target consumers' buying habits?				6
What advertising mediums will you use to promote your business' image and/or message? ____________________ ____________________ ____________________				6 and 7
How will you reach your customers? ____________________ ____________________ ____________________				6 and 7

THE COMPETITION	Yes	No	N/A	Find it in Chapter...
Do you know who your competitors are?				1, 6, and 7
How does your business measure against the competition (i.e. higher quality or lower price)? ____________________ ____________________ ____________________				1, 6, and 7
What sets your business apart from the competitors? ____________________ ____________________ ____________________				6 and 7
Will your product or service meet a need for an underserved market?				6 and 7
How do you plan to communicate your business' uniqueness? ____________________ ____________________ ____________________ ____________________				6 and 7

YOUR FINANCES	Yes	No	N/A	Find it in Chapter...
Where will your start-up funds come from? ____________				7 and 8
Do you know of the numerous federal and state government loans available to your type of small business?				8
Are you aware of how many months (or years) it will take before you start to see a profit?				7, 8, and 9
Do you know the cost of sales (merchandise, freight, labor, etc.)?				6
Have you calculated the monthly fixed costs of your business, including rent, utilities, and insurance?				9
Do you know what your monthly net profits will be?				9
Will you use money from profits or other sources to fund expansion of your business?				7 and 9
Do you know where to get a loan for your start-up or expansion efforts?				9
Have you developed a pricing strategy for your product or service?				6
Do you know the costs associated with obtaining insurance and bonds to cover your business' liability issues?				11
Are you familiar with the basic proforma financial statements — balance sheet, income statement, and cash flow analysis?				7 and 9
Can you interpret your proforma statements?				9
Have you found a bank that will meet your business' needs?				9
Are you aware of how your business structure is taxed?				2 and 3

START-UP EXPENSES	Yes	No	N/A	Find it in Chapter…
Do you know the down payment for leasing or purchasing office space? (Keep in mind, negotiating the lease or purchase price of property is usually an option.)				9 and 12
Have you calculated the expenses of equipment leases, inventory needs, fixtures, and office furniture and supplies?				9 and 12
Are you aware of all the necessary deposits you must make for things like sales tax, utilities, credit card acceptance, and leases?				3 and 12
Do you have enough funds to cover your start-up employee salaries?				10
Do you know the costs associated with paying estimated taxes, and obtaining permits and licenses to operate?				3 and 4
Are you familiar with the financial requirements for withholding taxes, unemployment tax, and workers' compensation?				4
Have you projected your initial advertising budget?				6
Have you thought of allotting money toward paying a professional, like a lawyer or accountant?				9
Do you know the cost of setting up a FAX machine, getting on the Internet, and establishing an email address or Web site?				12
How many phone lines will you require? ____________				12
Will you need a separate post office box for incoming mail?				12
Do you know the fees for setting up your business' legal form (sole proprietorship, partnership, corporation, or LLC)? (Keep in mind, if these expenses become overwhelming, then only calculate the major priorities now and budget the other expenses later.)				2

EMPLOYMENT ISSUES	Yes	No	N/A	Find it in Chapter...
Will you need to hire employees?				4 and 10
Have you considered using independent contractors or leasing employees instead of hiring permanent employees?				4 and 10
Are you familiar with the wages for your industry?				13
Do you know your state's minimum wage laws?				4
Does the area in which you wish to locate have a skilled labor pool from which you can hire and retain the best qualified employees?				13
Do you know the federal and state regulations that govern employee and employer rights (i.e. fair employment practices and anti-discrimination issues)?				4 and 10
Will you offer a benefits package to your employees?				10
Have you written a clear set of company policies and procedures for your employees?				10
Do you have all employer posters required for display (minimum wage, equal opportunity, etc.)?				4 and 10

INSURANCE ISSUES	Yes	No	N/A	Find it in Chapter...
Do you know what kind of property coverage your business will need (i.e. fire, burglary, robbery, business interruptions)?				11
Do you know what kind of casualty insurance your business requires (i.e. liability, automobile, employee theft)?				11

LOCATION	Yes	No	N/A	Find it in Chapter...
Are you aware of any environmental issues relating to your business?				3 and 4
How will you address safety and health issues, and do you know how to stay in compliance with both federal and state OSHA laws?				4
Does your product or service require specific location needs?				12
Have you checked the makeup of the population and the number and type of competitors in the area?				12
Can the area support a business like the one you propose?				12
Do traffic count, parking facilities, and other business establishments play an important part in location?				12
Do you know the four critical factors for locating your business?				12
Do you know the zoning restrictions and permit requirements for the area in which you will locate?				3

CHAPTER 2

Your Business' Structure

No matter what you've read, regardless of what you've learned in school, your best approach to smartstart your business is to prepare yourself for the multitude of decisions that lie ahead. As a small business owner, one of the first major decisions you will make is to choose a legal form under which to operate your business. You can prepare to tackle this task by understanding the four basic legal forms — sole proprietorship, partnership, corporation, and limited liability company — and then by weighing the advantages and disadvantages of each.

Variations of these four entities are available to most business owners in most states. These variations, such as the S corporation and the limited liability partnership, are discussed in greater detail in this chapter. Further, the major advantages and disadvantages of each entity are covered to help you better evaluate which one may be right for your situation. Consult your attorney or accountant, or both, to find out which form makes most sense for your business' financial condition.

To get your feet wet, look at some of the main criteria that you must take into account before making your decision.

FIVE FACTORS

Five critical factors will influence which way you decide to go. You must consider:

Legal liability. Determine whether your business has potential liability and if you can afford that risk.

Tax implications. Look at your business goals and individual situation to find out how you can best minimize your tax burden.

Cost of formation and recordkeeping. If you choose a structure that offers more legal protection to you as an individual, you can bet on increased administrative time and costs to ensure that liability protection.

Flexibility. You want to choose a form that maximizes the flexibility of the ownership structure — achieving both short-term and long-term goals.

Future needs. Even during the start-up phase, you will need to look down the road to what will happen when you retire, die, or sell the business.

With these key factors fresh in your mind, jump into the shallow end of the pool and learn the pros and cons of each form.

SOLE PROPRIETORSHIP

A sole proprietorship is the simplest, most common form of business organization. It is defined as a business that is owned by a single individual. It is the easiest and least costly means of getting into business. As the owner of a sole proprietorship, you are personally responsible for all business debts and liabilities. All your business profits will be considered as income to you and will be taxed at the personal income level. Refer to the discussion below on tax situations for Maryland sole proprietors. Conversely, all personal assets and properties are at risk if a sole proprietorship incurs debts beyond its ability to pay.

Advantages of a Sole Proprietorship

- It is easy and inexpensive to establish.
- A sole proprietor has full control over all business decisions.
- There are minimal legal restrictions or requirements.
- A sole proprietor owns all profits and reaps all benefits of ownership.

- There is no requirement to pay unemployment taxes.
- Depending upon the state in which you do business, there may not be a requirement to pay into the workers' compensation insurance fund.

Disadvantages of a Sole Proprietorship

- A sole proprietor is personally liable for all business debts.
- A sole proprietor may have difficulty obtaining long-term financing.
- The success of the business depends wholly on the efforts of the sole proprietor.
- Illness, injury, or death of the sole proprietor will directly threaten his or her business.
- There are no unemployment benefits if the business fails.
- Sole proprietors have only limited tax savings for the cost of fringe benefits.

If you will operate your sole proprietorship under a name other than your own, you should register the business name (commonly known as "doing business as" or "d.b.a.") with the Maryland State Department of Assessments and Taxation. You must file a *Trade Name Application* in writing and under oath. The filing fee is $11. You must also register your sole proprietorship with the clerk of the circuit court in the county where the business will be located. For more information, refer to the discussion on naming your business in Chapter 3.

If you are the owner of a sole proprietorship in Maryland, your business profits and losses will be subject to your personal income tax. You will be required to report these earnings or losses on your individual income tax return.

For more information on sole proprietorships in Maryland, contact the Maryland State Department of Assessments and Taxation, Corporate Charter Division. You can find this address in Appendix C.

GENERAL PARTNERSHIP

A general partnership is the association of two or more persons whom have agreed to operate a business. You can form a general partnership by a simple verbal agreement of the partners. However, it is in your best interest and the best interest of all parties that you have an attorney prepare, or at least review, a formal, written partnership agreement that addresses such issues as:

- The amount, type, and valuation of property each partner will contribute.
- The method for disbursement of profits and liabilities among the partners.
- A plan for sharing any gains, losses, deductions, and credits.
- A provision for changing the conditions of the partnership.
- A provision for dealing with the loss or death of one of the partners.

In a general partnership, any partner may hire or fire employees, contract for services, commit to sales, or accomplish any activity required to operate the business independently from the other partners. The actions of a single partner are binding upon all partners.

Advantages of a General Partnership

- A partnership is easy to establish.
- There is more than one person to shoulder the workload and responsibilities.
- Financing is easier to obtain than for a sole proprietorship.
- The partners share all profits and reap all benefits of ownership.

Disadvantages of a General Partnership

- A partnership may be more expensive to initially set up.

- The partners are exposed to unlimited liability for business expenses.
- Each partner is bound by the actions of the other partner.
- Decision-making authority is divided.
- The loss of one partner may dissolve the business.
- The partnership may be difficult to end.

A general partnership does not pay state or federal taxes. The partnership is, however, required to report income and expenses of the partnership on federal and state information returns. Your Maryland partnership will need to file *Form 1065, Partner's Share of Income, Credits, and Losses* for federal reporting.

In addition to federal requirements, you must file *Form 510, Maryland Pass-Through Entity Income Tax Return,* with the Revenue Administration Division of the Maryland Comptroller of the Treasury on an annual basis. You and your partner(s) are also required to report your share of the partnership's profit and loss on your personal individual income tax returns. A partnership with nonresident partners must pay a withholding tax on allocable income of those partners and report it on *Form 510D* on a quarterly basis.

LIMITED PARTNERSHIP

If a partnership sounds appealing to you but you fear the liability issues associated with a general partnership, you may want to consider a limited partnership. A limited partnership is similar to a general partnership and has most of the same advantages and disadvantages. However, be aware of a few significant differences between the roles of the limited and general partners. In a limited partnership, you must always have at least one general and one limited partner. If you are a limited partner you will invest assets into the business and your risk will be typically limited to the amount of capital you have invested. As a limited partner, you will not be otherwise involved in the management of the business and, therefore, will not share in liability for its debts or losses.

If you are an operating or general partner in a business, you are responsible for the liability and operation of the business. You assume responsibility for all management decisions and debts. As in a general partnership, as an operating partner your personal assets are not protected from the creditors of the business.

Advantages of a Limited Partnership

- A limited partnership is relatively easy to establish.
- There is more than one person to share in start-up expenses.
- It is easier for a partnership to get financing than it is for a sole proprietorship.
- The partners share all profits and reap all benefits of ownership.
- The limited partner's personal assets are not at risk from creditors.

Disadvantages of a Limited Partnership

- A partnership is more expensive to set up initially, due to the requirement for a written agreement.
- An operating (general) partner is exposed to unlimited liability for business expenses.
- The loss of one partner may dissolve the business.
- A partnership may be difficult to end.

As a limited partnership in Maryland you are required to file a *Certificate of Limited Partnership* and pay a $50 fee to the Maryland State Department of Assessments and Taxation. The certificate must include the name of the partnership, the address of its principal office, the name and address of each general partner, the date the partnership will dissolve, and any other relevant matters. Further, you are required by law to draft a formal, written agreement when setting up a limited partnership.

Foreign limited partnerships must pay a $50 registration fee to the Maryland State Department of Assessments and Taxation.

CORPORATIONS

A corporation is the most complex type of business organization. It is formed by law as a separate legal entity, fully distinct from its owners — also called stockholders or shareholders. As such, it exists independently from its owners and endures as a legal entity even at the death, retirement, or resignation of a stockholder. Thus, the corporation, not the individuals, handles the responsibilities of the organization, the corporation is taxed, and the corporation can be held legally liable for its actions. Any person or group of people operating a business of any size may incorporate. Similarly, any group engaged in religious, civil, nonprofit, or charitable endeavors may incorporate and enjoy the legal and financial benefits of incorporation.

You may find that incorporating offers your business a number of benefits. For example, your corporation may be able to more easily raise capital through the sale of stock. Also, as an owner of stock you do not have to be publicly listed, affording you and other stockholders a degree of anonymity. Further, the cost of fringe benefits such as life and health insurance, travel expenses, and retirement plans are tax-deductible.

Corporations can take on several different forms depending on the individual business situation. For the most part, if you decide to incorporate your business, you will need to know the differences between a:

- General (C) corporation — also referred to as a domestic corporation,
- S corporation,
- Foreign corporation,
- Close corporation,
- Professional corporation, and
- Not-for-profit corporation — also called a nonprofit corporation.

GENERAL (C) CORPORATION

A general business corporation is the most formalized type of business structure and is usually formed for profit-making organizations. A general corporation is the most common type of corporation. In a general corporation, its owners are stockholders, and ownership is based on shares of stock. There is no limitation to the number of stockholders. Since the corporation operates as a separate entity, each stockholder's personal assets are protected from attachment by creditors of the corporation. Thus, as a stockholder, your liability is limited to the capital that you have invested in the purchase of stock.

Advantages of a General Corporation

- A corporation has a lifespan independent from its owners (stockholders).
- Fringe benefit costs are tax-deductible;
- Personal assets are protected from business liability.
- Ownership can be transferred through the sale of stock.
- It is easy to raise operating capital through the sale of stock.
- Ownership of a corporation can change without affecting its day-to-day management.

Disadvantages of a General Corporation

- Incorporating involves considerable start-up expenses.
- Corporations are subject to more state and federal legislation.
- Profits are subject to dual taxation — as profits and again as dividends.
- Many legal formalities exist when filing and trying to maintain corporate status.
- Activities are limited to those defined in the corporate charter.

S CORPORATION

The S corporation is a form of the general corporation that has a special tax status with the IRS and many states. The most attractive benefit of an S corporation is the avoidance of double taxation. You have learned that if a dividend is declared, then shareholders must declare that dividend as income and it is taxed again — hence, the double taxation stigma. S corporations avoid this dual taxation because all losses and profits are "passed through" the corporation to the shareholders and are declared only once to the IRS as part of each shareholder's income. As in other forms of incorporation, each shareholder's personal assets are protected from the business' debts.

If you want to form as an S corporation, your general corporation must meet specific requirements before applying for or being granted S corporation status by the IRS. To qualify for federal S corporation status, your business must:

- Already exist as a corporation;
- Have no more than 75 shareholders;
- Count beneficiaries and shareholders of a small business trust toward the maximum 75 shareholders;
- Be headquartered in the United States;
- Issue only one class of stock;
- Not have nonresident aliens who are shareholders;
- Not be a financial institution that takes deposits or makes loans, an insurance company taxed under subchapter L, or a Domestic International Sales Corporation (DISC);
- Not be one that takes a tax credit for doing business in a U.S. possession; and
- Not have more than 25% of the corporation's gross receipts from passive sources, such as interest, dividends, rent, royalties or proceeds from the sale of securities. This provision has several conditions, so be sure to clearly understand how it may affect you if your company expects income from these sources.

If your corporation meets the above criteria, you may then apply for S corporation status if all shareholders consent to the election of S corporation status and your business files IRS *Form 2553, Election by a Small Business Corporation.* A copy of this form is located in Appendix A.

Keeping S Corporation Status

S corporation status is subject to many IRS regulations and qualifications. The special tax advantages of S corporation status will be lost if your corporation fails to maintain eligibility. Once S corporation status is terminated, it cannot be reactivated for five years. Your S corporation status can be terminated if your corporation:

- Exceeds 75 shareholders;
- Transfers S corporation stock to a corporation, partnership, ineligible trust, or nonresident alien;
- Creates a second class of stock;
- Acquires an operational subsidiary; or
- Loses corporate status.

Maryland recognizes the federal S corporation provision. To qualify, you must complete an informational return on *Form 510.* Nonresidents must pay a withholding tax on allocable income. Contact the Maryland State Department of Assessments and Taxation for more information.

Take a bigger picture perspective when considering S corporation status for your business. You will avoid double taxation, yet may not be able to participate in health and accident plans and other fringe benefits that are normally allowed to the general (C) corporation. For more information about S corporations, get a copy of IRS *Publication 589, Tax Information on S Corporations* from your accountant or local IRS office.

FOREIGN CORPORATION

When your corporation does business outside the state in which it was incorporated, it is considered a foreign corporation. For instance, suppose you originally incorporate in the state of

Maryland but later find you want to do business in New Jersey. Your company, a domestic corporation in Maryland, will become a foreign corporation in New Jersey. If your business will operate as a foreign corporation, it will be subject to potential liabilities, penalties, and problems unless it is qualified to operate in that state. If your business fails to qualify, you may be subject to corporate fines, criminal charges, or a lack of legal recognition in a court of law.

To qualify as a foreign corporation in Maryland, you must register with the Maryland State Department of Assessments and Taxation by filing an application for certificate of qualification. Contact the Corporate Charter Division of the Maryland State Department of Assessments and Taxation to obtain the necessary forms and filing procedures. The address and phone number are located in Appendix C.

CLOSE CORPORATION

A close corporation is similar to a general corporation, but contains certain restrictions in its certificate of incorporation. Close corporations are not available in all states and the restrictions on close corporations vary from state to state. Restrictions may include:

- A limit on the number of allowable stockholders;
- A prohibition against the public offering of stock; and
- Limitations on the transfer of stock outside the corporation.

Frequently, close corporations appeal to entrepreneurs and family businesses in that they offer the advantages of incorporation without the risk of surprise takeovers. Close corporations also offer freedom from most of the formalities of incorporation, such as holding annual directors' meetings and handling extensive recordkeeping.

Advantages of a Close Corporation

- Close corporations have the option of eliminating the need for a board of directors.
- A close corporation can use proxies for directors.

- Stock transfers can be restricted so that those outside the original group of shareholders cannot purchase stock of the company.

Disadvantages of a Close Corporation

- Shareholders must shoulder greater responsibilities if a board of directors is not assigned.

- Close corporation regulations vary from state to state, making interstate trade somewhat more difficult to handle.

Maryland has a close corporation statute. To learn more about filing as a close corporation in Maryland, contact the Maryland State Department of Assessments and Taxation.

PROFESSIONAL CORPORATION

Professional corporations are for individuals whose service requires a professional license. Examples of these professionals include doctors, lawyers, and accountants, but may include others depending on individual state law.

Licensed professionals who incorporate enjoy tax benefits for the costs associated with fringe benefits. However, the shareholders of a professional corporation are personally liable to their clients. Liability spreads to all shareholders even if only one was negligent or accused of wrongdoing.

Advantages of a Professional Corporation

- Personal assets are protected from business debts.

- There are certain tax breaks or deferments for the cost of fringe benefits.

Disadvantages of a Professional Corporation

- The corporation is limited to a single profession.

- Only licensed professionals may be shareholders.

- Shares may only be sold to a licensed member of the same profession.
- Shareholders are liable to their clients as a group.

Maryland allows the formation of professional corporations. For more information, contact the Maryland State Department of Assessments and Taxation.

Make sure you contact your lawyer or accountant to understand the tax law changes that will affect your business. Further, compare the pros and cons of the limited liability partnership (LLP) — the kinsman to the limited liability company (LLC). LLCs and LLPs are discussed in greater detail later in this chapter.

NOT-FOR-PROFIT CORPORATION

Not-for-profit corporations, also called nonprofit organizations, are usually formed by religious, civil, or social groups. Profits cannot be distributed to members, officers, or directors of a corporation, but instead must be disbursed in support of the beneficial purposes outlined in its articles of incorporation.

A nonprofit corporation does not issue stock, and all activities are controlled by a self-perpetuating board of directors. If your business will operate as a nonprofit corporation, clearly spell out all business operations in your articles of incorporation.

A tax-exempt organization is closely related to a nonprofit organization. Most nonprofit organizations try to qualify as tax-exempt under Section 501(c)(3) of the Internal Revenue Code. To qualify as a tax-exempt organization your business must be formed for:

- Religious, charitable, scientific, literary, or educational purposes;
- The testing of public safety;
- Fostering amateur sports competition; or
- The prevention of cruelty to animals or children.

Advantages of a Nonprofit Corporation

- A nonprofit organization can benefit from tax-exempt status because all contributions are tax-exempt.
- There is some flexibility in operations of the business.

Disadvantages of a Nonprofit Corporation

- All income must go to the not-for-profit purpose.
- Members, officers, or directors cannot benefit from dissolution of the corporation.
- A nonprofit corporation cannot merge with another corporation unless it is also classified as nonprofit.

For more information on tax-exempt organizations, contact your local IRS office for a copy of *Publication 557, Tax-Exempt Status for Your Organization.*

HANDLING CORPORATE FORMALITIES

You have heard about the major benefit of incorporation — personal asset protection. Now consider some of the responsibilities of corporations to maintain their corporate status. So that the IRS will not find good cause to pierce your corporate veil, your corporation must:

- Draft, approve, and file articles of incorporation. You file your articles with the Maryland State Department of Assessments and Taxation along with a $20 recording fee, plus a $20 organization and capitalization fee if the par value of your stock is not more than $100,000;
- File an annual report with the Maryland State Department of Assessments and Taxation by April 15 and pay a $100 fee;
- Pay corporate taxes. The base for the state corporate income tax is taxable income, determined under the Internal Revenue Code;
- Keep bylaws and minutes;

- Issue official stock certificates; and
- Maintain an official corporate seal.

Although time consuming, incorporating your business is a simple process. In fact, the trend for many small business owners is do-it-yourself incorporation. Although you may want to consult with your accountant regarding the tax consequences of switching from doing business as a sole proprietor to doing business as a corporation.

Two helpful resources are available to assist your do-it-yourself incorporation efforts. The first is *InstaCorp: Incorporate in Any State* by Corporate Agents, Inc. This user-friendly guide offers eight simple steps to incorporation and even has compatible software to help expedite the process. For sample documents — articles, bylaws, shareholders' agreements, and stock certificates — check out *The Essential Corporation Handbook* by Carl R. J. Sniffen. This nuts-and-bolts guide contains checklists that will help you keep track of the numerous formalities. To learn more about these helpful guides, refer to the Useful Resources section at the end of this chapter.

LIMITED LIABILITY COMPANY (LLC)

A limited liability company (LLC) is a relatively new and highly touted business entity. Limited liability companies have been adopted into legislation in all 50 states and the District of Columbia.

The LLC is a hybrid business form that draws advantageous characteristics from both corporations and partnerships. It is similar to an S corporation without its restrictions. Like a partnership, an LLC's existence rests with its owners — in an LLC, owners are referred to as members. The loss of a member through death, retirement, or resignation can result in the dissolution of the business. However, like a corporation, a limited liability company offers some protection for personal assets from business creditors. Due to its dual qualities — corporate protection and partnership tax treatment — many feel the LLC could replace general partnerships, limited partnerships, and even S corporations as the future entity of choice.

An interesting LLC characteristic is the lack of limitation on the number and nature of its members. However, most states will require at least two members to form an LLC. Members may be foreign persons or nonresidents, or even partnerships, corporations, trusts, estates, or other limited liability companies. An LLC is a good choice for real estate ventures that involve corporations, trusts, or foreign investors, or for new business ventures that involve existing corporations. Also, an LLC is an excellent estate planning vehicle for investment between you and your family corporation, trust, or partnership.

Advantages of a Limited Liability Company

- Profits and losses pass through the company to its owners for tax purposes.
- Personal assets are protected from business liability.
- There is no limitation on the number or nature of owners.
- An LLC is simpler to operate than a corporation.
- LLCs are not subject to corporate formalities.
- Owners may participate in management of the business.
- Some tax advantages result from business losses or high profits.

Disadvantages of a Limited Liability Company

- An LLC may be recognized differently in different states.
- Limits of liability have not been extensively tested in litigation.
- Legal assistance is needed to properly set up and structure an LLC.
- Professionals, such as lawyers, accountants, and doctors, are prohibited from registering as an LLC.

Simplicity and great flexibility are the hallmarks of the LLC. To start an LLC in Maryland, two or more people are required. An LLC must file articles of organization with the Maryland State Department of Assessments and Taxation. One original and one copy of the articles of organization must be filed with the department. A $50 LLC formation fee is required, as well as a $7 name registration fee for 30 days. A $50 reporting fee must be filed every five years. You must pay an additional $10 fee if you change the name or address of the principal agent's office. In addition, the name of your business must include the term "Limited Liability Company" or "LLC" and must not cause confusion with any other name on file with the Maryland State Department of Assessments and Taxation.

To register a foreign LLC in Maryland, you must pay a $50 fee and an additional $10 fee if you are changing the name or address of the principal agent's office.

Also, as an owner — or member — of an LLC in Maryland, you will need to draft an operating agreement. Similar to a corporation's bylaws, this agreement will define the rights, powers, and duties of members and managers. For example, you would want to spell out how investments in the entity — or contributions — can be made.

Keep in mind, because an LLC is a new entity, little legal precedent for it exists. Congress has recently passed tax legislation in 1997 that establishes the LLC with more than one member (or owner) as a partnership for tax purposes. The S corporation, as previously discussed, has more legal precedent than the LLC and is considered a more established business and tax entity. Talk to your accountant of lawyer regarding which form is best for your situation.

For more information about limited liability companies, consider getting a copy of *The Essential Limited Liability Company Handbook: The Newest Alternative in Business* by Corporate Agents, Inc. To learn more about this comprehensive guide, refer to the Useful Resources section at the end of this chapter.

LIMITED LIABILITY PARTNERSHIP

Yet another new entity, the limited liability partnership (LLP), is now available to small business owners in more than 40 states. In an LLP, partners are afforded the same limited liability protection as professional corporations.

Advantages of an LLP

- As a partner in an LLP you can enjoy the tax advantage of flow-through tax treatment.
- An LLP is not subject to the numerous limitations regarding ownership, capital structure, and division of profits.
- It is simple and familiar for an existing partnership to elect to become an LLP.

Disadvantages of an LLP

- A sole owner cannot set up an LLP since, as a partnership, an LLP must have at least two partners to exist.
- LLPs are not available in all states.
- It is a relatively new legal form, thus, little legal precedent has been set.

Maryland allows the formation of domestic and foreign LLPs. To start an LLP in Maryland, you must register with the Maryland State Department of Assessments and Taxation and pay a $50 fee. For more information on LLPs, log on to The Oasis Press Web site at *http://www.psi-research.com.*

CHAPTER WRAP-UP

Choosing the legal form for your business is the first of many decisions you will make as you smartstart your Maryland business. As you attempt to make sense out of the various legal forms, determine which of the five important factors — legal liability, tax implications, formation costs and recordkeeping requirements, ownership flexibility, and future goals — are the most critical for your business' needs.

Are you most concerned with protecting your personal assets from your business' creditors? Then you may want to avoid forming a sole proprietorship and set up a corporation or limited liability company (LLC). What about the tax situation for your business? You may be interested in forming a corporation, but unless you form as an S corporation or LLC you will suffer the dreaded double taxation. You may have an excellent opportunity to start a partnership with an associate whom you respect. Do you know the ups and downs of a general versus limited partnership and how these legal forms affect your ownership flexibility and future needs? And, finally, although the LLC and S corporation remain the most talked about legal forms, make sure you understand the potentially overwhelming recordkeeping rules and formation costs associated with starting your business as either of these two entities.

Keep this chapter handy as you weigh the pros and cons of each legal form. Make sure your decision involves a consultation with your attorney or accountant, or both! Also, contact Maryland State Department of Assessments and Taxation for any published material that will give you advice on structuring your business in Maryland.

USEFUL RESOURCES

The Essential Corporation Handbook by Carl R. J. Sniffen. This comprehensive reference will give you legal requirements for forming a corporation in all 50 states and the District of Columbia. Includes several sample corporate documents and explains how to keep your corporation in good standing.

The Essential Limited Liability Company Handbook: The Newest Alternative in Business by Corporate Agents, Inc. Written in layperson language, this helpful book gives you all the details you need to know to set up a new LLC or convert your existing business to an LLC. Includes a certificate of formation and sample operating agreement as well as a list of state requirements for all 50 states plus Washington, D.C.

InstaCorp: Incorporate in Any State by Corporate Agents, Inc. This complete step-by-step guide reveals do-it-yourself incorporation techniques for each of the 50 states. This money-saving tool will also help you understand the basic legal and tax ramifications of the various corporate structures. Easy-to-use *Windows 95*™ compatible software is available also.

LEGAL FORM CHECKLIST

- ❑ If you will operate as a general partnership, draft a partnership agreement that outlines business issues.
- ❑ If you will operate as a limited partnership, write a limited partnership agreement (required by law) and file a *Certificate of Limited Partnership* with the Maryland State Department of Assessments and Taxation, and pay a $50 fee.
- ❑ If your business will be a corporation, file your articles of incorporation with the Maryland State Department of Assessments and Taxation and pay a $20 recording fee plus a $20 organization and capitalization fee if the par value of your stock is not over $100,000.
- ❑ If you will do business as a foreign corporation, make sure you file an application for certificate of qualification with the Maryland State Department of Assessments and Taxation and pay a $50 fee.
- ❑ If you will file as a limited liability company (LLC), then draft your business' operating agreement and file with the Maryland State Department of Assessments and Taxation and pay a fee of $50.
- ❑ If you will file as a limited liability partnership (LLP), register with the Maryland State Department of Assessments and Taxation and pay a $50 fee.

CHAPTER 3

Business Start-Up Details

You have gotten your feet wet and conquered your first major task as a new small business owner. Your decision regarding the legal form for your business is the first of many decisions you will make as you continue to smartstart your enterprise. Now it's time to get out of the shallow end of the pool — get your head wet and learn how to swim. You are ready to tackle the maze of business start-up details that face the approximately seven million people in the United States who are actively pursuing starting their own businesses.

You are responsible for a number of start-up activities that center around licensing and registrations and may include:

- Naming your business, possibly under a trade name;
- Applying for a trade name, trademark, or servicemark;
- Contacting the one-stop business assistance center in the state in which you will do business;
- Obtaining the necessary state and local licenses and permits to get your business running; and
- Learning which taxes your business will be responsible to pay.

This chapter will guide you through the bureaucratic snarls that entangle many startups. In short, this information will give you the confidence you need to approach the various state and federal agencies and the know-how to effectively deal with the mounds of paperwork you may encounter. In addition, once you have completed these start-up tasks, your business will become more of a reality — giving you a sense of being an official business owner. Who knows...you may even be ready to try a dive into the deep end!

Once you have survived this phase of startup, and you know that you will have employees, then look to the following chapter to learn about your duties as an employer.

NAMING YOUR BUSINESS

The name you choose for your business is another important step you will take as a business owner. Many entrepreneurs underestimate the significance of naming their businesses. In choosing a name, you may want to consider the following tips.

- Select a name that is easy to understand, spell, pronounce, and remember.
- Make sure it is a name that can be easily located in a telephone directory.
- Ensure that it portrays the image you want for your business. For example, if quick turnaround and quality service are part of your marketing strategy, then choose identifiers that will convey these aspects.
- Stay away from individual letters or acronyms that may confuse the potential customer trying to locate your business in the telephone directory.
- Steer clear of names that are similar or identical to those used by another business.
- Avoid unusual spellings that may cause your customer difficulty in finding your business name or listing.

If you need assistance with selecting a name for your business, consult a public relations, advertising, or marketing consultant.

TRADE NAME

Any business entity can operate under a trade name. If you will operate your business under your actual name, you need not file a

Trade Name Application — also called d.b.a. or doing business as. In fact, most sole proprietors operate under their own actual names. However, if you operate your business under any other name, you are required to file an application and pay an $11 fee, plus $1 for each additional owner. The trade name provides a public record of all owners of the business. Contact the Maryland State Department of Assessments and Taxation for complete requirements. You can find the address in Appendix C.

Maryland has an office that will help you determine whether the name you have in mind has already been registered. For more information, contact the Trade Name Search and Registration Office of the Maryland State Department of Assessments and Taxation.

Most businesses operate under a trade name, often referred to as a fictitious business name or an assumed business name. By doing so, they protect themselves from frivolous lawsuits and other legal wranglings. For example, The Book Nook may be the name of a local bookstore, but this name does not reveal anything about the ownership of the business. It may be owned by a sole proprietor, a partner, a corporation, or a limited liability company. (If it is a corporation, it may contain the word, "Inc." in its name.) To operate the store as The Book Nook, the corporation, Books, Inc. will have to file with county recorder in The Book Nook's county of residence or a trade name application with the Maryland State Department of Assessments and Taxation so the public can determine the true ownership of The Book Nook. Anyone wanting to serve legal papers to the business would need to determine the true owners, and in this case, the address and officers of Books, Inc.

TRADEMARKS OR SERVICEMARKS

You can protect your business name by registering it as a trademark, trade name, or servicemark. Trade name or trademark protection is usually good for a specified period of time, usually five to ten years. Once that time period has elapsed, you will be responsible for reregistering your business.

To register your trademark or servicemark, contact the Maryland Secretary of State at the address in Appendix C. You may search the trademark and servicemark database of the Maryland Secretary of State to find out if your mark has been taken.

If you will do business in other states, it may be to your benefit to obtain a federal trademark registration. Your trademark will distinguish your product or service from those of others that offer similar products or services. To find out more about federal trademark registration, obtain the free booklet *Basic Facts About Trademarks*. To order this booklet, use the address and phone number in Appendix B.

For a more in-depth look at trademarks and servicemarks, consider getting a copy of *Develop and Market Your Creative Ideas* by Dale A. Davis. To learn more about this tried and proven textbook, see the Useful Resources section at the end of this chapter.

NAME RESERVATION FOR CORPORATIONS AND LLCS

If you will operate your business as an LLC or a corporation, you will need to reserve your company name. Most states charge a minimal fee to reserve a name for a specific period of time, usually 60 to 180 days. Maryland LLCs and corporations must pay a $7 name reservation fee per name for 30 days.

For more information contact the Corporate Name Availability Search Office of the Maryland State Department of Assessments and Taxation.

ONE-STOP CENTER

Many states have formed centralized business assistance offices to help business owners who are starting, expanding, or relocating to their state. Referred to as a one-stop center or business assistance center, this office works in coordination with the numerous other state agencies that will regulate your business.

Maryland has a one-stop center called the Dingman Center for Entrepreneurship where you can obtain registration and other information you will need to keep your business legally operating in Maryland. More than likely, the center will contact other state agencies like the tax department or the secretary of state to make them aware of your venture. Once these agencies are aware of your business' existence, they will usually contact you regarding any filing requirement. However, be aware of their reporting requirements because you may not be excused from reporting even though you were not sent reporting forms. A method to contact the center is provided in Appendix C. See Chapter 5 for more information on the Dingman Center for Entrepreneurship.

STATE LICENSES

Many businesses and professions require special licenses to operate their specific types of businesses. A license is always needed for professionals like doctors, lawyers, and dentists. A license is usually necessary for occupations like cosmetologists, morticians, and contractors. A license may be granted by a state, county, or city agency. Some of the more frequently licensed occupations in Maryland are:

- Bankers;
- Child care providers;
- Food manufacturers, distributors, and retailers;
- Pharmacists;
- Professional athletes; and
- Traders.

This is not an inclusive list, but if you are in a profession that is licensed, you likely already know that the requirement exists. Most state licenses must be renewed on an annual basis. Because there are different agencies that license different occupations, first contact the state licensing bureau. If you are uncertain of the status of licensing requirements for your business, contact the Maryland State Licensing Bureau. Refer to Appendix C for this office's address and phone number.

It is unlikely that your small business will need a federal license to operate. Licenses from the federal government generally are required for businesses that deal with securities, firearms, and use of the airwaves for transmission of information, such as television and radio. If you deal with firearms or ammunition, the consumption or sale of alcoholic beverages or tobacco, or transportation by taxi or bus service, be sure to know the licensing requirements.

LOCAL COUNTY AND CITY PERMITS

If you plan to operate a retail or manufacturing business you will probably be required to get permits either for construction or to open your particular type of business. There are often requirements or restrictions regarding signage, parking, or the type of business allowed in a particular area. Check with the local city and county governments regarding any special zoning ordinances.

Maryland may require an additional local license to operate a business. Check with the municipal offices of the city in which your business is located to see if a local business license is required.

ENVIRONMENTAL PERMITS

Permits often are required to conduct a business that may be regulated by a local or state government. Some federal agencies such the Environmental Protection Agency (EPA) or the Occupational Safety and Health Administration (OSHA) have state equivalents. In Maryland, the state equivalent of the federal EPA is the Maryland Department of Environment (DOE), and the state equivalent of OSHA is the Maryland Occupational Safety and Health (MOSH) Training and Education Unit of the Maryland Department of Labor, Licensing, and Regulation.

Do not make the assumption that since you are a new or small business you will have little or no contact with these agencies. Due to the requirements of the Clean Air Act of 1991, local, federal, and state laws and regulations affect even one-person operations. You may find that new regulations are put into effect after you start your business, so you must be aware of changes in the laws for which these agencies are responsible.

If your business will use any solvent or substance that could become airborne or get into the water in the form or seepage or runoff, you will have reason to contact these agencies. Even if you don't operate a business that may release controlled substances, you may sell equipment that has a harmful effect on the environment. So it is best to know what the rules are when you represent your product or service.

Also, if you are buying an existing business, make sure you thoroughly investigate any potential environmental liabilities. It is not uncommon for the buyer of an existing business to be held liable for environmental problems caused by the business' previous owners. You are encouraged to contact a licensed environmental professional to perform an environmental assessment of the business. This assessment will show you any liabilities before it is too late.

Maryland has enacted laws that regulate the quality of air, water, noise pollution, sewage and solid waste disposal, and mining. Contact the Maryland State Department of Natural Resources for more information. See Appendix C for the listing.

Maryland has a program that can assist you in determining if you need to contact environmental agencies. If you do have an environmental problem, the DOE Small Business Assistance Program should assist you in determining what your options are and how you should proceed.

REGISTERING TO PAY TAXES

Once you have officially obtained the necessary licenses and permits for your business, you will be responsible to notify Uncle Sam. In many cases, you can simply contact a central tax agency, which in turn will get you started with the appropriate forms and filing requirements. Once your business is listed in their database, you may receive periodic inquiries about your business or forms that you must complete to comply with state or federal laws, or both. The main taxes you will need to be aware of include:

- Estimated federal and state individual income taxes;
- Estimated federal and state corporate income taxes;
- A sales and use tax; and
- Property taxes.

Oftentimes, there may be a single form or tax application that will get you registered with several agencies regarding several different taxes. The Maryland Comptroller of the Treasury has a single form called the *Combined Registration Application, Form COT/ST-705,* that will help you determine for which taxes your business will be liable.

GET AN EMPLOYER IDENTIFICATION NUMBER

Unless you form a sole proprietorship, you must obtain an employer identification number (EIN), even if you do not have employees. The first registration you should make is to file *Form SS-4, Application for Employer Identification Number,* with the federal government. You will receive an employer identification number that you will need in many cases to complete other registrations. It is somewhat similar to your personal Social Security number, only it relates to your business.

You can obtain *Form SS-4* from your local IRS office or your accountant. For your convenience, a copy of this form is included in Appendix A. Once you have the form, you can apply for an EIN either by mail or by telephone. If you want an EIN immediately, call the Tele-TIN phone number for the service center for your state. The Tele-TIN phone and address are located in Appendix B. If you are not in a hurry, you can apply for your EIN through the mail. Keep in mind, you will need to complete *Form SS-4* at least four to five weeks before you will need your EIN.

After you receive your EIN, you will need to register with the state agency that governs employees and employers. See Chapter 4 for more information on filing employee taxes.

ESTIMATED INCOME TAX

As a small business owner in Maryland, you will need to estimate the amount of money your business will make and pay taxes on these estimates. Regardless of the form of business you have chosen, you will be responsible for paying estimated income taxes several times throughout the year — usually on a quarterly basis. And, if you have underpaid, you will be required to pay underpayment penalties at the end of the year. Make sure you calculate these amounts or any underpayment penalties in your monthly cash flow projections. Your accountant may be able to advise you on how best to plan for paying estimated income taxes.

Individual Federal Income Tax

When you are a sole proprietor, a partner, or a shareholder in an S corporation, you are considered self-employed. Since there is no employer to deduct federal income tax from your wages, you must make quarterly advance payments against your estimated federal income tax. You must report this business income even if it wasn't actually distributed to you. File your payments along with IRS *Form 1040-ES.* You will then file *Form 1040* at the end of the year along with *Schedule C* — which itemizes your business expenses for the year. Check with your accountant to make sure you know how to estimate, file, and pay correctly.

Individual State Income Tax

In Maryland, you must also pay against your estimated state income tax. You must file *Form 502, Individual Tax Return.* You must also file *Form 502D, Individual Estimated Tax Payment,* if your state and local taxes exceed $250. You must declare on the 15th of April, June, September, and January. You need not declare on January 15 if you file a return and pay all tax due by January 31. Contact the Maryland Comptroller of the Treasury for more information

As a business owner, it is your responsibility to remain informed of these requirements. Contact your local small business administration (SBA) office, small business development center (SBDC), or the Maryland Comptroller of the Treasury for more information. The addresses and phone numbers of these resources are listed in Appendix B and Appendix C. Further information and Internet links are available through The Oasis Press via its Internet Web site at *http://www.psi-research.com.*

In addition to estimated tax payments you must pay a self-employment tax, which is your contribution to Social Security and Medicare. This tax is paid quarterly and is included in your estimated tax payment. Since you are self-employed, you are responsible for the full amount of the contribution, rather than the 50% you would pay as an employee. One-half of the self-employment tax is deductible as a business expense on federal *Form 1040.* See Chapter 4 for more information on FICA, SSI, and Medicare.

CORPORATE INCOME TAX

If your business is a corporation you will be required to submit a separate business tax form with your personal tax report. In Maryland, corporate income taxes are imposed at the state level and administered by the Maryland Comptroller of the Treasury. You must submit *Form 500D, Estimated Tax Payment,* if your tax liability is more than $1,000. Quarterly payments are due on the 15th of April, June, September, and December.

Your corporation will be required to make quarterly federal payments based on its estimated tax using *Form 1120-W, Federal Estimated Tax Payment.* Corporate taxes are typically due on April 15, June 15, September 15, and December 15, unless your corporation operates on a different fiscal year. In this case, your taxes will be due on the 15th day of the 4th month following the end of the fiscal year.

SALES AND USE TAX

Maryland imposes a sales tax on merchandise sold within the state. If you operate a retail business or provide certain services, you will be required to collect and pay this sales tax to the Maryland Comptroller of the Treasury. Also, you will be required to obtain a seller's permit from the Taxpayer Service Section, which will register your firm as a retail business that is authorized to collect sales tax.

Maryland charges a use tax for items that were exempt from sales tax, such as items bought for resale that you decide to use instead. The state does not tax property or services bought outside the state before bringing the property or service into Maryland. If you paid less tax in the other state than you would have in Maryland, a formula is supplied.

You are exempt from paying sales tax on merchandise your business will resell, lease, or rent to others if you give the seller a resale certificate. Separate resale certificates usually must be obtained for each transaction, unless the seller accepts a blanket certificate.

In most cases you will not be required to pay sales taxes to wholesalers and distributors so long as you provide them with resale certificates on the goods you purchase. In like manner, as a wholesaler, distributor, or manufacturer, you will not be required to collect sales tax on the goods you sell provided the buyer is a retailer purchasing those goods for resale and provides you with resale certificates at the time of sale. For example, if you sell exclusively to other resellers or if your primary business is mail order, you may only be required to collect the tax for items sold and delivered within the state. However, this area of the law is being challenged, so you will find it wise to stay informed about how these changes affect you.

You will be assessed additional taxes on certain types of goods provided for resale. The federal government and most states assess pass-through taxes on certain goods such as gasoline, tobacco, and alcohol. As a retailer, you will pay taxes on these goods at the time of purchase and pass the tax through to the consumer. In the case of these taxes, you do not have to pay them separately to the state. The manufacturer, wholesaler, or distributor does this for you. However, you will still be required to maintain thorough records on all sales.

You are required to keep detailed records of your gross receipts regardless of whether those receipts are taxable or not. These receipts will justify the taxes you pay and the deductions you take on gross sales throughout the year. You will be required to file a seller's permit indicating that you know how much you sold was taxable and how much was not taxable.

Be careful to report on a timely basis. Maryland should send copies of reporting forms in advance of the due date. A late or incorrect form can result in heavy penalties or fines. Keep in mind, if you don't receive your forms, don't assume that you have no tax liability. You are responsible for getting the forms, filing them, and paying the tax.

You can get useful IRS publications, tax forms, and instructions through the Internal Revenue Information Services (IRIS) via a government bulletin board called FedWorld. You can access IRIS directly via telephone or via the Internet. For more information, see Appendix B.

PROPERTY TAX

Property taxes are assessed to pay the operating expenses of your locality, pay for bonds, and provide for special projects at the county and community level. Taxes are usually paid on an annual basis to the county treasurer. In most cases the county tax assessor will automatically bill you as the owner of record, so you will not need to contact this office when purchasing property for your business.

The Maryland State Department of Assessments and Taxation will mail you a personal property return at the beginning of each year. Personal property includes furniture, fixtures, office and industrial equipment, machinery, tools, supplies, and inventory.

Corporations, LLCs, LLPs, and limited partnerships must file a personal property return, *Form 1, Personal Property Tax Return*, by April 15 and pay a $100 fee, whether they own property or not. You will be billed later for your actual tax liability. Nonstock corporations are not required to pay the fee. Sole proprietorships and general partnerships must file a return only if they possess (own, lease, rent, use, or borrow) business personal property or need a business license. If you are unsure whether you are required to file, call the state department of assessments and taxation.

Interests and penalties will be assessed on unpaid property taxes as of October 1. Payments should be made to the local tax collector. Delinquent real estate taxes become liens on the property as of the date the tax was due.

CHAPTER WRAP-UP

As you will soon find out, the details of running a small business can be overwhelming. Your best line of defense is to educate yourself about the many requirements placed on your new Maryland business.

This chapter has introduced you to most of the start-up details that today's small businesses face. Some of these details are related to federal laws that affect businesses in all 50 states and Washington, D.C. However, many of these details will vary according to Maryland state laws — and, in some cases, are superseded by state laws. In addition, you will need to be aware of the city and county rules and regulations that govern your small business. From choosing a name for your business to applying for a trademark or trade name; from getting state permits and licenses to registering to pay taxes, as a small business owner you will be responsible for making sure your business is "official."

To help you stay educated and informed of the latest rules and regulations that affect your Maryland business, stay in close communication with your state's one-stop center — the Dingman Center for Entrepreneurship. This office may be able to put you on its mailing list for updates regarding issues that relate to not only starting, but operating a small business in Maryland. Also, if you have Internet capability, make sure you check out your state's home page. Contact the Maryland State Department of Assessments and Taxation and the Maryland Comptroller of the Treasury to learn how you can easily log on to their Web sites for the most current information for your business. Refer to Chapter 5 for more information on the role of your state's department of business and economic development.

USEFUL RESOURCES

Develop and Market Your Creative Ideas by Dale A. Davis. From patenting your invention to constructing a prototype, this step-by-step manual guides today's inventors through all the stages of new product development. Provides valuable information on financing, distribution test marketing, and finding licenses. The easy-to-read book also includes many resources for prototypes, trade shows, funding, and more.

The Business Environmental Handbook by Martin Westerman. This all-in-one resource manual gives small business owners simple techniques for recycling, precycling, and conservation. Shows business owners how they can save money and help preserve resources — while creating a positive public relations image with their customers. Takes the mystery out of some of the more complex environmental issues facing businesses today.

START-UP DETAILS CHECKLIST

- ❑ Contact the Maryland State Department of Assessments and Taxation to determine whether you need to register your business name as a trade name.
- ❑ Register any trademark, trade name, or servicemark you feel is necessary with the Maryland Secretary of State.
- ❑ Contact the Dingman Center for Entrepreneurship to find out if it can help you register your business or it can send you a start-up kit.
- ❑ Contact the Maryland State Licensing Bureau to find out whether your business or profession is subject to any special state licensing requirements.
- ❑ Find out whether your business will be required to obtain a city sales or local business/occupation license.
- ❑ Make sure your operations are consistent with current zoning and environmental regulations.
- ❑ Get a local certification of occupancy, if applicable.
- ❑ Obtain a federal employer identification number (EIN) by completing *Form SS-4*.

- ❑ Contact the Maryland Comptroller of the Treasury for information on how and when to pay your state estimated taxes, and contact the IRS for federal estimated tax information.
- ❑ If you will operate as a corporation, determine your corporate income tax obligations.
- ❑ Register with the Maryland Comptroller of the treasury to pay the state sales and use tax, admissions and amusement tax, alcohol tax, income tax withholding, motor fuel tax, use tax, tobacco tax, and unemployment insurance tax by using *Combined Registration, Form COT/ST-705* and determine how and when you will pay the tax to the state.
- ❑ Obtain a seller's permit and display it at your place of business.
- ❑ Find out your property tax (city and county) obligations and make sure you project these figures into your monthly cash flow statements.

CHAPTER 4

Your Duties as an Employer

Minimum wage. Affirmative action. ADA. Immigration. FUTA. FICA. OSHA. No, you won't have to completely learn a new language; but, you will need to add more than a few dozen acronyms, buzzwords, and phrases to your vocabulary. Welcome to the world of employment!

Your duties as an entrepreneur will seem like a walk in the park compared to your responsibilities as an employer. In fact, your ability to conquer the multi-faceted job of employer can cause your business to sink or stay afloat in both lean and profitable times. Your best course of action is to thoroughly understand and apply the numerous requirements of being an employer in Maryland. You will be responsible for complying with federal and state laws that govern fair employment, anti-discrimination, withholding taxes, workers' compensation, and safety in the workplace. Some of the responsibilities that lie ahead include:

- The minimum amount you will pay your employees, the amount you will pay if they work in excess of a certain timeframe, and what you will pay to minors;
- How you will report these wages and, in so doing, which taxes you will withhold;
- The anti-discriminatory manner in which to hire, promote, and retain your employees;

- Your obligations to grant various types of employee leave requests and how to accommodate individuals with disabilities;
- How to properly hire and use independent contractors for your business; and
- The safety and health programs that you must implement to comply with the multitude of regulations.

Everything you need to understand what being an employer is all about is contained in this chapter. And, to help you further, you are given a checklist at the end of the chapter to help you remember your duties.

FAIR EMPLOYMENT PRACTICES

One of the first things you must do as an employer in Maryland — and that means before you hire employees — is to understand both the federal and state laws that govern fair employment practices. Much of these fair practices centers around the laws that cover payment of wages and working conditions, including number of hours worked.

A good place to start is understanding the beginning of what is today called fair employment practices. Drastic changes to employment standards came about in 1938 as a result of the Great Depression. Also known as the Fair Labor Standards Act (FLSA), this federal law requires overtime for hours worked in excess of 40 hours in a week and sets minimum wages. In addition, the law includes child labor and recordkeeping provisions.

In August 1996, the Fair Labor Standards Act was amended to provide a two-step increase in the minimum wage and a subminimum rate for youth during their first 90 days of employment. The amendments also:

- Change certain provisions of the FLSA with respect to the tip credit that can be claimed by employers of "tipped employees;"
- Provide an exemption for certain computer professionals; and

- Redefine home-to-work travel time in employer-provided vehicles.

Every employer of employees subject to the Fair Labor Standards Act's wage-hour provisions must post, and keep posted, a notice explaining the act in a conspicuous place in all of their establishments to permit employees to easily read it. The content of the notice is prescribed by the wage and hour division of the U.S. Department of Labor. An approved copy of the minimum wage poster is available for informational purposes or for employers to use as posters via the Internet. For more information, contact *http://www.dol.gov.*

MINIMUM WAGE

The federal government has a minimum wage law. On September 1, 1997, the federal minimum wage increased from $4.75 per hour to $5.15 per hour, pursuant to the Minimum Wage Increase Act of 1996.

Maryland has a state minimum wage law that requires all qualified employers to pay at least $5.15 per hour. This rate is the same as the federal minimum wage law. Administrative and professional employees are excluded from minimum wage requirements. Further, Baltimore City has its own wage hour law. You must follow the federal, state, or city law, depending upon which law provides the best result for your employee.

Generally, the state minimum wage law relates to employees who work in companies that are exempt from the federal minimum wage law, or those that primarily involve intrastate commerce. To find out if your business can be categorized as involving interstate or intrastate commerce, contact the Department of Labor, Licensing, and Regulation to be certain which minimum wage amount applies to your business.

OVERTIME PAY

Be aware that in addition to minimum wage, there are federal and state laws that govern overtime pay. If you pay your employees hourly, you are probably required to pay overtime. However, executive, administrative, and professional employees who are paid on a salaried basis are not covered by the FLSA. To determine if your employees fall within one of these categories, consider the following:

- Executive means your employee spends a majority of time in management activities, exercises some discretion and independent judgment, and supervises at least two full-time employees.
- Administrative means your employee exercises some discretion and independent judgment in performing nonclerical office work directly related to management policies or business operations.
- Professional means your employee exercises discretion and independent judgment in a position requiring knowledge of an advanced type in a field of science or learning, or the employee works in a position requiring invention, imagination, or talent in a recognized field of artistic endeavor.

Generally, you should compute pay on a weekly basis to determine if overtime pay is payable to an employee. An employee may work more than eight hours in a day without earning overtime pay. However, if an employee works in excess of 40 hours in a week, the additional hours must be paid at one and one-half times that employee's normal rate. Even if you reduce an employee's hours in the previous or following week so as to average 40 hours over two or more weeks, you must pay overtime pay for the week when more than 40 hours of work was conducted.

There are different requirements for exempt and nonexempt employees. You do not have to pay overtime for exempt employees, but you should be aware of the definition of an exempt employee. The above requirements apply to nonexempt employees.

Retain payroll records in the event someone claims that overtime pay was not paid.

Maryland has an overtime pay law in addition to the federal law. The state law requires you to pay your non-salaried employees at a rate of one and one-half times their regular rate for all hours worked in excess of 40 hours per week. Employees of bowling alleys and residential institutions other than hospitals, who are engaged in the care of the sick, mentally ill, or aged, are paid at an overtime rate after working in excess of 48 hours per week. Administrative and professional employees, as well as employees of recreational establishments, hotels, and motels, are exempt from overtime requirements.

EQUAL PAY

A part of the Fair Labor Standards Act, the Equal Pay Act requires equal pay to men and women doing substantially the same work with similar skill levels, responsibilities, and effort under similar working conditions. It applies to all local, state, and federal agencies and to any business engaged in interstate commerce. It is regulated by the wage and hour division of the U.S. Department of Labor. If you don't comply with equal pay statutes, you may receive a claim based on wage or sex discrimination. If you are found liable, you may be forced to pay back wages or fines up to $10,000 and may possibly face imprisonment.

EMPLOYMENT OF MINORS

The federal government as well as Maryland regulate the employment of children. These laws usually define the type of work done, the maximum number of hours and days worked and other conditions that may affect a minor's ability to complete his or her education. If you plan to employ anyone under the age of 18, be sure to contact the Division of Labor and Industry of the Maryland Department of Labor, Licensing, and Regulation for the rules and exceptions that apply to your Maryland business. The type of work a minor will perform is a major determinant in whether or not you can employ that individual. There are some exemptions for work such as delivering newspapers.

Children between ages 14 and 17 may work a certain number of hours in particular types of employment if they obtain work permits. Applications are available at local secondary schools.

Special permits for children under age 14 who work as models, performers, or entertainers are issued through the Division of Labor and Industry. See Appendix C for contact information.

REPORTING WAGES

You are required to provide each employee who worked for your business during the previous year a completed IRS *Form W-2, Annual Wage and Tax Statement.* The *W-2* is the form that the employee files with his or her state and federal tax reports to show the amount earned at your business. It also shows the state and federal withholdings. More on withholding taxes is located at the end of this chapter.

All *W-2* forms and a summary form (*W-3*) must be sent to the IRS no later than February 28 of each year. When you apply for your employer identification number (EIN) on *Form SS-4, Application for Employer Identification Number,* you will receive the appropriate documents and instructions on how to properly report yearly wages. (See Chapter 3 for details on applying for an EIN and Appendix A for a copy of the form.) Strict regulations for sending *W-2*s to your employees exist, so be sure to read and understand the information provided by the IRS.

ANTI-DISCRIMINATION LAWS

The last century brought much change to the ways employers can treat their employees and prospective employees. Legislation that prevents discriminatory practices now pervades the day-to-day operations of U.S. businesses — touching the practices of both big and small businesses. It is critical that you know the various anti-discrimination laws that affect your business, which may include one or more of the following:

- The Civil Rights Act of 1964
- The Civil Rights Act of 1991
- Affirmative Action
- Rehabilitation Act
- Age Discrimination in Employment Act
- The Americans with Disabilities Act
- The Immigration and Reform Act of 1986
- The Family and Medical Leave Act of 1993
- The Uniformed Services Employment and Re-employment Rights Act of 1994
- The National Labor Relations Act of 1935

Don't let the lengthy and official titles scare you. Compliance with all of these laws is simple to understand and even simpler to accomplish.

THE CIVIL RIGHTS ACT OF 1964

The Civil Rights Act of 1964 (CRA) is the principal federal legislation governing employment discrimination. The CRA protects individuals attempting to exercise equal employment opportunity rights from discriminatory practices. Title VII of the CRA prohibits employers from discriminating against employees and job applicants based on race, religion, sex, color, or national origin. In addition, it prohibits discrimination in recruiting, hiring, job advertising, testing, pre-hire investigations, pay and compensation, benefits plans, promotion, seniority, and retirement.

The CRA is regulated by the Equal Employment Opportunity Commission (EEOC). The act applies to:

- Public and private employers with 15 or more employees,
- Public and private employment agencies, and
- Hiring halls or labor unions with 15 or more members.

Employers that fail to comply with the CRA face severe penalties including court-decreed affirmative action programs and court-ordered back pay to the victim.

Sexual harassment is prohibited under Title VII of the Civil Rights Act of 1964. Unwelcome sexual advances, requests for sexual favors, or verbal or physical conduct of a sexual nature are all forms of sexual harassment. Specifically, these behaviors cannot be presented as a condition of employment or as the basis for employment decisions, nor can they create an environment that is hostile, intimidating, or offensive. To learn more about one of the most talked about issues confronting today's employers, read *Draw the Line: A Sexual-Harassment-Free Workplace* by Frances M. Lynch. For more information on this helpful handbook, see the Useful Resources section at the end of this chapter.

THE CIVIL RIGHTS ACT OF 1991

The Civil Rights Act of 1991 extends punitive actions and jury trials to victims of employment discrimination based on the employee's sex, religion, disability, and race. Under previous legislation (the CRA of 1964), employees could only seek back pay. The new act is regulated by the EEOC and applies to all businesses with 15 or more employees. Punitive damage awards are limited to $50,000 for businesses with 100 or fewer employees; $100,000 for businesses with 101 to 500 employees; and $300,000 for businesses with more than 500 employees.

AFFIRMATIVE ACTION

The concept of affirmative action was born when, in 1965, President Lyndon B. Johnson signed an executive order that placed strict requirements on companies that provided goods or services to the federal government. This legislation made all employers practice affirmative action by actively recruiting and promoting qualified veterans, minorities, women, and individuals with disabilities. The law requires these companies to achieve and maintain an equitable distribution of each group within their workplaces.

Affirmative action is regulated by the Office of Federal Contract Compliance Programs (OFCCP) and the Civil Service Commission. It applies to companies with federal contracts of $10,000 or more per year as well as all federal agencies and the U.S. Postal Service. Companies with more than $50,000 per year in federal contracts must additionally file a written affirmative action plan with the OFCCP. Failure to comply with these requirements could result in cancellation of the company's federal contract(s).

REHABILITATION ACT

Similar to the President Johnson's executive order requiring affirmative action, this act requires firms providing goods and services to the federal government to hire and promote qualified individuals with disabilities. This act is regulated by the OFCCP and the Civil Service Commission and applies to companies with more than $2,500 per year in federal contracts. Failure to comply with these requirements could result in cancellation of your company's federal contract(s).

AGE DISCRIMINATION IN EMPLOYMENT ACT

This act prohibits employers from age discrimination when hiring, retaining, and promoting employees who are 40 years of age or older. It encourages the hiring of older persons based on ability rather than age and it provides a basis for resolving age-related employment problems. The Age Discrimination in Employment Act is regulated by the EEOC and applies to all:

- Government employers,
- Private employers of 20 or more persons, and
- Employment agencies or unions with 25 or more members.

Employers who don't comply may face court-ordered affirmative action programs, court-ordered back pay, fines of up to $10,000, and possible imprisonment.

AMERICANS WITH DISABILITIES ACT (ADA)

The Americans with Disabilities Act (ADA) prohibits discrimination against qualified employees and job applicants with disabilities regarding job application procedures, hiring, firing, advancement, compensation, job training, discharge, retirement, and other benefits or terms of employment. The ADA is enforced by the Equal Employment Opportunity Commission and applies to all employers with 15 or more employees during 20 weeks of any calendar year. Penalties for noncompliance can include administrative enforcement, back pay, and injunctive relief.

The ADA is a very complex act and can be costly if you don't understand it. Unfortunately, not even attorneys can provide definitive information about the act. It was written to help disabled workers find employment, but has been broadened to cover many physical and mental problems of potential employees. Some restrictions are:

- Employers must make reasonable accommodation for modifying a position to employ a disabled person. The term "reasonable accommodation" has not been well defined and is the source of much confusion and potential employer liability.
- Employers may not ask job applicants about the existence, nature, or severity of a disability.
- The act does not apply to employees or potential employees with temporary disabilities.

- The act protects persons with AIDS and HIV from discrimination.
- It provides limited protection for recovering drug addicts and alcoholics.

There are also tax benefits for making changes in your company to accommodate the disabled. To find out how to receive tax breaks for accommodating employees with disabilities, contact the IRS. To learn more about your responsibilities relative to the ADA, contact the Equal Employment Opportunity Commission. See Appendix B for contact information for these two agencies.

IMMIGRATION POLICY

The Immigration Reform and Control Act of 1986 (IRCA) is legislation designed to prevent illegal immigrants from easily finding employment in the United States. The law protects your right to hire legal immigrants and prohibits the hiring of illegal immigrants. You are subject to fines up to $20,000 for each illegal alien that you hire.

To comply with the law you should request identification from everyone you hire and have each employee complete a *Form I-9, Employment Eligibility Verification* prior to hiring. *Form I-9* was developed to help you verify an employee's right to work in the United States. A copy of this form is in Appendix A. You may photocopy this form or buy it from a supplier of business forms.

Although you may not refuse to hire anyone because you think the person may be an illegal alien, you must obtain identification that is specified on *Form I-9*. Overall, as an employer you must:

- Have new employees fill out Part I of *Form I-9* within three days of being hired;
- Have new employees present documents that prove eligibility to work in the United States;
- Complete Part II of *Form I-9;*
- Retain *Form I-9* on file for each employee for at least three years, or for at least one year after the employee is terminated, whichever is longer;

- Present *Form I-9* upon request to an officer of the U.S. Immigration and Naturalization Service (INS) or the U.S. Department of Labor (DOL). You will get at least three days notice before being required to do so; and

- Employers can use *Form I-766* to verify employment as of January 1977. This form is used by aliens who are approved by the INS to work in the United States.

Detailed instructions are printed on *Form I-9*. For further information refer to the 17-page booklet entitled *Handbook for Employers: Instructions for Completing Form I-9,* which is available from the INS. Use Appendix B to find out contact information for the INS employer relations officer closest to you.

FAMILY LEAVE

The U.S. Department of Labor's Employment Standards Administration, Wage and Hour Division, administers and enforces the Family and Medical Leave Act (FMLA) for all private, state, and local government employees, and some federal employees. The FMLA became effective on August 5, 1993, for most employers.

The act permits employees to take up to twelve weeks of unpaid leave each year:

- For the birth of a son or daughter, and to care for the newborn child;

- For the placement with the employee of a child for adoption or foster care, and to care for the newly placed child;

- To care for an immediate family member (spouse, child, or parent, but not a parent "in-law") with a serious health condition; or

- When the employee is unable to work because of a serious health condition.

As an employer you must guarantee that your employee can return to the same job or a comparable job and you must continue health care coverage, if provided, during the leave period.

This law is regulated by the EEOC and applies to employers with 50 or more employees within a 75-mile radius. The law does not apply to employees with less than one year on the job or to employees who have not worked at least 1,250 hours or at least 25 hours per week in the past year. Workers who are on family leave are not eligible for unemployment benefits or other government compensation.

The Family and Medical Leave Act can be another source of problems for the unwary employer. Be sure you understand all the provisions of the act before you disallow a request by an employee who wants to take advantage of the provisions of the act.

Maryland does not have a family leave act independent of the federal law. Contact the U.S. Department of Labor, Wage and Hour Division, for more information. Refer to Appendix B for the division's address and phone number.

All covered employers are required to display and keep displayed a poster prepared by the U.S. Department of Labor that summarizes the major provisions of The Family and Medical Leave Act (FMLA) and tells employees how to file a complaint. The poster must be displayed in a conspicuous place where employees and applicants for employment can see it. A poster must be displayed at all locations even if there are no eligible employees. You can download a copy of this poster via the Internet. For more information, log on to *www.dol.gov.*

MILITARY LEAVE

The Uniformed Services Employment and Re-employment Rights Act of 1994 requires that military leave must be granted for up to five years. Thus, as an employer you must rehire an employee if that person was inducted into or voluntarily enlisted in the armed forces of the United States. The law also protects reservists who are called to active duty.

The law also grants insurance benefits if your company provides company insurance. Further, it applies to voluntary as well as involuntary military service — in peacetime as well as wartime. However, it does not apply to a state activation of the National Guard for disaster relief or riots. The protection for such duty must be provided by the laws of the state involved.

If you have questions regarding your rights and responsibilities regarding military leave, you can obtain additional information from a volunteer organization called Employer Support of the Guard and Reserve. This organization also provides assistance to employers on a local basis if problems develop between a guardsman or reservist and the employer. See Appendix B for contact information.

UNION ORGANIZATION

The National Labor Relations Act of 1935, also known as the Wagner Act, established a national policy that encourages collective bargaining and guarantees certain employee rights. This legislation was amended by the Labor Management Relations (Taft-Hartley) Act of 1947 and the Labor Management Reporting and Disclosure (Landrum-Griffin) Act of 1959. Together these laws establish a balance between management and union power to protect public interest and provide regulations for internal union affairs.

These laws apply to all private employers and unions and are governed by the National Labor Relations Board (NLRB). The NLRB has the power to investigate, dismiss charges, hold hearings, issue cease and desist orders, or pursue cases via the Circuit Court of Appeals or the U.S. Supreme Court.

RIGHT-TO-WORK

Many states have right-to-work laws that prohibit employers from denying employment to individuals who have refused to join a union. These laws also make it illegal for an employer to force mandatory payment of union dues by nonunion workers so as to keep their jobs. If your business will not need a unionized workforce, you may want to seek to do business in a state that has a right-to-work law.

Maryland does not have a right-to-work law and allows companies and unions to enter into “union shop” or “agency shop” agreements. A union shop agreement would allow you to hire employees who don’t belong to a union with the stipulation that those employees join the union within a certain timeframe — usually 30 days. An agency shop agreement would not make it necessary for an employee to join the union but would stipulate that the employee must pay union dues in order to retain employment.

INDEPENDENT CONTRACTORS

Many small business owners use independent contractors to complete certain tasks necessary for their businesses rather than go through the process of hiring additional employees. There are several advantages to contracting an independent worker. First, instead of paying the significant overhead costs for an employee — including taxes, benefits, and insurance — you pay a contractor only for the end result. Second, hiring a contractor involves a much smaller administrative workload. You need only file IRS *Form MISC-1099* as opposed to handling the numerous forms and deductions required for a regular employee.

When using an independent contractor, it is crucial that you don't treat that individual as an employee. Be cautious that the contractor meets the FLSA's definition of contract labor. For instance, if you provide office space or equipment and set specific work hours, the IRS may consider the contractor to be an employee. You must then collect and file taxes for that person.

The IRS uses a 20-factor test to determine whether a worker is an employee or an independent contractor. See below for the 20 factors that help determine independent contractor status. Generally, an employee works for you at your place of business. You set working hours and conditions and provide the equipment, materials, and resources to get the job done. Contractors set their own hours, determine their own work practices, perform their services away from your place of business, have other clients besides you, and have their own business name, cards, and stationery. Frequently, a contractor is a licensed professional.

20-FACTOR TEST

For the following questions, a "yes" answer usually means the worker is an employee.

- ❑ Does the principal provide instructions to the worker about when, where, and how he or she is to perform the work?
- ❑ Does the principal provide training to the worker?
- ❑ Are the services provided by the worker integrated into the principal's business operations?
- ❑ Must the services be rendered personally by the worker?

- ❑ Does the principal hire, supervise and pay assistants to the worker?
- ❑ Is there a continuing relationship between the principal and the worker?
- ❑ Does the principal set the work hours and schedule?
- ❑ Does the worker devote substantially full time to the business of the principal?
- ❑ Is the work performed on the principal's premises?
- ❑ Is the worker required to perform the services in an order or sequence set by the principal?
- ❑ Is the worker required to submit oral or written reports to the principal?
- ❑ Is the worker paid by the hour, week, or month?
- ❑ Does the principal have the right to discharge the worker at will?
- ❑ Can the worker terminate his or her relationship with the principal any time he or she wishes without incurring liability to the principal?
- ❑ Does the principal pay the business or traveling expenses of the worker?

For the following questions, a "yes" answer generally means the worker is an independent contractor.

- ❑ Does the worker furnish significant tools, materials and equipment?
- ❑ Does the worker have a significant investment in facilities?
- ❑ Can the worker realize a profit or loss as a result of his or her services?
- ❑ Does the worker provide services for more than one firm at a time?
- ❑ Does the worker make his or her services available to the general public?

The penalties for incorrectly labeling a worker as a contractor can be expensive. You are liable for the employer taxes that you failed to withhold as well as a portion of the employee's taxes that were not paid. You must file *MISC-1099* for each contractor that you paid in excess of $600 during the year. Failure to file could double your percentage of the employee taxes you may owe should the IRS determine that your contractor was actually an employee. In like manner, contractors will report the income on *Schedule C* or *Schedule F* along with their personal income tax returns.

A written agreement with any independent contractor you will use will help to define your relationship with the contractor for the IRS. The agreement should define the work being accomplished and clearly state that the contractor is responsible for paying self-employment taxes. Further, the agreement can:

- Determine start and stop dates but not working hours;
- Make payment dependent on results, not the amount of time spent to get them; and
- Make the working relationship clear and base it strictly on a given result.

For more information about employer-employee relationships, refer to IRS *Circular E, Employer's Tax Guide.* Also, Congress is considering a revision to the 20-factor test. Keep yourself informed of this important issue via the Internet or industry associations. For more information, log on at *http://www.psi-research.com.*

WITHHOLDING TAXES

When your business has employees, you must withhold federal income tax from their wages. In addition, you must contribute to Social Security, Medicare, and unemployment funds.

FEDERAL UNEMPLOYMENT TAXES (FUTA)

Unemployment benefits are paid from state unemployment taxes and unemployment insurance. The cost of administering the unemployment program is paid from Federal Unemployment Tax Act (FUTA) funds.

The federal unemployment tax is your company's contribution to the unemployment insurance fund. You are required to pay 6.2% on the first $7,000 of each employee's annual pay. The actual rate you pay is normally 0.8% because you receive a 5.4% credit for the state unemployment taxes you pay.

You will be required to pay FUTA if you employ one or more persons (not farm or household workers) for at least one day in each of 20 calendar weeks (not necessarily consecutive) and if you pay wages of $1,500 or more during the year. You may be required to pay federal unemployment tax even if you are exempt from paying state taxes. If your FUTA liability is more than $100 in any quarter, you are required to make a federal tax deposit for the amount owing.

FUTA tax is reported annually on *Form 940, Employer's Annual Federal Unemployment Tax Return,* which is due by January 31 of the next calendar year. If you have made timely deposits, however, you have until February 10 to file. In addition, if at the end of any calendar quarter you owe more than $100 FUTA tax for the year, you must make a deposit by the end of the next month.

Some employers can qualify to file a simplified FUTA return. To be eligible to file *Form 940-EZ,* you must:

- Pay unemployment tax to only one state;
- Pay state unemployment taxes by the due date on *Form 940-EZ;* and
- Have wages that are subject to FUTA and are also taxable for state unemployment tax purposes.

To find out more about this simplified filing, get the following publications:

- *Publication #334, Tax Guide for Small Business*
- *Publication #15, Circular E, Employer's Tax Guide*
- *Publication #509, Tax Calendar and Checklist*

The locations and phone numbers of regional IRS offices are listed in Appendix B.

STATE UNEMPLOYMENT TAXES

As an employer in Maryland, you are responsible for paying unemployment tax at the state level if:

- You employ one or more persons in each of 52 weeks during any calendar year; or
- Your payroll totals $8,500 in any calendar quarter.

Although the tax is on your employees' covered wages, you are not allowed to deduct this tax from their wages. The burden of paying the state unemployment tax lies on your shoulders as the employer.

If you operate as a sole proprietor or partner, you won't be required to pay unemployment tax because you will not be considered an actual employee of your business.

To register to pay unemployment tax in Maryland, file *Form COT/ST 705, Combined Registration Application.* Remit your taxes using *Form DEED/OUI 15, Contribution Report.* At the end of each quarter, a listing report, *Form DEED/OUI 16,* will be sent to you by the Maryland Department of Business and Economic Development. You must list each employee's Social Security number, name, and gross wages. A penalty of $35 is charged for each form filed late.

Contact Employer Assistance at the Office of Unemployment Insurance, Maryland Department of Labor, Licensing, and Regulation, to receive the booklet *What You Should Know About Unemployment Insurance in Maryland.* This office also provides posters and notices you must post in your business to inform employees of their unemployment benefits and health care coverage rights. See Appendix C for contact information.

TAX EXPERIENCE RATING

The unemployment tax rate for your business is related to the overall experience your company has had with benefits claims over a certain number of years; hence, the name tax experience rating. For example, if you have had many employees who have claimed benefits, your business will probably have a higher experience rating. On the flip side, if you have had few employees claiming benefits in the past, you will have a lower experience rating.

As a new employer, Maryland will assign your business a standard rate. Your experience with unemployment claims and benefits from the point you start your business or purchase an existing business will dictate whether your rate will increase or decrease. If the seller of the business has an excellent rating, talk to the Maryland

Department of Business and Economic Development to learn how you can take over that rate.

As a precautionary measure, if you are buying an existing business make sure the seller is current and has filed all necessary unemployment taxes and reports. If you don't, you may be held responsible for unpaid taxes. You are encouraged to get an unemployment tax release from the department of business and economic development. Discuss this important aspect of the sale with your attorney. If you do find unemployment taxes owing, make sure this amount is negotiated in the sale price of the business.

SOCIAL SECURITY AND MEDICARE (FICA)

Passed into law by Congress in 1935 as the Federal Insurance Contribution Act (FICA), all employers are required to pay Social Security taxes to the government to provide for old age, survivor, and disability benefits as well as hospital insurance (Medicare). Payments are made in equal amounts by an employee and his or her employer, with collection responsibilities falling on the employer. The current rate is 7.65% for the employer and each employee up to $65,400 of each employee's annual pay. For more details, refer to IRS *Circular E.*

FEDERAL INCOME TAX WITHHOLDING

You must withhold federal income tax from the wages of any employee who meets threshold wage levels. This requirement applies to all employees who do not claim an exemption from withholding.

The amount withheld is recomputed each pay period. Federal income tax is based on gross wages before deductions for FICA, retirement funds, or insurance. Most employers base income tax withholding on percentage or wage brackets. Refer to IRS *Publication 15, Employer's Tax Guide* for detailed descriptions of these withholding methods.

STATE INCOME TAX WITHHOLDING

You must also withhold a portion of an employee's wages for the state income tax. Again, this requirement applies to all employees who do not claim an exemption from withholding. You are required to have a withholding identification number, which is obtained from the Maryland Comptroller of the Treasury. Make sure you contact this agency for the appropriate forms and filing procedures.

Maryland income tax withholding is reported on *Form MW 506.* You are required to file quarterly if your tax liability will be less than $400 in any quarter, and monthly if your tax liability will be $400 or more. All *Forms MW 506* submitted for the previous calendar year must be reconciled and reported on *Form 508* yearly by February 28.

WORKERS' COMPENSATION

Before 1911, if an employee was injured on the job that employee was forced to take legal action against the employer to collect compensation. This led to a high risk of lawsuits against employers. But, in 1911, Wisconsin passed the first workers' compensation laws — paving the way for complex yet beneficial state-by-state workers' compensation laws.

Although the general trend is to expand coverage to protect as many workers as possible, each state's mandated coverage is based on the perceived risks of their employees. For instance, manufacturing-based states have more comprehensive coverage whereas agricultural-based states are not as comprehensive. Because of these variations, workers' compensation laws don't cover all occupations in all states.

If you have an employee in your Maryland business, you are required to obtain workers' compensation insurance. This type of insurance pays the benefits for covered employees for job-related illnesses, injuries, and deaths. Benefits include medical expenses, death benefits, lost wages, and vocational rehabilitation. If you fail to carry workers' compensation coverage, you will be vulnerable to paying all of the benefits and possible fines.

Workers' compensation is offered in most states in one of three ways.

- A wholly state owned insurance company — or monopoly state fund — is the only insurance available.
- A wholly state owned insurance company — or state fund — competes with other insurance companies to provide coverage.

- No state owned insurance company offers coverage, only private insurance companies.

Maryland is one of thirteen states that has a state fund that competes with other insurance companies. Thus, you have the option to use either type of insurer, or you may apply to the Maryland Workers' Compensation Commission to be a designated self-insurer.

As an employer in Maryland, your business is not responsible for workers' compensation coverage for:

- Individuals who elect to be exempt from coverage if you are a principal contractor;
- Domestic servants who earn less than $750 in a calendar quarter;
- Individuals engaged in independent farming operations who also perform farmwork for you; or
- Owner-operators of specified Class E vehicles who enter into specified agreements with you.

Also, if you are the owner of a sole proprietor or a partner in a partnership, you are not required by law to obtain coverage for yourself. Keep in mind, you cannot substitute workers' compensation insurance with other types of insurance like general liability and health and accident insurance.

For more information on the workers' compensation requirements for Maryland, contact the Workers' Compensation Commission. For state insurance information, contact the Injured Workers' Insurance Fund. See Appendix C for contact information. Chapter 11 provides more in-depth information about workers' compensation as well as information on how you can reduce your costs. To more fully understand the ins and outs of workers' compensation, obtain a copy of *CompControl: The Secrets of Reducing Workers' Compensation Costs* by Edward J. Priz. To learn more about this book, see the Useful Resources section at the end of this chapter.

SAFETY AND HEALTH REGULATIONS

As part of the U.S. Department of Labor, the Occupational Safety and Health Administration (OSHA) creates regulations and enforcement practices to render the nation's workplaces safe and healthy for employees. Basically, any business engaging in interstate commerce that has one or more employees is responsible for complying with OSHA standards.

A few types of businesses are exempt from OSHA compliance and include:

- Self-employed persons;
- Farms on which only immediate members of the farm employer's family are employed; and
- Working conditions regulated by other federal agencies under other federal statutes.

Since many of the OSHA standards are specific to certain types of industry, equipment, substances, environments, or conditions, it is important to have a clear understanding of OSHA regulations that apply to your business. The administration has established and is continually upgrading legally enforceable standards that fall into four major industry categories — general industry, maritime, construction, and agriculture. To help you better understand the federal OSHA standards that may apply to your business, consider hiring a professional safety consultant or refer to a comprehensive reference on workplace safety programs. Your local OSHA division of the U.S. Department of Labor can provide you with two helpful publications, including:

- *All About OSHA, OSHA 2056*
- *Employer Rights and Responsibilities Following an OSHA Inspection, OSHA 3000*

Check Appendix C to find out how you can contact the OSHA office nearest you.

One requirement that you should be aware of is the need to keep a record of industrial injuries and illnesses. All employers with 11 or more employees are required to maintain specified records of all occupational injuries and illnesses as they occur on *Log and Summary of Occupational Injuries and Illnesses, OSHA 200.* However, this recordkeeping is not required for employers in retail trade, finance, insurance, real estate, and service industries. Further, employers must complete a detailed report for each occupational death, injury, or illness on *Supplementary Record of Injuries and*

Illnesses, OSHA 101. You can request the booklet, *Recordkeeping Requirements for the Occupational Injuries and Illnesses,* from the U.S. Department of Labor. Although you will not be required to send the reports to the government, they should be available should OSHA inspect your business.

Some states have their own occupational safety and health programs and Maryland is one of them. The Maryland Occupational Safety and Health (MOSH) Training and Education Unit of the Maryland Department of Labor, Licensing, and Regulation offers numerous booklets, fact sheets, and posters available to educate employers on state requirements.

Maryland has enacted state laws that differ from federal standards for the following areas:

- Lead exposures in construction;
- Right-to-know;
- Field sanitation; and
- Personnel platforms suspended from cranes, derricks, and hoists in general industry.

Regulations are enforced through unannounced inspections that could result in civil penalties. You may also comply voluntarily by requesting and filling out a state consultation survey.

To learn more about state OSHA rules, contact Maryland Occupational Safety and Health (MOSH) Training and Education Unit of the Maryland Department of Labor, Licensing, and Regulation.

ENVIRONMENTAL REGULATIONS

Environmental protection is one of the fastest growing areas of legislation relating to small business today. If your business handles hazardous materials, uses natural resources, or expels anything to air, water or land, you could be subject to dozens of federal, state, and local laws that will regulate how you do business. You should become familiar with the laws that may affect your business regarding clean air and water.

Just as important, conserving, recycling, reducing waste, and becoming environmentally friendly will save you hundreds to thousands of dollars each year. These "green" policies will establish your reputation with your customers as a socially responsible, environmentally sound businessperson.

The Environmental Protection Agency (EPA) is the federal agency that enforces environmental laws and regulations. Like OSHA, Maryland has a state agency called the Department of Environment that represents the EPA in your state. Through the department's Small Business Assistance Program, you can receive information about its services and publications. See Appendix B for the address and phone number of the EPA regional office that serves Maryland and Appendix C for contact information on the department of environment.

Further, your state ombudsman may help you stay informed about potential problems you may encounter because of the federal or state legislation regarding the environment.

To learn how your business can create a cost-effective, comprehensive environmental plan, get a copy of *The Business Environmental Handbook* by Martin Westerman. For more information, refer to back to the Useful Resources section in Chapter 3.

CHAPTER WRAP-UP

To get a jump-start on your duties as an employer means to understand what lies ahead before you post your first job opening. As an employer in Maryland, you will be subject to numerous state and federal laws that govern employment. Although it probably wasn't part of your original job description, you must function as a personnel manager until your business grows to a size that warrants hiring such an individual. Don't be alarmed — a multitude of Maryland state agencies as well as federal agencies relating to employing individuals exist that will assist your attempts at personnel management.

Your main concerns will center around what is dubbed as fair employment practices. Fair employment means that you will comply with both federal and state laws regarding things like minimum wage, overtime pay, equal pay, employing minors, and wage reporting. In addition to these practices, you will be required to have a basic knowledge of what are known as anti-discrimination laws. The various acts described in this chapter — dealing with affirmative action, ADA, immigration, and family leave, to name a few — just scratch the surface. However, as you get to know these common federal laws, you will gain a bigger picture perspective that will help you better understand the sometimes elusive phrase "personnel management."

Further, as an employer in Maryland, you must withhold federal and state unemployment taxes, Social Security and Medicare (also known as FICA), and federal and state income taxes from the wages you pay to all covered employees. To protect your business and your employees, you must also comply with state workers' compensation requirements.

Of course, as a new business you may not need to hire anyone for awhile. However, if you do need employees to get your business running, it is essential that you understand what it means to be an employer in Maryland. Use this chapter as a quick reference for future employment issues. Also, refer to Chapter 10 for a more detailed discussion of human resources management.

USEFUL RESOURCES

CompControl: The Secrets of Reducing Workers' Compensation Costs by Edward J. Priz. This invaluable guide will help you get a handle on your state's workers' compensation requirements. Written in easy-to-understand language, this book provides information on payroll audits, rating bureaus, and loss-sensitive points. By using case studies drawn from real businesses of all sizes, the author takes the mystery out of dealing with the often confusing world of workers' compensation laws.

Draw the Line: A Sexual-Harassment-Free Workplace by Frances Lynch. Written for managers and business owners, this handy guide tells exactly where to draw the line regarding sexual harassment in your workplace. Gives helpful hints on how to communicate your business' sexual harassment policy and make sure your employees understand and respect the policy.

EMPLOYER DUTIES CHECKLIST

- ❑ Register with the Maryland Comptroller of the Treasury to withhold state and federal income taxes from the compensation paid to your employees and learn the requirements for submitting quarterly reports.
- ❑ Contact the Maryland Comptroller of the Treasury to register to pay state taxes and submit quarterly reports for the unemployment coverage for your employees.
- ❑ File with the Internal Revenue Service (IRS) to pay federal unemployment taxes and submit quarterly reports.
- ❑ Determine your obligations to carry workers' compensation insurance coverage.
- ❑ Review state and federal labor laws to determine the personnel-related policies your business will follow.
- ❑ Check with the Maryland Department of Environment to identify the environmental regulations your business must follow regarding all air, water, and solid waste standards.

CHAPTER 5

Sources of Business Assistance

As you've learned so far, starting a business is hard work. You can make your life easier by getting to know the resources available to you and, more importantly, by learning how to use them effectively in your start-up endeavors. In fact, at the heart of your venture are knowledge and know-how — and these amount to power. If you want the power to smartstart your business, you will seek help from qualified business experts. For today's burgeoning entrepreneur, this help is closer than you think.

Numerous federal, state, and private agencies and organizations are available to assist you. This chapter introduces you to the most important and most helpful organizations. Take the time to familiarize yourself with each resource — you will double your investment in time once you know how and where to get the answers you need to start and grow your business.

FEDERAL RESOURCES

Surprisingly enough, your biggest source of help comes from the federal government. Big Brother is definitely watching out for small business and wants to see small businesses grow and prosper into the twenty-first century. For every federal regulation and legal requirement that the federal government places on America's small businesses, there exists at least one federal agency that will go the extra mile to help those same business owners get their businesses started on the right track. Thus, your first points of contact should be one or more of the following agencies:

- The U.S. Small Business Administration (SBA), which includes the Service Corps of Retired Executives (SCORE), business information centers (BICs), and small business incubators;

- The U.S. Department of Commerce, which includes numerous bureaus and administrations like the Census Bureau and the Economic Development Administration;

- The Internal Revenue Service (IRS); and

- The Equal Employment Opportunity Commission (EEOC).

You will find that many of these agencies offer state-specific business assistance and have their own state-level offices to better serve your business' needs.

U.S. SMALL BUSINESS ADMINISTRATION

Formed in 1953, the U.S. Small Business Administration (SBA) provides assistance to entrepreneurs who are starting and expanding their own businesses. Many of the SBA programs and services are free-of-charge and include:

- Financial assistance through numerous loan and loan guarantee programs;

- Assistance with government procurement of small business products and services;

- Minority business assistance programs;

- Counseling on a variety of topics from marketing your products and services to managing your business to developing a business plan; and

- Educating entrepreneurs about international trade, technology, and research.

The SBA is easy to reach and is praised by numerous business owners as being one of the easiest government agencies to deal with. There is an SBA district office and a regional office in Maryland to serve your needs. (See Appendix B.) Also, you can quickly access a storage house of information by using one of the SBA's telephone hotline or computer online services.

A computerized telephone message system is available from SBA Answer Desk and can be accessed 24 hours a day, seven days a week. This toll-free number will put you in touch with operators who will answer your start-up questions and give you guidance on how to get additional assistance. Operators are available Monday through Friday from 9:00 A.M. to 5:00 P.M. (eastern standard time).

Another way to get help from the SBA is by using *SBA OnLine* — an electronic bulletin board that provides the most current and accurate information on starting and running a business in Maryland. You may also request a free copy of *The Resource Directory for Small Business Management*, which lists a number of publications and videotapes at an inexpensive cost. To access *SBA OnLine* you must have a modem and computer.

The SBA has an Internet home page that contains detailed information on its services and other business services and provides a direct link to *SBA OnLine*. For more information, log on at *http://www.sba.gov*. If you prefer to contact the SBA Answer Desk or *SBA OnLine* direct, use the phone numbers listed in Appendix B.

In addition to offering a myriad of services for the new or expanding business owner, the U.S. SBA provides business counseling and training through other service programs as described below.

Service Corps of Retired Executives (SCORE)

Sponsored by the SBA, the Service Corps of Retired Executives (SCORE) has 12,400 volunteers in nearly 400 offices throughout the nation. These retired businesspeople offer expert advice based on their many years of firsthand experience in virtually every phase of starting and operating a business. To set up a free appointment with a SCORE counselor nearest you, call your SBA field office or contact your nearest small business development center (SBDC). SBDCs are covered in more detail later in this chapter.

Business Information Centers

Business Information Centers (BICs) are joint ventures between the U.S. SBA and private partners. They provide the latest in high-tech hardware, software, and telecommunications to help start-up and expanding businesses. BICs also offer a wide array of counseling services and training opportunities.

Whether you are considering starting a new business or need assistance in expanding or improving an existing business, BICs can help. BICs provide the tools and advice necessary to evaluate and improve your marketing and sales techniques, price your products, or investigate the possibilities of exporting. The research tools and invaluable advice can help your new business get off the ground or help your existing business grow.

BICs combine the latest in state-of-the-art personal computers, graphic work stations, CD-ROM technology, and interactive videos through on-site counseling and helpful training courses. Using a BIC's resources can result in a well-crafted, comprehensive business plan, which can be used to guide you through the first steps of business ownership or through product or service expansion.

Maryland has a business information center (BIC) that provides free assistance and advice, on-site counseling, and self-help information. To find the address and phone number of the BIC in Maryland, refer to Appendix B.

Small Business Incubators

Although relatively new, small business incubators have become a breeding ground for a number of start-up businesses throughout the United States. Business incubation is a dynamic process of business enterprise development. Incubators nurture young firms, helping them to survive and grow during the start-up period when they are most vulnerable. These incubators sometimes offer a lower than market rate rent and shared housing with a number of other new enterprises in one facility. These businesses can then share conference rooms, secretarial help, accounting expertise, research personnel, and on-site financial management counseling. Then, once a business is ready stand on its own and wants to relocate, the incubator program will assist the business in finding a new location.

To qualify for participation in a small business incubator program, your business will have to go through a selection process. As part of this process, qualified individuals will review your business plan to determine if your business will fit into their program. To find out if there is an SBA-sponsored incubator program in Maryland, contact your local SBA office.

The National Business Incubation Association (NBIA) provides members with the resources needed to develop and manage successful business incubators. Whether you are exploring the concept of a business incubator for your community or already have an established incubation program, NBIA services are designed to keep you apprised of industry best practices and save you time and money.

With approximately 800 members worldwide, NBIA is the largest membership organization of incubator developers and managers. Servicing technology, industrial, mixed-use, economic empowerment, and industry-specific incubators since 1985, the association provides members with critical tools and promotes awareness of incubators' value for economic development. The NBIA's overall objectives include:

- Providing information, research, and networking resources to help members develop and manage successful incubation programs;
- Sponsoring annual conferences and training programs;
- Building awareness of business incubation as a valuable business development tool; and
- Informing and educating leaders, potential supporters, and stakeholders of the significant benefits of incubation.

To find out about private sector incubators, contact NBIA. See Appendix B for address and phone information for this organization.

Minority Enterprise Development

The SBA offers two main programs through its Minority Enterprise Development (MED) that seek to foster business ownership for those that are socially and economically disadvantaged.

8(a) Small Disadvantaged Business Development. Qualified minority small business owners can take advantage of the 8(a) program which offers business development assistance through federal procurement opportunities.

7(j) Management and Technical Assistance. The 7(j) program provides management and technical training in four main areas:

accounting, marketing, proposal/bid preparation, and industry-specific technical assistance.

U.S. DEPARTMENT OF COMMERCE

The U.S. Department of Commerce has developed a number of programs that assist small business owners. These programs are headed up by several different bureaus and administrations.

- Bureau of Economic Analysis, which reports on the state of the U.S. economy and provides technical information that helps calculate the gross national product figures.
- Consumer Affairs, which develops cooperative projects with companies, trade and professional associations, consumer organizations, and federal, state and local agencies to help businesses improve customer relations.
- Census Bureau, which produces statistical information in the forms of catalogs, guides, and directories that cover things like U.S. population and housing, agriculture, state and local expenditures, transportation, and industries.
- Economic Development Administration, which helps generate new jobs, protect existing jobs, and stimulates commercial and industrial growth in economically distressed areas.
- International Trade Administration, which helps American exporters find assistance in locating, gaining access to, and developing foreign markets.
- Minority and Business Development Agency, which helps minority business owners in their attempts to overcome the social and economic disadvantages that may have limited past participation in business.
- Patent and Trademark Office, which will help protect new products and unusual trade names.

Although the department doesn't have the one-on-one relationship with small business owners that the SBA does, it does provide information that can help your business profit. To learn more about the U.S. Department of Commerce, contact it via phone or mail at the address listed in Appendix B.

U.S. CHAMBER OF COMMERCE

The U.S. Chamber of Commerce was established in 1912 at the suggestion of President William Howard Taft to provide a strong link between business and government. Since then it has played a vital role in helping businesses, especially small businesses, succeed and prosper. In addition, the chamber represents businesses on critical legislative and regulatory issues.

One of the primary roles of the U.S. Chamber of Commerce is to help the public understand the danger that results from excessive government intervention in the economy. Costly and far-reaching federal programs and mandates on businesses raise the costs of doing business and weaken the U.S. competitive position in the global marketplace. To serve the needs of this small business sector, the U.S. Chamber of Commerce has developed programs that are both affordable and effective. As a small business member of the U.S. Chamber of Commerce, you can:

- Obtain access to a wide-range of affordable and leading-edge training tools and products developed exclusively for small and growing businesses through the chamber's Small Business Institute;

- Receive *Nation's Business,* the organization's own magazine that serves as a vital resource to the owners and top management of small businesses by providing practical, how-to information about growing and running a business;

- Access information on small business legislative issues and SBA loans through the chamber's Small Business Center;

- Attend leading technology expositions, conferences, and seminars for small business offered by the chamber's Small Business Institute; and

- Gain your competitive edge in the morning with "First Business," a daily, live, half hour business-news television program that focuses on the interests of small businesspeople.

More than 96 percent of the U.S. Chamber's members are small businesses with 100 or fewer employees. Seventy-one percent of this total have ten or fewer employees. Further, virtually all of the nation's largest companies are also active members of the U.S. Chamber of Commerce. To learn how to join the U.S. Chamber of Commerce, use Appendix B.

Local Chambers of Commerce

If you want to learn more about the region or community where you plan to locate your business, then turn to your local chamber of commerce for assistance. Your local chamber of commerce will give you information about general business conditions, available space and rentals, and local business organizations and associations. Usually chambers of commerce are a good place for referrals. To locate the chamber nearest you, look in the White Pages of your telephone directory.

The Maryland Chamber of Commerce provides services, insurance programs, and publications to members at a discount. For more information, see the listing in Appendix C.

INTERNAL REVENUE SERVICE (IRS)

The thought of a visit from Uncle Sam may frighten you — and it should. But there is good news! The Internal Revenue Service (IRS) has developed several programs to help you stay informed and one step ahead of the taxes for which you are responsible as a small business owner. Through its Tele-Tax program, the IRS offers quick and easy access to tax help and forms on about 150 tax topics. In fact, you can order forms, instructions, and publications toll-free by phone between 7:30 A.M. and 5:30 P.M., Monday through Friday.

If you prefer, use your personal computer and modem to get the forms and information you need. The IRS's Internet Web site not only contains forms, instructions, and publications, but educational materials, IRS press releases and fact sheets, and answers to frequently asked questions.

The IRS has a program called the Small Business Tax Education Program (STEP). STEP consists of workshops, seminars, and other courses for small business owners. These educational seminars are held at local community educational facilities. To facilitate awareness of this program as well as offer general help to small business owners, each state has its own taxpayer education coordinator. For more information on IRS assistance for your business, refer to Appendix B.

EQUAL EMPLOYMENT OPPORTUNITY COMMISSION (EEOC)

As discussed in Chapter 4, a multitude of duties awaits employers in Maryland. If you will employ individuals in your business you will need to understand the laws that cover civil rights, age discrimination, and equal pay. These laws were created and are enforced by the Equal Employment Opportunity Commission (EEOC). Created by Congress, the EEOC enforces Title VII of the Civil Rights Act of 1964. In addition, since 1979 the EEOC has also enforced the Age Discrimination in Employment Act of 1967, the Equal Pay Act of 1963, and Section 501 of the Rehabilitation Act of 1973. In 1992, the EEOC began enforcing the Americans with Disabilities Act — more commonly known as ADA.

Every employer in the United States, including all employment agencies, labor organizations, and joint labor-management committees must post and keep posted in a conspicuous place upon their premises, a notice that describes the applicable provisions of Title VII and the ADA. Such notice must be posted in a prominent and accessible place where notices to employees, applicants, and members are customarily maintained. Failure to comply may result in fines to your business. To obtain a poster or to learn how the laws mentioned above affect your business, consider obtaining a copy of *Laws Enforced by the U.S. Equal Employment Opportunity Commission.* To order this free publication and poster, use the toll-free phone number listed in Appendix B.

STATE RESOURCES

In order to attract new business and keep existing business, most states have adopted a "small business-friendly" philosophy. In line with this philosophy, you will find numerous state agency programs and services — most of them free-of-charge — simply for the asking. Take a moment get to know what Maryland agencies are available to you and how you can best utilize their services.

MARYLAND SECRETARY OF STATE

The Maryland Secretary of State is responsible for registering all trademarks and servicemarks within the state. The secretary of state will issue your business a certificate of registration, if you meet the statutory requirements. You are entitled to a hearing before the secretary of state or the secretary's designee before a decision is made to deny your application.

DINGMAN CENTER FOR ENTREPRENEURSHIP

The Dingman Center for Entrepreneurship — Maryland's one-stop center — is part of the Maryland Business School at the University of Maryland in College Park. The center offers a variety of services to entrepreneurs, including access to networking opportunities, professional guidance, and identifying potential funding sources. Among the more popular programs is the Baltimore-Washington Venture Group (B-WVG).

This program facilitates contacts that may lead to financing, joint ventures, consulting relationships, and management team additions. The B-WVG has also formed a partnership with the Private Investors Network (PIN), an organization comprised of the region's active private equity investors. The partnership maximizes the opportunity for young companies to gain financing.

MARYLAND DEPARTMENT OF BUSINESS AND ECONOMIC DEVELOPMENT

The Maryland Department of Business and Economic Development (DBED) works with regional and local economic development organizations to provide information, services, and publications to support the economic health and growth of communities throughout the state. The department has divisions of finance, marketing, tourism and promotion, and regional development. The department offers a free publication called *Financing Overview for Business.* To obtain a copy, contact the Division of Regional Development (listed in Appendix C). Also, see Appendix D for information on the various loan programs offered through DBED.

MARYLAND COMPTROLLER OF THE TREASURY

The comptroller of the treasury collects sales and use, corporate and personal income, state unemployment, admissions and amusement, and other taxes. The comptroller also handles the taxation of tobacco, alcohol, and motor fuels. The office provides free assistance and filing tips as well. See the listing in Appendix C.

MARYLAND DEPARTMENT OF LABOR, LICENSING, AND REGULATION

The Labor and Industry Division of the Maryland Department of Labor, Licensing, and Regulation enacts laws to prevent accidents and incidents that could result in on-the-job fatalities and injuries. The division also assists in regulating industries and employers in complying with state laws and regulations. The division administers the Maryland Occupational Safety and Health (MOSH) Training and Education Unit and provides information on state wage laws and employment standards.

MARYLAND STATE DEPARTMENT OF ASSESSMENTS AND TAXATION

The state department of assessments and taxation administers and enforces the property assessment and property tax laws of Maryland. The Corporate Charter Division registers sole proprietorships, limited liability partnerships, and limited liability companies, corporations, and business trade names.

MARYLAND DEPARTMENT OF ENVIRONMENT

The department of environment enforces environmental laws and regulations for the state. It provides information on environmental and safety and health issues throughout the state. The Small Business Assistance Program provides regulation and compliance information to businesses.

MARYLAND STATE LICENSING BUREAU

The state licensing bureau provides information and licensing requirements for your business or occupation and instructs you on which agency you will need to contact for licensing.

WORKER'S COMPENSATION COMMISSION

The Worker's Compensation Commission provides employers with state workers' compensation information and requirements and handles questions and claims from employees.

SMALL BUSINESS DEVELOPMENT CENTERS

The small business development center (SBDC) network is a cooperative effort of the U.S. SBA, the state academic community, the private sector, and state and local governments. Over 900 SBDCs are located in colleges and universities throughout the nation. Similar to a SCORE counselor, your local SBDC can offer advice on a variety of start-up issues. Frequently, your local SBDC will sponsor business-oriented seminars. In 1993 alone, SBDCs provided direct counseling to 230,483 businesses and training to 326,289 small business owners and managers. To find the nearest SBDC, contact the lead center listed in Appendix C.

The Maryland SBDC Network is a partnership of the Maryland Business School's Dingman Center for Entrepreneurship and the U.S. Small Business Administration.

PRIVATE SOURCES OF HELP

In addition to the various state and federal resources, you will find a wealth of business information from private organizations and agencies. Keep in mind, the private resources listed here represent some of the most popular and well-established organizations and by no means represent all the private resources available in Maryland. To learn about other private sources of help, do an Internet search or contact your local library for assistance.

STATE BUSINESS PUBLICATIONS

Maryland has a number of trade and business journals that will help you stay current on business activities and issues in Maryland. For a list of these helpful business publications, see Appendix C.

NATIONAL FEDERATION OF INDEPENDENT BUSINESSES (NFIB)

The National Federation of Independent Businesses (NFIB) is the oldest and largest small business advocacy group in the nation. This nonprofit organization is the only business organization with the strength of a combined federal and state lobbying program. Representing approximately 600,000 small and independent business owners, NFIB has offices in every state capital and in Washington, D.C.

You can become a member of NFIB. As a member you will receive:

- A monthly newsletter called *Capitol Coverage* that will keep you current on the issues discussed at each level of government;
- A bimonthly publication called *Independent Business Magazine*, which features articles geared toward the interests of small business owners;
- Copies of state and federal mandate ballots that show you how NFIB's legislative lobbying agenda is established; and
- An annual publication entitled *How Congress Voted* which gives details of the Congressional voting record and how these votes affected and will affect you as a small business owner.

To learn more about NFIB, see Appendix C.

NATIONAL ASSOCIATION FOR THE SELF-EMPLOYED (NASE)

Another helpful membership organization is the National Association for the Self-Employed (NASE). Since 1981, NASE has established one of the largest business associations of its kind. Attributing its success to the "strength in numbers" theory, NASE now has 320,000 members with 3,000 new members joining each week. As a member of NASE, you will receive a variety of benefits, including:

- Free access to knowledgeable small business consultants via ShopTalk 800® — a toll-free hotline where you can get advice on issues that affect your business;
- Free Internet software; and
- A monthly newsletter called *Self-Employed America®*, which gives you valuable information on how small businesses can survive and prosper in today's competitive environment.

NASE offers its members a chance to get involved with small business advocacy issues through its Legislative Action Network (LAN). Further, members will have access to medical and dental plan savings, travel savings, and discounts on special business training, eye care and legal services. To contact NASE, use the address and phone number in Appendix C.

CHAPTER 6

Successfully Marketing Your Product or Service

Most new business owners understand that they will have to partake in some degree of marketing and promotion to make their businesses' products or services visible to the world. But all too often, these same business owners forego developing a solid marketing and public relations strategy so they can deal with the more immediate aspects of starting a business, such as obtaining financing or filing the right paperwork with state and federal offices.

Regardless of the type of business you plan to open — whether it be a retail shop or a home-based consulting business — you will need to know how to attract and retain customers to ensure your business remains profitable. By choosing to look at your market before you open your business you will be able to:

- Understand the specific habits and characteristics of your business' clientele;
- Safely evaluate your pricing based on your production demands versus your market demands;
- Be better prepared for the cycles of your business' field or industry; and
- Know what are your business' best methods of communication.

All of this information will give you the keen insight to be more responsive to your business' needs and financial stability.

This chapter will help you gather information about your business and formulate it into a meaningful marketing and public relations plan. One of the first steps to building a sturdy framework to your plan is to understand some basic principles behind marketing and public relations. If you are familiar with this field of business already, you know that there are innumerable books, articles, and seminars on marketing and public relations. Unfortunately, not all of them follow the same definitions or standards. So, to maintain some sense of clarity, this chapter treats marketing and public relations as two separate vehicles of communication.

PUBLIC RELATIONS OR MARKETING FIRST?

Public relations is the practice of ensuring that your company is desirable or viewed in a favorable light. A favorable review of your business in a local newspaper or sponsoring a student in a 4-H program both qualify as good public relations. The options in which you position your business in a favorable light are limitless. Marketing on the other hand, defines and perpetuates demand and is directly related to the goal of "making a sale" or creating revenue for your business. Advertising your products or services on television or even deciding to have a sidewalk sale are functions of marketing.

Many business owners decide to jump into the world of marketing and advertising before dealing with how the public perceives them. Obviously, if you can first establish an awareness that you will soon be open for business and ready to meet your customers' demands, then your marketing efforts to make sales will be more effective and show better returns. In other words, by first establishing healthy public relations, you will clear the way to make sound decisions about marketing and generate money back to your business.

Don't be misled by the lure of marketing and advertising professionals. You would be amazed at how quickly salespeople will catch wind of your new business. Not far from the snake oil peddlers of decades past, they will want to sell you on a variety of schemes to bring in immediate revenue. Whether it is selling advertising space in phone books, designing a Web site for your company, or selling you a blimp emblazoned with your company name to hover about your city's skyline, you are in no position to determine what will actually work unless you understand how the general public will perceive these promotional attempts — assuming the public will even notice. Until you can identify who your best customers are and who can help you further your business' exposure, you are at the mercy of salespeople and general advice-givers. Since it is unlikely that your startup will be able to afford a marketing and public relations staff, much of this responsibility will be on your shoulders.

DEFINE YOUR KEY AUDIENCES

Your public relations and marketing efforts will be much easier if you start off by identifying the groups of people that will (or could) affect the livelihood of your business. Your key audiences might include:

- The general public
- Your customers
- Your employees
- Your investors
- Government and civic leaders
- The media

Keep in mind, this is a general list of potential audiences and you should take time to think about any additional groups of people that may influence the success of your specific type of business. For example, keeping unionized truckers on your side may be a top priority if you plan to start a big-rig transportation brokerage, but certainly not if you intend to run a typing service for college students. You will definitely want to add those specific groups to the more obvious key audiences in your public relations strategy.

THE GENERAL PUBLIC

Regardless of the type of business you own, it is important that the general public supports (or at least tolerates) your company. If the general public does not support your business, the likelihood is strong that even your best customers or clients will be swayed to support another business. You may want to focus primarily on your money-spending customers; however, the general public should always be on your mind too. Developing a favorable standing with the general public is sometimes referred to as community relations. The idea is to establish your company as a "good neighbor," not a money-hungry entity with little regard to the environment or community.

To illustrate the importance of community relations, consider the following scenario. Suppose you want to open a skateboard shop that targets teenagers. You take a lot of time to cater to the likes of your young customers, and as a result they view your store as a hangout. On the other hand, the general public is far from being fascinated by the sport and may view your shop as an eyesore— "full of kids out front with nothing better to do." This does not bother you because you have established a loyal following among your customers and are reaping the financial rewards. That is, until one day a skateboarder accidentally knocks down an elderly woman in front of your shop. Suddenly you are faced with a crisis as the media takes hold of the negative publicity this brings to your store as an indirect cause of the accident, not to mention the impending lawsuit filed by the woman. Because you have not maintained a positive image among the general public, you must spend a great deal of effort to reclaim your business from rumors, angry parents who no longer want their children to support your store, and negative media reports.

If on the other hand, your business had promoted a "responsible use campaign" before the accident — without alienating the kids that support it — you would have been in a better position to recover from the crisis. You could have accomplished this by offering free "responsible use" workshops or by bringing a well-known personality in the skateboarding world to demonstrate safer places to skate. By writing press releases, you might lure the local newspaper or television stations to cover the event.

Although the time and money spent on such a campaign may not show any financial return — as the same amount applied to advertising a sale might — being aware of your business' overall perception and its place in the community can be help you prevent or at least recover from situations that could dramatically affect future sales.

YOUR CUSTOMERS

Naturally, you will want your business to be the first choice of your potential clientele. This means you will have to conduct some research as to who specifically will be your best type of customer. Determine the common characteristics — age, ethnic group, gender, income level, education level, interests, and buying habits of the public who want your goods or services. This will be a crucial element to any of your future marketing needs. Specific methods for defining your best customers are discussed in greater detail in the marketing section of this chapter.

As soon as you have a good idea of who your customers are, you should always put your best foot forward when you choose to communicate to them. Your customers keep your business going. You want to create a comfortable experience for your customers to buy and use your products or services. Begin thinking about what will appeal to your customers on a subconscious level and what steps you can take to meet their interests. Will they identify and be drawn toward the design of your company logo or letterhead? Will the fixtures, furniture, and colors in your office or store appeal to your customers? All of these small details affect the big picture of your business and their importance should not be overlooked.

YOUR EMPLOYEES

If you will have employees, train them on the importance of portraying your company image in a favorable fashion. That includes how your business' customers or clients are greeted when they call on the phone, walk in the door, or how they are received when they have a problem with a product or service. Inform employees about your company's goals and objectives and motivate them to make the business work. If you include your employees in your efforts and get them excited and proud of their roles, you are more likely to see the positive effects trickle over to your customers. Being concerned about staying in a favorable standing with your employees can improve morale, lessen employee turnover, cut down on rumors and gossip, as well as offer crucial information about company policies. For more information on establishing a healthy relationship with your employees, refer to Chapter 10.

YOUR INVESTORS

Although your business is not publicly held and you will not have to worry about how shareholders and security analysts view your business, you may want to make an effort to establish a healthy relationship and company image with your banker or other financial consultants. Of course you will focus the message that is relevant to your investors from a different standpoint than you would project to another key audience, like your customers. In other words, you will want to take steps to ensure that your business appears financially sound to your investors. Taking time to educate yourself and project your willingness to work and communicate with your investors are preliminary steps to reaching lasting healthy relations with your investors. This time spent may be just as, if not more important than the efforts you make with other key audiences, especially when you need funding. See Chapter 8 for more details on working with your bank.

GOVERNMENT AND CIVIC LEADERS

Developing a good relationship with local, state, federal, and even international officials can be crucial. Simply put, since these officials have a direct hand in creating legislation that could affect your business, make certain they know about your business and industry. By maintaining a productive and active voice with the various levels of government, you are more likely to improve or maintain the working standards, taxes, and other government interventions that your business faces. If your business has a voice and a strong image, you are more likely to be respected and heard.

THE MEDIA

Last, but certainly not the least important to your public relations efforts, is the role of the media. Work with the media to build your image. The media can include everything from your local newspaper, an international cable news network like CNN, and even the World Wide Web. By sending a press release about your company to editors and journalists, the chances are you can influence positive coverage of your business in news stories. If journalists can rely on you or your business for advice or pertinent information for their news stories, then the chances are they are more likely to listen to you when you have something to say about your business.

The Media Can Be More Than an Audience

The media cannot only serve as an audience, but as a definable conduit to communicate to several of your key audiences. Because the media — whether it is television, radio, or magazine — can reach so many different quantities and types of people, you can use this to your advantage and pinpoint press releases to better serve your business' different key audiences. For example, you may discover through interviews that your customers primarily watch the evening news on television for information about the community. With this insight, you know that you should direct news releases to the television news programs with a focus on your customers' interests and needs. But you can also position that same news story for a different medium with elements that would interest your financial backers, if for example, you know they prefer to read the local business journal. By continually learning about your key audiences' habits and characteristics, you will also be better able to assume which is the best medium for the key audience you want to reach.

Keep in mind, a third-party endorsement from the media can often be more effective than a high-priced advertisement. In fact, the Wirthlin Group for Allen Communications, a New York-based public relations firm, found that 28 percent of its 1,023 respondents said a news article would impact their buying decisions, as compared to 8 percent who said they would be influenced more by an advertisement. The respondents also said that they felt magazines and newspapers were more reliable for information than television or the Internet.

Take Time to Build Relationships with the Media

Carefully establish a relationship with any useful media contacts. Make it as easy as possible for them to know you're available to provide insight into a particular issue and available for their needs. They want resources to rely upon — experts in a variety of fields — and if they can determine that you are an acceptable resource, the chances of promoting your company are greater too. Don't expect to submit a press release then watch the story unfold on the six o'clock news. Avoid a press release that is just a strong sales pitch. Instead, try to gauge what the media is likely to want to report — what would make a newsworthy story. If you can provide the lead to a good story within the realm of your business, then you may very well have an "in." If not, it's probably better to wait until you do, rather than alienate essential media contacts.

Use the Internet as a Media Tool

Although it is subject to a lot of current media attention itself, the Internet is proving to be an invaluable medium for all types of business communication. Beyond developing a Web site for your business, you can monitor discussion groups about your business and industry that might generate ideas for press releases and potential news stories. Use email to communicate with journalists and send press releases, if that is an acceptable form of submission for them. You can even use the Internet as a medium itself to reach specific segments of your key audiences to communicate your message and further your business' image, rather than push your blatant marketing or sales pitches. To learn more about the Internet as a public relations tool, check out *Connecting Online: Creating a Successful Image on the Internet* by Greg Sherwin and Emily Avila. See the Useful Resources section at the end of this chapter for details.

BUILD A PUBLIC RELATIONS STRATEGY

Now that you have information about your key audiences, you are ready for a more formal plan of attack — a public relations strategy.

Your first step is to look at the overall picture — or your business' place in the world. Paint a portrait of your business in the marketplace by finding articles about similar businesses, statistics or information about your customers and the community in which your business will serve, or any other indicators that will help you overcome potential image problems and stay in good standing with all your key audiences. You can find this information in the library, in magazines and trade journals, on the Internet, and even by surveying the public about its attitudes and opinions. To assist your survey efforts, use a software program like *The Survey Genie.* See the end of this chapter for information about this invaluable tool.

ANALYZE YOUR INFORMATION

When you feel you have gathered enough information to start with, write down what you believe to be an accurate representation of your new business in relation to its competitors and the issues that face you and your competition. Consider what messages you need to communicate to what key audiences to position your business in a favorable light. Consider the limitations that your business has to face in order to communicate those messages to the key audiences. In addition, determine if there are government regulations that could affect your company or contribute to your problem.

IDENTIFY POTENTIAL PROBLEMS

You may discover that there are potential image problems that could affect your business' operations immediately or down the road. Although, you cannot predict the future, if you suspect an issue lingers ahead, it may be wise to publicly address the issue before it balloons into general consciousness, or even worse, a crisis. You should be as specific as possible in determining these problems and their source, as well as what might happen if you chose to ignore them.

For example, if you have decided to start a timber harvesting operation in the Pacific Northwest, you could face some fairly tough battles trying to keep your business' image favorable in both the eyes of people who consider your business destructive to the forest ecosystem and to the industry who relies on timber for income. By siding with one or the other, you could face repercussions such as environmentalist demonstrations or a loss of support from your vendors and other business allies. Ideally, you may want to take steps to remain acceptable with both parties to a certain degree, assuming that you don't want to take on the risk of boycotts or other actions. You may also discover that you can only bend so far to meet the demands of either extreme side to the issue in order to keep your business profitable. Of course, there may be simply nothing you can do in some cases, other than monitor the extremist noise-makers and hope they do not become the majority of your key audiences.

The process of identifying and monitoring problems should be ongoing from the point you decide to open your business to the day when you sell or close the business.

SET GOALS TO PREVENT AND RESOLVE PROBLEMS

Now you are ready to set goals and identify the methods to position your business in an agreeable manner. Once you have identified any problems, try to come up with ways to resolve them. Find solutions to your questions, based on research, surveys, and instinct. You might ask yourself some questions to find an answer. Will holding a grand opening meet your goals of more exposure for your business? Would coming up with a relevant news story for the media meet your goal? Could your goal be achieved if you find more time to identify and meet the needs to some of your identified audiences' needs? Would creating a newsletter or a Web site help?

Always keep in mind which members of your key audiences will be most affected by the problem and your solution. Your message should cater to their specific interests and needs. Using different types of media — such as a business journal that your vendors and distributors read or a national news program viewed by your general customers — will help you target your message.

Imagine your business develops a better way to reduce production costs and, in return, receive more profit. Information such as this, might be very newsworthy for a business journal that is read by your financial supporters. However, the information is not useful to your customers, since you are not passing a lower price for the goods on to them. From your research, you may have discovered that your customers are concerned about the environment, so instead of restating the news to them about your cut in costs, you can slant the focus of the story to show the added benefit for your customers of having less packaging to throw away.

Once you have identified your business' potential image problems, know your target audience, and know how you can shape the information to suit your audience's needs best, you will have to determine your strategy. You have four options:

Ignore the problem. You may not have the time to deal with the issue now or feel that it is simply too early to effectively address it.

React only if you absolutely have to. You may decide that it is best for the business if you don't address the problem unless one or more of your key audiences becomes concerned about it.

Prevent the problem. It may be best to be proactive before the problem becomes uncontrollable or too time consuming.

Involve others. You can sometimes involve groups like the media, government officials, or even media consultants to solve or head off an image problem for your business.

Do not be concerned, if you choose to ignore the problem, it may be in your best interest considering your other business demands. Weigh your decisions according to your workload, other demands, and the importance of keeping up with your business' image. There will always be a tradeoff, and it is okay to decide that dealing with an image problem may be the least of your worries at any given point. In a bigger picture context, do not write off the power of solid public relations throughout your business' lifespan.

If you choose to actively pursue a goal, you will want to outline exactly what you are going to do to reach your goal. You might determine that it is best to have an action event, such as holding a special event, an exhibit, or some other sort of community involvement project. The involvement of the news media will be crucial to publicize these sorts of events and to get your message across.

Of course, you may decide that it would be better to pursue communications tactics instead. This might include distributing a newsletter, brochure, press release, or direct mail advertisement. It might include coming up with a business logo, developing a Web site, or renting that blimp mentioned earlier with your company name across it.

MAKE A TIMELINE

Taking time to create a schedule will help you reach your planned goal. Suppose you are going to hold a grand opening for your business. You must determine when your business will be ready to hold the event, how long it will take to get a banner made that reads, "Grand Opening," when a string quartet can come and perform for your guests, and determine whether the day and time will be convenient for your key audiences. By planning ahead and doing some research, you can ensure a much more successful launch than if you went without any insight or planning.

ALLOT MONEY AND RESOURCES

Along with creating a timeline, you will also want to examine the cost and time it will take to meet your goals. It is wise to create a detailed line-item budget, especially for the larger events you may be planning. Be sure to look for hidden costs, as well.

EVALUATE YOUR EFFORTS

At some point, you will want to determine if your efforts were successful. You determine success based on your original goals, your initial strategy, and the methods you used to achieve these objectives. You can survey your customers or potential customers to find out if their perception of your business has changed. You may simply notice that a news story featuring information about your business' activities has brought in more curious customers. Whatever the case, you will want to weigh the effort it took to meet your objectives and what you have learned from the event. You may discover that your goals were not realistic or you may discover a very effective way to building a healthy image with your business. This process can provide some real, qualitative insight into your business and its market.

HOW TO MARKET YOUR POSITIVE IMAGE

Suppose you want to increase the public's awareness that your business is going to be open soon. By careful consideration, you decide that having a grand opening is the best method of meeting your objectives. You have flyers printed, you alert the media, you even booked the string quartet mentioned earlier to add some atmosphere. Your intent is to introduce yourself to your community and provide it with an enjoyable evening. And, after carefully orchestrating something close to the social event of the season, you can't help but feel your business is off to a great start.

Yet, in the weeks that follow, you may notice that interest in your business is waning. More importantly, you aren't earning enough money to keep your cash flow at a healthy level. What may have appeared to be the grandest of grand openings may leave you frantically searching for any means to attract customers.

It is important to establish your business with a positive image, but you will still need a certain amount of sales to keep your business alive and profitable. It is now time to transition your company's positive image into healthy sales. In short, you are ready to work on marketing your product or service.

Marketing is the pursuit of keeping your business financially stable through promotion. This could include running an advertisement in a magazine or taking the time to identify your best potential customers and use resources to communicate to their interests and needs through the type of business you operate.

By taking steps prior to opening your business, you will be better equipped to meet the needs of your best customers and help ensure that they continue to support your business throughout the months and years that follow.

DEFINE YOUR IDEAL CUSTOMERS

Go back to the key audiences you identified earlier in this chapter. Out of these groups, who do you see as your cash-spending customers? Base your assumption on indicators like:

- What you already know about the industry and its consumers;
- What your competitors have done and continue to do to market to specific groups of people; and
- What business journals, association newsletters, industry magazines, and other resources are saying about your ideal customers.

Although a new business should try to profit as much as it can, your business' marketing efforts — which will take time and revenue — should be calculated and precise. You want to hit the right segment of people who are likely to support your business and hopefully support it loyally.

Of course to achieve this, you may want to pinpoint your general customers even further. To find your best customers, learn as much as you can about them. One excellent way to do this is through interviews or surveys. You can choose to do them on the street, near a competitor's store, or even over the telephone. By developing useful questions about your potential customers' likes and dislikes, you develop a better understanding of what exactly makes your customers tick. By getting to know their habits, knowing what types of entertainment they like, and understanding their motives for seeking out your business, you will be much more capable of making decisions about how to communicate to your best customers. You may even discover a segment of customers that is otherwise ignored by your competition that you could successfully cater to.

For example, if you are planning to open an automotive parts store, you might assume that your primary customers are middle-aged men, who are either mechanics or do-it-yourselfers. However, through your surveys of the general public, you discover that many women would be interested in supporting a retail store that offers automotive parts. By examining your competition, you realize that this segment of the general market is virtually ignored. You decide that it is worth allocating some money toward trying to develop women as a primary customer segment in your store. By taking steps to appeal to this group's interests and needs, you are building additional sales and have a one-up on your competition.

USE YOUR COMPETITION'S STRATEGY TO YOUR BENEFIT

Although it may seem strange at first, you can learn a lot from your competitors. Observing how they run and promote their businesses and who visits their stores can give you insight as to who might migrate to your business.

Examine their prices. Document the pros and cons of their products or services. Find out as much as you can what their operating costs might be. Visit their Web site and determine what type of customer they are trying to reach. Find out who their distributors and suppliers are, if any. Determine whether their location is convenient and to their benefit. You have the luxury of evaluating their work and deciding that they are or are not doing something as well as they should — and you can implement a better way of performing the functions of the business in your store.

DISTINGUISH YOURSELF FROM YOUR COMPETITORS

After you have finished obtaining as much publicly available information as you can from your competition, compile it and analyze it. Compare your results with what you intend to do as a new business. Compare everything from your customers to what costs will affect daily operations. From this information, you can build ways to give you an advantage over your competition. Maybe you can operate at a lower cost and reduced prices. Maybe your business is in a better location. Whatever the difference, your business will need to develop some unique selling points to lure customers. These can be as subtle as you want, like providing a more comfortable atmosphere in your business. Or, they can be as blatant as you want, such as heavy promotions on your rock-bottom prices that may resemble a promotion for a monster-truck rally at the local fairgrounds.

BLAZE YOUR OWN CREATIVE MARKETING TRAIL

Unfortunately, as a new business you are not likely to have a great sum of money for any major marketing efforts. Certainly don't try to keep up with your competition if they are large and can sink millions into highly targeted advertising campaigns — you will likely just drain what resources you do have and put your business in financial jeopardy. But certainly don't be discouraged by fighting Goliath corporate competitors. Your creativity, research, and public image can give you an advantage to sway your customers "to support the community" rather than some corporate giant.

DETERMINE THE FACTORS THAT WILL AFFECT SALES

Of course, before you can really partake in a creative marketing idea to bring in customers, you need to examine some essential factors that could influence your overall marketing and sales. You will need to find inexpensive, yet quality ways to produce your message. You may have to find a reputable printer or television production crew to produce your marketing message. However, before you commit to creating and producing a marketing idea, you need to be firm on what your internal cost demands are, the revenue you can commit to marketing, and how much you can invest to maintain a quick return on your money.

BEWARE OF THE IMPACTS OF PRICING

Your operating costs may play a larger role in your marketing decisions than you may think. You may discover that your potential customers seek a business with lower prices. So it may seem best to reduce your prices. Without prior examination, you may be doing more business, but not able to keep your production or operating costs in check.

Pricing your product or service will have an extraordinary impact on the success of your business. If you price your product or service too low, you will experience low profits and may even experience significant losses. Price your product or service too high and your customer base will migrate to your competitors or never form at all. So setting the right price for your product entails certain risks.

Analyze Costs

Fortunately, most of the mystery associated with pricing can be easily dispelled with a simple analysis of your costs. Once you know the cost of goods and cost of sales, you have most of the information you need to determine the correct pricing for your product.

For example, suppose you plan to start a tie-dye T-shirt business. Each shirt you make requires $2.50 of raw material and costs $1.50 to dye and treat properly, including all of the overhead manufacturing expenses. After discovering it is more lucrative to run a mail-order business, you determine that the average shipping cost of a shirt is another $0.50. Your distributor near Haight-Ashbury in San Francisco warehouses your shirts by the thousands and ships them to clothing stores throughout the nation on demand. The distributor's average handling cost is $1.25 per shirt. The clothing stores determine the final price for the shirts based on a standard markup that takes into account many of the sales costs. So the total for your tie-dye shirts works out like this:

Raw material	$2.50
Manufacturing	$1.50
Shipping	$0.50
Cost of Goods	$4.50
Distribution	$1.25
Your profit	$0.50
Cost to Store	$6.25
Markup @ 50%	$6.25
Final Selling Price	**$12.50**

The final price the customer pays is $12.50. If the price is slightly lower than or equal to your competitors' prices, you're in business. If, however, the final price is higher than your competitors' pricing, there is something wrong with your process and you will need to rethink your production.

PRODUCTION CONSIDERATIONS

When you set prices for your goods or services, consider what costs will be after you get into full production or to a production level that you consider adequate to support your business. Do not price your product or service solely with low overhead costs built in if you may have to rent other space or obtain equipment and hire employees to deliver your product or service. As production increases, you will obtain some efficiencies of sale. If you could purchase ten items at a unit price to make up a product, purchasing 500 will probably substantially decrease your unit cost.

However, the need for cash will also increase as production increases and you risk the chance of not being able to deliver to meet demand. You may not get paid for a finished product until several months after you have produced it and shipped it to your customer. You may also find that your vendors cannot meet the increased demand on the timeframe you expect. You should have alternative sources of all materials when possible.

Get your suppliers to guarantee prices and supplies of material. Discuss potential orders with suppliers in plenty of time for them to obtain the material they need to deliver to you. In today's global market, you can expect that foreign-made items will constitute some of your manufactured goods. Unless the materials can be easily air shipped, you may have a significant delay in getting items from manufacturers who depend on raw material or finished goods from other countries. You may also find that price and quality vary considerably from one shipment to another, so you will probably want to guarantees relating to different deliveries and the ability to return defective or substandard quality materials.

Use Sales to Drive Production Goals

Production goals are directly driven by sales. It does no good to make 10,000 tie-dye T-shirts if nobody buys them. Conversely, if you are unable to provide T-shirts on demand, your customers may choose to take their business elsewhere.

Your goal then, is to manufacture T-shirts at full capacity and sell 100% of your inventory as it is made. Of course, the reality of actually doing this is very difficult, but certainly not impossible.

DETERMINE OTHER FACTORS THAT WILL AFFECT SALES

Other factors may also influence your best methods to market your business. You may want to consider the economy of the community you serve, looking at the population of the community you serve, and where your business is located in comparison to other competitors or other businesses that your customers may support. If you are catering to only a small population or to a small percentage who desire or can afford your product, you may want to be very careful about what money you spend to communicate to that select group.

Your business' location can play a big role in your sales too. If you are located near a competitor, you may find that you can draw upon its customers who may be comparison shopping. You may also discover that if you are not near any other business that your customers may support, that they have to find more reason than impulse to come to your business. Also, see Chapter 12 about other considerations for choosing your business' site or refer to *Location, Location, Location: How to Select the Best Site for Your Business* by Luigi Salvaneschi.

DEVISE A WORKABLE SALES AND MARKETING PLAN

By taking into account the information you have gathered about your customers, competition, and your operating costs, you should be able to determine how much money you can devote to reaching your customers. Document your objectives and goals in a similar fashion to any public relations strategy you had done earlier.

For example, you may set a goal of bringing in four new clients to your consulting practice each month. How you choose to bring in those clients will be based on what you know about the demand for your services, how you can communicate to potential customers, and what money you have available to do so. Putting photocopied flyers under potential customers' windshield wipers may be your best option at this point. After the month is up, then evaluate this method's success. Unfortunately, you only brought in three new clients, but you have determined a fairly low-cost method to bring in new clients.

The process of coming up with an idea to increase sales is never a sure-fire thing, despite what salespeople's gimmicks may tell you. Realize that you will be taking a risk — although necessary to build your sales and profits — anytime you partake in a marketing effort. Fortunately, with some early planning and some research as to who your best customers are and what they are seeking in a business, you can feel a little more assured that your decisions will show positive results. Keep in mind, that the process of marketing and gathering information about your market is ongoing. You may start out small and gradually build enough additional revenue to market your business with more expensive methods, such as television advertising or renting that blimp.

CHAPTER WRAP-UP

How you choose to promote your business will largely depend on your costs and your time. But keep in mind that all of these factors are interconnected. Your marketing will be based largely on your production costs, the economy, your location, and the size of your market. Your company's image is just as important to your banker or financial lender as it is to your customers or other key audiences at various times. Although the desire may be strong to put off your marketing and public relations until after you have opened your doors for business, the ability to be more responsive to the demands and costs of your business will come much quicker if you start considering your market now.

USEFUL RESOURCES

Marketing Mastery: Your Seven Step Guide to Success by Harriet Stephenson and Dorothy Otterson. Learn to capitalize on your customers' feelings of satisfaction with your product and business.

Power Marketing for Small Business by Jody Hornor. A wealth of basic, step-by-step marketing information that easily takes a new or experienced business owner through the essentials of marketing and sales strategies.

Successful Network Marketing for the 21st Century by Rod Nichols. Shows how network marketing fits the home-based business trend for self-directed success.

TargetSmart: Database Marketing for the Small Business by Jay Newberg and Claudio Marcus. This illustrated book clearly explains how a small business can effectively understand and implement a database to capitalize on its results.

Know Your Market: How to do Low-Cost Market Research by David Frigstad. This exciting workbook explains how a small business can conduct its own market research.

Connecting Online: Creating a Successful Image on the Internet by Greg Sherwin and Emily Avila. Cuts through the hype, to show how the Internet and all of its tools can be effectively implemented to build a company's image.

NOTES FOR MARKETING:

CHAPTER 7

Your Smart Business Plan

Before undertaking any endeavor, you must have a plan. This is true whether you are embarking on a skiing trip or launching a new business. Even if you haven't yet written a business plan, you probably have at least a general idea about your business goals, your customers, and your product. But have you considered such things as business expansion, second or third year profits, or financing?

Writing a business plan will force you to consider the management of your business for the next three to five years. A top-notch business plan will take a lot of work. You must think through your entire business at least once. Drafting a business plan causes you to think about yourself, your product or service, your market, your customers, and your finances — at least once before you get into business. A smart business plan will convey prospects and growth potential. As a savvy entrepreneur you can use you business plan to give you greater control of your business.

Frequently, new business owners do not write a business plan until forced to do so by a bank or financial institution as a part of a loan application package. By taking this approach, they miss out on some of the most important benefits associated with having a business plan. If you write a business plan, you will have:

- A clear picture of the financial condition of your business projected over the next five years;
- Critical marketing information related to your business;

- Specific business goals and milestones for the foreseeable future;
- Key information for business goal-related decision making; and
- Ready documentation available, if needed, for business financing.

You have a story to tell — that is not enough. The way you present the story is crucial to your success. This chapter will help you present your story in the best possible light to attract the investors and give you the control you need.

GET HELP BEFORE YOU BEGIN

A business plan is not difficult to create. Most plans follow a specific format that has been largely standardized throughout the business community. This specific format is not to be used as a boiler plate for your plan; rather, use it as a guideline to incorporate your business' unique characteristics. The basic elements are the same for all plans. Feel free to modify or expand on the basic elements of the business plan to better describe your business.

In preparing your business plan, you may refer to any number of resource materials on the market, including *The Successful Business Plan: Secrets & Strategies* by Rhonda M. Abrams. In addition, there are several quality software packages on the market that will lead you through the process of preparing your business plan.

One such product is KMT Software's Softkey *Power Business Plans* software. This application is an add-on to Microsoft *Office* and integrates documents from *Office* applications into a single, business plan document that is very effective. The software is powerful yet simple to comprehend and use and it is available for both *Windows* and Macintosh versions of Microsoft *Office.*

See the Useful Resources section at the end of this chapter for more information on both products.

ESSENTIAL COMPONENTS OF A SMART PLAN

Several examples from KMT Software's *Power Business Plans* are used throughout this chapter and in the sample business plan at the end of this chapter to illustrate the essential components of a successful business plan, including:

- Section I: Executive Summary
- Section II: Company Background
- Section III: Owner/Management Background
- Section IV: Market Analysis
- Section V: Product/Service Offering
- Section VI: Marketing Plan
- Section VII: Financial Plan and Analysis

Be sure you read through these essential components and the sample business plan before you start your own plan. You may include other aspects of your business that you feel are important to understanding the business, but may not be in the outline above. Modify your plan to depict your business or business idea and clarify in the reader's mind why you think the business idea is viable. Feel free to add or delete parts of the business plan described in this chapter. However, be careful not to delete important parts of the plan that will limit the understanding of your business. You can also provide too much information that may not be read or digested by the reader. The outline provided here is modified in the sample plan and in the other plans in the KMT Software plans to better accommodate the needs of the business.

SECTION I – EXECUTIVE SUMMARY

The executive summary is considered by many experts to be the most important part of a business plan. It functions as the front door to your plan and presents your entire business in condensed form. Many lending officials read the executive summary first. If it doesn't make the best impression, the rest of the business plan is often ignored. The end result: your loan proposal doesn't receive the level of attention it may deserve.

Because writing the executive summary requires you to have an extremely clear picture of your business, many business planners advise writing this section of the business plan last. In this way, you benefit from the information and knowledge gleaned by writing the rest of the plan, and all aspects of your business are fresh in your mind.

Even when the business plan is prepared for internal use only, the executive summary plays an important role. As the representation of your entire business concept, all of your goals, your marketing plans, and your financial predictions, the executive summary provides you with a big-picture look at your business. This big-picture look of your business will include:

- Type of business;
- Company business summary;
- Financial objectives, including the highlights of your operating performance;
- Management overview; and
- Product/service and competition.

If you will be using your business plan to obtain financing, include two additional sections — funds requested and use of proceeds. This big picture is available at all times, in a single place, for reference when making important decisions regarding the direction and growth of your business.

If you feel intimidated about writing a plan you may decide to obtain outside help from a consultant or a small business development center. You should actively participate in the development of the plan and clearly understand all the financial calculations and what is said in the text sections. If a lender asks a question about the plan and you indicate that you don't have an answer because the consultant wrote the plan, or that section of the plan, the lender will not be impressed with what you know about your business or prospective business.

Content

Because the executive summary is such an important part of your business plan, its content and tone must clearly convey to the reader the unique structure, capabilities, and expertise of your business and its management. Accordingly, show that:

- Your business is well planned.
- Your business is competently managed.

- Your market has been researched and a clear market exists.
- Your business is competitive against similar businesses.
- Your business is financially sound and is likely to remain so.

By convention, these points are generally made in the order listed, following the content of the business plan. Literally then, the executive summary summarizes the remaining sections of the business plan. If it is well written, it will motivate the reader to examine the remaining sections in detail.

Style

Writing the executive summary requires a little skill. As a narrative discussion of your business, it must have all of the compelling elements of the opening pages of a novel, yet be firmly based in reality. A well-written executive summary will tell the story of your business, and it will entice, excite, and motivate the reader. At the same time, it will avoid exaggeration and outright fantasy. Rather than an example of creative writing, an executive summary is business writing at its best.

When writing an executive summary, use language that presents a positive, confident business attitude. Write in an active voice, presenting your points in a clear and logical manner. If you don't feel confident writing the summary yourself, hire a professional writer or prevail upon a friend or family member with strong writing skills to write it for you.

Ideally, the executive summary is short, one to three pages in length. "White space is my friend" is a common mantra for professional business writers. What this means is that you should avoid having huge blocks of text dominating your page. Break up text with space between paragraphs and by using bold headings and bulleted points in much the same way that this book is designed.

Refer to the executive summary portion of the sample business plan at the end of this chapter. This summary is very well written and uses a compelling, easy-to-read page layout.

SECTION II – COMPANY BACKGROUND

This section of your business plan discusses the basic structure of your business as well as your business goals. It provides your readers with a detailed description of your business, preparing them for later discussion of your product line and marketing strategy. The company background section includes the following basic information:

- Your mission statement or purpose of your business;
- A brief history of your business or business concept;
- A discussion of your personal business goals, including anticipated growth and financial objectives;
- The legal form of your business and its ownership structure;
- A discussion of your business location and facilities;
- A discussion of the financial status of your company, including how you will finance the operation; and
- Other information that has a bearing on your company.

Your Mission Statement

The mission statement briefly describes the character, purpose, and goals of your business. In short, the statement tells about your business and business philosophy. Part declaration, part philosophy, part rallying cry, a well-thought-out mission statement provides the focus for all major business decisions. An example of a well-written mission statement might be:

> "Fortune Branch Market is a mom-and-pop convenience store specializing in friendly, neighborly service to an isolated, rural customer base. We concentrate on serving our customers' needs and work to maintain a diverse inventory, which includes special order items requested by individual customers. Our goal is to maintain moderate annual growth through good, old-fashioned service, a friendly smile, and word-of-mouth advertising."

If you prefer, you can use this section to point out to your readers that you have clearly identified your market and the opportunity for steady sales and future growth.

Business History

Next describe the history of your business, including when it was founded, milestones achieved, such as a break-even date, and the completion of specific goals. State which phase of development your company is in — whether it be in the start-up or expansion phases.

If you are developing a new product, this is the place to discuss the extent of its development, such as:

- The completion of product testing,
- The acquisition of patents, copyrights, or trademarks, or
- The acceptance of initial orders.

For a start-up business, an important thing to include in this section is a discussion of the basis for the business concept. The business could be an original idea aimed at an all-new market niche or it could be based on an existing, successful business concept where you will employ a unique approach or advantage. It could also be a proven business concept being introduced into an untapped or underserviced market.

Business Goals

In this section of the business plan, describe your business' future, including sales, growth, and expansion plans. To bolster this information, include charts, tables, and figures that show your sales, profit, and income projections. If there are industry-standard sales figures for your business, use them to back up your assertions regarding projected sales and growth. Use this section to describe how you will take advantage of your unique niche or concept.

Legal Form of Business

Describe the legal form of your business. Is it a sole proprietorship, partnership, corporation, or limited liability company? Explain why you chose the form for your business. Identify the state where your business is registered and any other state in which you are operating. Identify the owners, managers, or corporate officers. If your business is a corporation, identify major shareholders and discuss the number of shares that are outstanding.

Location and Facilities

You can describe the location of your business and explain why the location is particularly suitable for your business. Include demographic and psychographic factors that contribute to the location's suitability. For example, list the number of potential customers within a ten-minute drive based on income, education, interests or other factors that you identified in your assessment of why your business will be successful. List any branch offices or multiple locations. Identify the geographical area serviced by your business.

If your company requires specialized facilities for its operation, include a description of the facilities. Some examples may include machinery, equipment, computer software, display counters, cash registers, alarm systems, a loading dock, storage facilities, or even a railhead for loading and shipping by train.

Financial Status

Briefly discuss the financial state of your business, including funding sources to date, profitability, outstanding loans, owner equity (the amount of ownership you have in the business), the number of employees, and the character of the workforce (experience, education, or other important characteristics).

If you are currently seeking additional funding, briefly describe how much money is being sought and why, as well as how much of the required funding will be provided through owner equity and personal investment. Save detailed discussion of your financial condition and loan requirements for the financial section of your business plan.

Other Information

You may have agreements to distribute or manufacture products that will give your company a competitive edge. Or you may have applied for patents or have copyrights that are important in the development of the business. Also include leases, options, or letters of intent that materially affect your business. Include copies of prospective catalogs or other printed material that will advertise your business. Include a brief description of any of these documents in your Executive Summary and include complete copies at the end of your plan.

SECTION III – OWNER/MANAGEMENT BACKGROUND

The purpose of this section of the business plan is to describe the abilities, experience, and qualifications of the people who will run the business. The greater the wealth of experience being brought to bear on the success of the business, the higher the level of confidence potential investors will feel when considering your business' investment potential.

The Management Team

While your business concept, service, or product is the core of your venture, it is the people who work for you that personify that business concept. For this reason, it is appropriate to provide an overview of the key people who will be representing your business to your customers. Describe the attributes of each key person, emphasizing their experience, background, and education as they pertain to your business.

Identify any professionals and consultants whose specialized expertise you will utilize or require. Examples of these professionals include technical consultants, accountants, equipment specialists, and attorneys. In those cases where you have planned to add specialists or additional management to your team, identify those skills you will be seeking and when you plan to bring them on board.

Management Retention

When your business relies on the expertise of key employees, it is a good business practice to provide those key players with appropriate incentives to remain with your company.

Potential investors will be interested in the steps you have taken to retain your most valuable employees. The following incentives provide tangible evidence of your efforts:

> **Salary.** Salary is the amount of money paid to your employees on an annual basis, regardless of performance. If you pay a higher salary than your competitors, indicate how much higher and reflect this in percentage form.

Bonuses, commissions, and profit sharing. A bonus is extra cash, generally paid at the end of the quarter or year, in recognition of superior performance at the company or at the individual level. A commission is cash payment in addition to salary, based on a percentage of total sales made. Profit sharing is a cash distribution to all employees based on the annual profitability of the company.

Stock. Corporations can issue shares of stock to employees as a performance incentive, in effect making the employees part owners and giving them a stake in the financial success of the business. Alternately, employees can be given stock options that will allow them the opportunity to purchase stock in the future at today's prices.

SECTION IV – MARKET ANALYSIS

The market analysis section of your business plan is your opportunity to demonstrate a thorough understanding of your customer base. Developing a thorough knowledge of your market will require some research, but the effort expended here pays big dividends and it will show that you have done your homework. This homework will entail a comprehensive analysis of your industry, target market, customer profile, major competitors, and a description of your product.

Summary

Start out with a summary. Keep in mind, the person reading your plan is probably in a hurry and is likely to be scanning rapidly through your document, so give the good news first, and then back it up with the facts. Give the reader an interest in the subject and a desire to learn the details presented in the next sections of your business plan.

Your goal in this section is to identify the most beneficial aspects of the market and present them in a positive, convincing manner. Some example paragraphs may be:

> "Industry statistics indicate that this form of retail business requires a minimum population base of 10,000 people to achieve break-even sales. ABC Mousetraps serves a much larger population base of 25,000 people."

> "There has been a growing concern for controlling mice infestations more humanely than by the using poisons or the old spring trap method. ABC Mousetrap's new trap design is a direct response to this issue."

Industry Analysis

Industrial growth or decline is an important consideration in determining the health of your business. Use this section to discuss trends in your industry as they apply to your market sector. Your particular industry may be enjoying an annual growth rate of ten percent nationwide, while experiencing a growth rate of only six percent in your market sector.

There may be underlying factors that affect the growth of your industry. Identify these factors and explain them here. For instance, a decline in the economy on either a national or a local level may have a significant impact on your business. Other factors may include seasonal influences, technological advances, government regulation, or environmental or ecological concerns. Include these factors and state them in a format like this:

> "A department of agriculture study predicts that mice populations in urban areas will increase approximately twelve percent per year during the next ten years."
>
> "The mousetrap industry is seasonal by nature, with peak sales occurring in early to late fall. ABC Mousetraps has efficiently responded to this industry-wide condition through the implementation of innovative production methods and the extensive use of temporary labor resources."

Target Market

Identify your target market in this section. Describe the type of people you expect your customers to be and why. Include those specific aspects of your product or service that will appeal to those customers and the marketing approach you will use to direct sales to them. You will use demographic statistics to help you determine the characteristics of your market sector. This information is available at your local library, small business development centers (SBDCs), and through some Internet resources. If you have Internet access, refer to *http://www.psi-research.com* for links to more information.

Some of the characteristics of your target market that might be significant include income bracket, educational level, gender, lifestyle, and family makeup. You must describe the characteristics of your target market in a way that demonstrates that you can reach potential customers in sufficient numbers to sustain your business. An example target market statement may read as follows:

> "The market that ABC Mousetraps will serve is the middle class, suburban, and rural consumer who desires to control mouse infestation humanely, at a competitively low cost. Additionally, rural customers who stock feed or grain for livestock will benefit from a control method that does not include poison or the expense of conventional extermination methods."

Customer Profile

Based on the target market analysis in the previous section, you will then develop a customer profile based on age, income, family status, geographic location, occupation, attitude, and motive for buying. Include any other factors that may be relevant to your product or service. Review the sample business plan at the end of this chapter for more information.

Major Competitors and Participants

If you are just starting out in business, more than likely your market is already being served by your competitors. Use this section of your business plan to identify those competitors. This will demonstrate that you have a full understanding of your market sector and the role your business will assume in it. Also, your research will help identify those parts of the market that are not being adequately serviced, and allow you to target your money, time, and advertising efforts accordingly.

Projected Market Growth

How will your business grow during the next year or during the next five years? Use this section to make some reasonable estimates regarding your projected market share for your product or service. Compare these figures against industry standards and adjust them according to the peculiarities of your market sector.

SECTION V – PRODUCT/SERVICE OFFERING

Describe your product or service in this section of your business plan. Use detailed, descriptive phrases that clearly identify what it is that you sell as well as any unique characteristics about your product that set you apart from the competition.

Product Summary

Describe your product or service in general terms, summarizing the detailed description that follows in much the same way that you first summarized your market analysis. Identify those other aspects of your business that enhance your product, such as personalized customer service, environmental considerations, or assistance after the sale. For example:

> "ABC Mousetraps manufactures and markets a unique mousetrap that does not kill the entrapped rodent. The trap is constructed of recycled paper. Once the trapped mouse is released to the wild or otherwise disposed of, the trap is fully disposable as normal paper waste. ABC Mousetraps also offers free trap placement advice and an industry-unique mouse disposal service that allows the customer to return the trap and rodent to the store for humane disposal at no additional cost — all without having to directly handle the rodent."

Detailed Description

When your business has more than one product line, describe each one in detail in this section of the business plan. Your purpose here is to give the person reading your business plan a thorough understanding of what you sell as well as any services you provide before or after the sale. Identify how your product or service compares and contrasts with that of your competitors.

Competitive Comparisons

Most businesses have some sort of competition. Even if you have a new product or service, there are usually alternative ways to the product or service you provide. Prospective customers will consider the alternatives and determine if yours has advantages either in price, convenience, design, or many characteristics that distinguish your product or service.

To help communicate your uniqueness amongst the competitors, list the strengths and weaknesses of your product or service against all those you can identify. Create a listing of the characteristics that you believe will identify your company and do the same for other companies that are likely to be your direct or indirect competitors. For example, if you plan to open a paintball field, your direct competitors may be the other paintball fields in your area — probably within a 30 or 40-mile drive from your location. You will also need to consider the alternative recreation opportunities that will attract the age or income group you think is interested in playing.

Product or Service Uniqueness

As you develop your list of competitive comparisons, you will probably identify characteristics that are unique about your business. If you own a restaurant, you may emphasize your speed of service, food quality, ambiance, price, taste, or friendliness of the staff.

Again, itemize these characteristics that make your product or service desirable to a specific group of people. You may want to interview customers or prospective customers to see if they agree with your assessment of the unique characteristics of your business. If you believe that you have a unique approach to a product or problem, but others don't recognize the value of it, there is little value to the perceived difference. In the long run, your customers' perceptions of what they believe is unique will hold the most weight.

Research and Development

Many businesses start with nothing but an investment in research and development (R&D). This investment usually leads to changes in the way something is manufactured or delivered. The value of R&D is difficult to measure until it is tested in the marketplace. However, R&D can give an important lead in obtaining business over other companies that have not invested in R&D.

Patents and Trademarks

Patents are processes for manufacture of an item that are protected by the U.S. government. In many cases the protection extends to other countries. The protection is for a limited time but there is normally enough time under patent protection to make a product commercially viable and for the patent holder to get a return on the investment required to take out a patent. Usually patents are obtained through the help of a patent attorney and can be very expensive to obtain. Once obtained, they can be an extremely valuable part of a business, due to the ability of the business to create a product under the patent, or license the patent for a royalty and allow other businesses to create the product.

Therefore, ownership of patents is an extremely important part of a business plan. However, just mentioning the patent's existence is not enough. You must describe how the patent can generate income for the business and add to its overall success.

Trademarks are identifiers of a product or service that is unique to a company and is protected by the U.S. government from anyone else using the same identification. Trademarks are not as expensive to obtain as patents but often require the help of an attorney to obtain.

Make sure you identify any trademarks owned by your business in your business plan. Trademarks can have a significant value to a business if they carry a positive image by the public. A trademark that has not been advertised or is not well known is of little value until it has proven its value in the marketplace.

SECTION VI – MARKETING PLAN

A marketing plan is different than a market analysis. With a marketing plan, you will map out a strategy for reaching your customers and bringing them to you. The purpose of marketing is to get your message out to your potential customers.

The Message

The first step in marketing is identifying your message. In addition to the product or service itself, determine what you are selling. It may be convenience, value, quality, safety, fun, youth, or even sex appeal. Whatever your message is, the advertising media you use must push your message and identify your business with the message. This part of your business plan describes your message and how advertising will be used to associate your business with your message. Overall, your message must be geared toward creating and retaining customers.

Product Pricing Strategy

Describe your pricing strategy and how it will allow you to compete with other businesses in your industry. Determine whether you will set your prices to be greater than, less than, or the same as your competitors. Each pricing strategy has inherent advantages, and the one that you use will depend directly on your message. It would make little sense, for instance, to emphasize value in your advertising while pricing your product higher than the competition.

Product Positioning

Positioning refers to the process of ideally presenting your product to the segment of the market you are specifically targeting as your customer base. For instance, camping gear is positioned to attract younger, recreational consumers while garden tractors are positioned to attract older, primarily male consumers. Positioning will influence which advertising mediums you use to market your product or service. Briefly describe your product positioning strategy in this section of the business plan.

Promotional Strategy

Promotion is the art of associating your company with your product in ways and under circumstances that wouldn't ordinarily occur. To promote your business, you can:

- Sponsor local amateur sporting teams,
- Contribute funds for public facilities,
- Provide scholarship funds to graduating seniors,
- Participate in charity events, or
- Pay for publishing church bulletins or newsletters.

All of these activities provide you with the opportunity to promote and advertise your business as well as contribute to goodwill.

SECTION VII – FINANCIAL PLAN AND ANALYSIS

The financial plan is the meat of your business plan. If you are preparing your business plan for the purpose of obtaining funding, this section will tell a lender whether the amount is reasonable and if you are capable of handling the additional debt. Most investors expect to see the information in this section presented in a specific format. Key parts will include:

- Start-up capital requirements, if any,
- Financial highlights,
- A 3- to 5-year income statement,
- A 3- to 5-year balance sheet,
- Cash budgets or cash flow statements, and
- A break-even analysis.

Initial Capital Requirements

This section is sometimes called sources and uses of funds. You first mentioned the amount of required capital in your Executive Summary (Section I) of your business plan. This is the section where you amplify and explain that amount.

Break down and identify the costs associated with the startup or improvements to your business, detailing where you expect the money to come from and how you expect to spend it once you receive it. Potential lenders will expect to see this information in a table format. If you have the capability to produce a graph of your information, it is acceptable to do so. Refer to Chapter 8 for details on how to obtain financing.

As a new business you won't be able to provide previous financial history. However, you can project your expenses and income based on some reasonable expectation. You should be able to defend your assumptions about sales as well as certain expenses. Too often, profits look very promising but fail to materialize because expenses, such as taxes, repairs, insurance and other miscellaneous expenses, are not included in the projections. It is not uncommon for a new business to show a loss for the first year of operation. What lenders want to know is how much loss you may project and how you will recover from the loss with profits in future years.

Financial Highlights

This section highlights key financial ratios calculated for the next five years. These ratios provide information at a glance as to the projected liquidity, leverage, efficiency, and profitability of your business for the planning period. Ideally, your debt-to-equity ratio should decrease over time while your gross margin should remain at or above the averages for your industry. For more information on how to prepare this section, consult your accountant.

3- to 5-Year Income Statement

The income statement is frequently referred to as the profit and loss (P&L) statement and shows how profitable your business is after all expenses are paid. Income statements are read from top to bottom, and entries are listed in the following order: income from sales, cost of sales, and gross profit. These are followed by a listing of general and administrative expenses. Subtracting total expenses from the gross profit reveals net profit before taxes. Finally, taxes are subtracted to leave net profit as the bottom line.

Your accountant may help you prepare this financial form for you. If your business is too small to warrant an accountant, a computer program such as *Quickbooks* will generate this report for you provided the information you enter into the program is accurate. Alternately, many popular spreadsheet programs such as *Lotus 1-2-3* or Microsoft *Excel* provide the basic tools necessary to produce these forms.

3- to 5-Year Balance Sheet

The balance sheet provides a snapshot of your business' financial position for each planning period. More than an income statement, the balance sheet includes such things as the value of equipment, facilities, and property. For this reason, it provides the potential investor with better information about the financial condition of your company than can be derived merely from your income statements.

The balance sheet compares all assets and liabilities. Excess value is the company's net worth. Net worth is distributed as equity or retained as earnings for the company to use. In either case, the net worth is listed as a liability. Once done, liabilities and assets should balance out, hence the name balance sheet.

Balance sheets may be difficult to prepare without professional assistance. Buildings, facilities, and equipment depreciate in value over a set period. Property improvements result in appreciation of property, and inventory values vary with time and acquisition costs.

Cash Flow or Cash Budget Statements

Cash flow statements, sometimes referred to as cash budgets, tell the story about your business' ability to conduct business on a daily basis. Most businesses are subject to seasonal or market fluctuations. It is important to be sufficiently liquid to survive lean times. This is also true of businesses that maintain large inventories or that operate with a large credit base.

The cash flow statement is similar to your checking account ledger. You work to maintain a positive balance in your account at all times. If you run out of cash, you no longer have the resources necessary to conduct business, even if your income statement shows a continuous net profit. Many businesses have closed because of success. By trying to produce more product than cash flow permits, a business may run out of cash and be unable to deliver products on time, thus losing contracts or not collecting receivables when expected.

Most lenders will be very interested in your cash flow statements and will check them against your policies for accounts receivable, aging, inventory turn and other indicators of your business health.

Break-Even Analysis

The break-even analysis tells you how much income in gross sales you must have to meet all expenses. Expenses include total fixed expenses plus the cost of goods. To arrive at a break-even figure, you divide total fixed expenses such as rent, utilities, and insurance by your gross profit margin.

Profit margin may fluctuate from product line to product line, so you will have to adjust your figures accordingly. The main reason for including a break-even analysis in your business plan is to show that you have sufficient income to continue operations.

CHAPTER WRAP-UP

Your smart business plan will give you the edge your business needs to prosper in today's competitive environment. The key to your business plan is preparation and research. Make sure you allot sufficient time to research the various aspects of your business plan. Use the basic outline in this chapter to help you stay organized in your research efforts.

Start now to focus on several critical aspects of your business. You will want to:

Clearly identify your business concept. What product or service will you sell and what type of business is it?

Know your industry. Become familiar with the ups and downs of your industry. Is it seasonal or are there cyclical economic influences that will affect your operation? How big is your industry and at what maturity level is it currently?

Understand your target market. Know the demographics and psychographics of your customer base. Find out what appeals to your customers and work those things into your sales and marketing strategy.

Familiarize yourself with your competitors. Take a close look at what you're up against. What are your competitors doing that you aren't doing? What things will you do better than your competitors?

Know what distinguishes your product or service. Investors will want to know what makes your business concept different and unique. Is it a new product or service? Did you improve on an existing idea? Are you serving a new market or filling a need in a market that has not yet been reached?

As you sit down and document the answers to these questions — and a slew of others — you will begin to see the blueprints of your business. You will use these blueprints to approach investors and lenders. You will also use them to build a successful business.

USEFUL RESOURCES

The Successful Business Plan: Secrets & Strategies by Rhonda M. Abrams. A step-by-step guide that gives insider tips on writing a business plan. Includes helpful financials to make it easier to compile your information. Complete business plan kit includes templates of the numerous worksheets included in the book or easy-to-use software for Microsoft *Windows* applications.

U.S. Small Business Administration (SBA). Check out *http://www.sba.gov* or call your local SBDC to learn how you can participate in a "Developing Your Business Plan Workshop." The Internet Web site contains a shareware library of programs, templates, software demos, and on-line workbooks to help you get started on your business plan.

Power Business Plans by KMT Software. (For use with *Windows 95*™ only.) This CD-ROM based software package can help you write your own business plan. It includes five sample business plans as well as templates to develop your financial and text portions of your business plan. You can obtain a free copy of the CD-ROM to review (there is a $5.00 shipping and handling charge). If you are satisfied with the software, call (800) 228-2275 and charge the remainder of the cost of the program, $39.95, to your credit card.

101 Wet Stone Hill Road
Wakefield, RI 02756
Telephone (401) 422-8888
evergreen@inter.net
Contact: Nolan Wentworth

SAMPLE BUSINESS PLAN

Evergreen Lawn Care

Professional Lawn Care

Proprietary Information: DO NOT DISTRIBUTE

TABLE OF CONTENTS

EverGreen Lawn Care
Business Plan

EXECUTIVE SUMMARY

Evergreen Lawn Care is a start-up company that will provide fertilizing and weed and insect control. The sole proprietor of the company is Mr. Nolan Wentworth who is contributing his own capital, significant lawn care experience, knowledge, and business skill. Mr. Wentworth is an area expert on lawn care with a very good reputation. His expertise and reputation give Evergreen a competitive service advantage. In addition to Mr. Wentworth's contributed capital, Evergreen will need another $75,000 for start-up capital. The business will operate in the South County, Rhode Island.

Evergreen's marketing plan was designed to initially attempt to convert a large portion of the more than 2,000 customers that Mr. Wentworth helped to service when he was employed by GreenThumb, an area lawn care company. Additional marketing and advertising strategies are designed to target the business executive/professional who doesn't have the time nor expertise to maintain a beautiful lawn but understand the value a nicely landscaped lawn adds to property values. Evergreen' particular niche and positioning will be to appeal to the environmentally conscious homeowners who are concerned about their kids, the long lasting health of their lawn and making a small contribution to mother earth.

Currently, the lawn care business in South County is dominated by one company — Mr. Wentworth's former employer, GreenThumb. Some landscapers and grass cutting companies also offer fertilizing services, but these providers hold an insignificant portion of the market. From all indicators, the South County lawn care market has experienced very little competition. Therefore, Evergreen has an excellent opportunity to create a large customer base if it can persuade people that it can offer greater expertise and value added services over the current supplier, Green Thumb.

While Evergreen will directly compete with GreenThumb, it is offering a service that is differentiated from that of GreenThumb's. Here are some of the ways that Evergreen's service will be different:

The 14 point lawn care evaluation. Evergreen will offer every prospective customer a free lawn evaluation that can be used to develop a custom designed six step lawn care program. GreenThumb does not offer a comparable analysis.

Evergreen's organic alternative. Evergreen will offer customers an organic alternative that is safer for the environment than the fertilizer used by GreenThumb. The facts will easily show how Evergreen's services will cost far less in the long run, while customers will appreciate the added safety the services afford their children and pets.

Evergreen's experience and expertise. Evergreen is the only area company to have Nolan Wentworth: a lawn care professional who is highly respected in the South County region.

TYPE OF BUSINESS

Evergreen Lawn Care is a service business specializing in fertilizing and weed and insect control.

COMPANY/BUSINESS SUMMARY

This is a start-up business that will be organized as a sole proprietorship; a business to be owned and operated by Nolan Wentworth. The firm will provide services for the care and maintenance of lawns, trees, and shrubs. The company will concentrate services on preventing plant life disease and promoting plant growth by utilizing natural alternatives.

FINANCIAL OBJECTIVES

The financial plan and analysis section of this business plan details the projected operating results, financial position, cash budgets, and break-even point. Below is a chart that summarizes the financial objectives for the five year planning period beginning in 1997.

Operating Performance Highlights

(all numbers in $000)

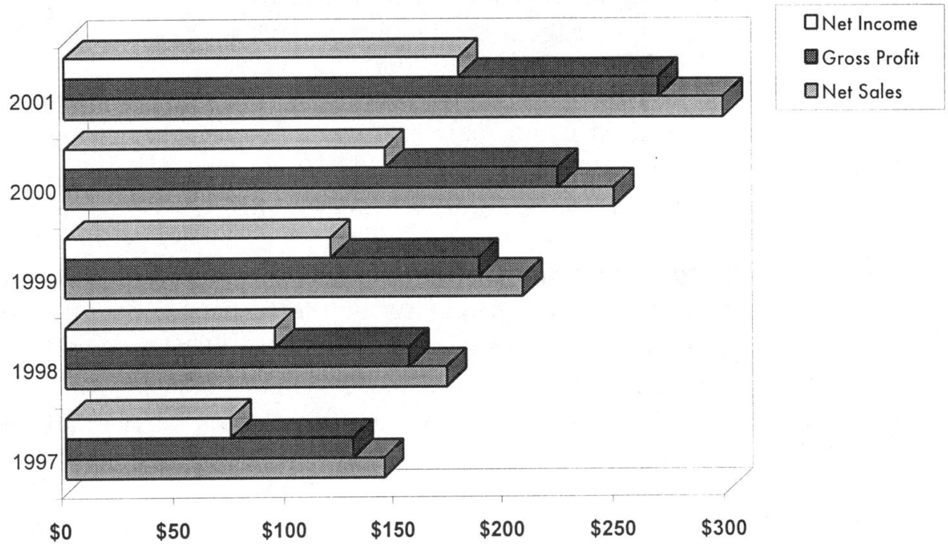

Above chart assumes 20% annual growth in sales.

Operating Performance Highlights

	1997	1998	1999	2000	2001
Net Sales	$144	$173	$208	$249	$298
Gross Profit	$130	$156	$188	$224	$269
Net Income	$74	$94	$120	$145	$179

Management Overview

Nolan Wentworth is a graduate of the University of Rhode Island's Turf Sciences program. Mr. Wentworth also worked for five years as a greenskeeper at a large public golf course in Massachusetts and worked for another five years as a landscape architect for a nursery in Rhode Island. For the last two years, Mr. Wentworth worked for GreenThumb as a lawn specialist, a position that required him to become company certified. Mr. Wentworth worked under the direction of an agronomist for over 6 months while he was with Green Thumb.

PRODUCT/SERVICE AND COMPETITION

Evergreen Lawn Care will offer a six application lawn care program. These applications will be custom designed for the particular grass type and location. Evergreen will be offering the homeowner safe, all-natural fertilizers and weed controllers.

FUNDS REQUESTED

Evergreen is requesting a five year $75,000 loan to finance the start-up. Collateral of about $65,000 is available to secure the loan.

USE OF PROCEEDS

The $75,000 loan proceeds will be used to purchase a truck and equipment that will cost approximately $65,000. The remaining loan proceeds will be used to purchase supplies (fertilizer and other related chemicals).

COMPANY BACKGROUND

Identification of Market Opportunity

Evergreen Lawn Care plans on providing fertilizing and weed and insect control services to the South County of Rhode Island. According to the statistics provided by the Small Business Development Center of Rhode Island, the lawn care business is a $750,000 market in South County. There are no Rhode Island statistics on the rate of growth in revenues for the lawn care industry, but according to *Lawn and Turf Magazine*, a trade association publication, the national growth rate for lawn care services has been 20% for the last 5 years and is forecasted to grow at that rate into the near future.

South County Rhode Island is an excellent market opportunity for this service with only one competitor, GreenThumb, a national company that has granted a franchise in South County.

The Professional Landscapers of America estimate that the homeowner's return at resale can be between $800 and $1,200 over the cost of lawn care improvements. However, there is no debate that the value of a home is enhanced through the use of lawn care services. The use of lawn care services tends to be common in areas where home values are relatively high and where home sales are vigorous.

While Mr. Wentworth was with Green Thumb, he observed several things that convinced him that his EverGreen start-up has excellent chances for success:

- There is an overwhelming desire by most customers for a safer alternative to the toxic chemicals that required flag notification at the end of a treatment.
- Traditional lawn treatment companies are wed to the past and have little opportunity to change methods because of equipment investment and reliance on old ways.
- Mr. Wentworth studied the organic trend closely and experimented with it extensively. He became convinced that his expertise, drive, and customer knowledge would stack the cards in his favor.

BUSINESS HISTORY

Evergreen is a start-up company. Mr. Wentworth has recently resigned from his position with GreenThumb to start his venture. To date, he has invested approximately $5,000 of his own capital.

GROWTH AND FINANCIAL OBJECTIVES

The first year goal of Evergreen is to have 275 customers by the end of the first 12 months with subsequent annual growth in revenues equal to the national projected rate of 20% per year.

5 Year Sales Forecast

(all numbers in $000)

	1997	1998	1999	2000	2001
Lawn Feed and Weed	$90	$108	$130	$156	$187
Tree & Shrub care	50	60	72	86	103
Other	4	5	6	7	8
Total Sales	$144	$173	$208	$249	$298

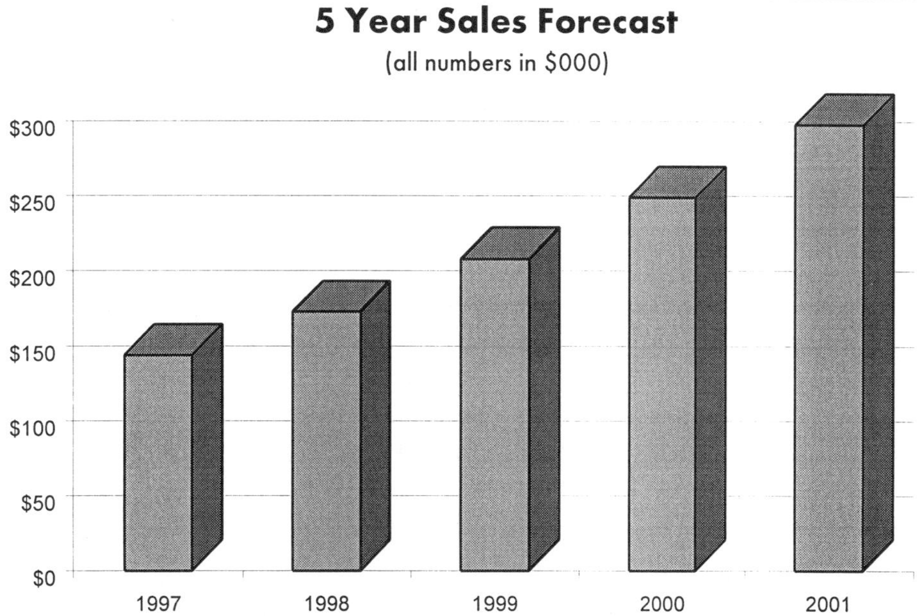

Sales forecast based on 275 customers the first year, followed by 20% growth

LEGAL STRUCTURE AND OWNERSHIP

The company is organized as a sole proprietorship. Mr. Wentworth has filed all the necessary paperwork to gain a d.b.a. certificate and all appropriate permits.

COMPANY LOCATION AND FACILITIES

Mr. Wentworth will conduct the business from his home office at 101 Wet Stone Hill Road, Wakefield, Rhode Island. The home office is equipped with a personal computer, laser printer, and fax machine. Mr. Wentworth has erected a 2,500 square foot barn on this residential property that will be used to store supplies and equipment, including the company truck.

PLANS FOR FINANCING THE BUSINESS

Mr. Wentworth has contributed $5,000 of his personal funds to the business venture. He plans to contribute an additional $20,000 from a maturing CD and another $10,000 from a loan from his father-in law. He will need an additional $75,000, in the form of a five year business loan, to purchase supplies, equipment, and a truck. The loan can be collateralized, at least to some extent, with the title to the truck and the equipment. The truck and equipment will have a combined cost of $65,000.

OWNER'S BACKGROUND

Since the business is organized as a sole proprietorship, there is no management team. Mr. Wentworth will be the sole manager.

BACKGROUND ON MR. WENTWORTH

Nolan Wentworth, who will run the business, is a graduate of the University of Rhode Island's Turf Sciences program. He has also had excellent practical experience, with much of this related to lawn care. Mr. Wentworth worked for five years as a greenskeeper at a large public golf course in Massachusetts and worked for another five years as a landscape architect for a nursery in Rhode Island. For the last two years, Mr. Wentworth worked for GreenThumb as a lawn specialist, a position for which he had to become company certified. While he was with GreenThumb, Mr. Wentworth worked under the direction of an agronomist for over 6 months.

Mr. Wentworth also keeps up with developments in the industry. He is very much aware of the April 1990 public hearings held by the U.S. Senate to acquire information on the environmental impact of the use of chemical insecticides and fertilizers. He is keenly aware that the government may impose increased government regulation on this business, and is constantly reevaluating any impact this might have on the industry. He has researched new fertilizers/ insecticides that are not harmful to the environment and is very much interested in organically based fertilizers. Mr. Wentworth plans to stay on top of the effects of new products on the environment through books, magazines, conferences, and workshops. His business knowledge will become a public relations tool.

OTHER EMPLOYEES

The company will have two part-time employees. Evergreen will utilize the skills of two other family members:

- Mr. Wentworth's wife, Jane, will manage the books for the company and manage customer renewal process.
- In the summer, Mr. Wentworth will employ his son Jimmy (age 20), who is attending the University of Massachusetts Amherst. Jimmy is studying Architectural Landscape Design.

MARKET ANALYSIS

SUMMARY

From all indications, the South County lawn care market is large enough to support several companies. At this time only one major player is in the market. The lack of competition in the market combined with Evergreen's unique expertise and approach make success highly probable. The overall market seems large enough and is growing fast enough to provide plenty of business to a company that can successfully service its target market. Evergreen's target market has three factors that will also contribute to success.

- They are sold on the idea that a beautiful lawn and fine looking shrubs and trees add significant value to a property.
- They lack the time needed to conduct their own lawn care program.
- They have the economic resources to afford a six step application program.
- While not essential, Wentworth believes that the large majority of customers will select the EverGreen alternative because of its organic approach.

INDUSTRY ANALYSIS

It is estimated that more than 15 million homes nationwide use lawn care services. The size of the South County, Rhode Island market for lawn care is estimated to be potentially $750,000 per year. This estimate is based on the industry statistics that disclose the number of suburban households per thousand that contracts for lawn care. Evergreen's projected share of the market is modest, at approximately 14% of the market by the end of year one.

TARGET MARKET

The market that Evergreen will be targeting is the suburban upper-middle to upper-class market with household annual incomes that range from $60,000 to $100,000 and higher. In South County, Rhode Island, there are approximately 22,000 households with annual incomes in the range defined above. The six application per year lawn care maintenance program, which costs an average of $360 (for a 7,000 square foot area), is affordable for this market. The defined market can be easily convinced of or already sees the merit of the six application process as a way of assuring a beautiful lawn. Statistics show that in neighborhoods where the average household income is $60,000 or above, 1 out of every 3 homes has a lawn care provider. However, market penetration in the South County area has not been great up till now with only one local vendor providing service. Estimates show that only 1 out of 10 homes in this demographic segment currently contract lawn care services.

CUSTOMER PROFILE

The demographics of the homeowner market that Evergreen will serve are as follows:

- Income Level: $60,000 + annual household income
- Occupation: Executive and professional
- Median property values: $130,000 +
- Neighborhoods: Suburban, upper-middle class
- More likely to have at least one child

MAJOR COMPETITORS AND PARTICIPANTS

The only major competitor at this time is GreenThumb. Other competitors are lawn maintenance (grass cutting) and landscapers who offer lawn care as secondary to their primary business. GreenThumb is a national company that has had a South County franchise for the past 4 years. GreenThumb has had the market virtually to itself. Evergreen will be in direct competition with GreenThumb. Mr. Wentworth was employed by GreenThumb for the last two years and will attempt to persuade GreenThumb customers to convert to EverGreen at 5% below their GreenThumb cost. GreenThumb has over 2,000 customers.

PROJECTED MARKET GROWTH AND MARKET SHARE OBJECTIVES

Mr. Wentworth's sales goals are very modest with a target of 275 customers by the end of year 1. It is estimated that Evergreen's market share will be approximately 14% of the existing market but under 5% of the potential market. Mr. Wentworth is predicting that half of these customers will come from the existing Green Thumb base and half will be new customers. Annual growth is assumed to be at least at the national projection of 20% for each of the next five years. These goals seem to be modest and achievable when compared with the customer list of over 2000 customers from GreenThumb.

PRODUCT/SERVICE OFFERING

PRODUCT/SERVICE SUMMARY

The service that Evergreen will offer is a six step lawn care program that involves fertilizing for growth and color and applications that will control weeds and insects. Each program will be custom designed based on a 14 point, no charge, evaluation.

PRODUCT/SERVICE UNIQUENESS

Evergreen's service is also unique because of the skill and knowledge that Mr. Wentworth brings to the business. In addition, Mr. Wentworth's customer relation skills help to make this venture unique and give a definite competitive advantage to the firm. Mr. Wentworth knows that being courteous to the clients and his expert qualifications are the most critical issues for this business. If a lawn care firm is unable to maintain a friendly, courteous relationship with its customers, it will not be successful.

PRODUCT/SERVICE DESCRIPTIONS

Evergreen will be in the business of selling a six part application process that will give the homeowner a beautiful lawn. The service consists of a six specifically designed and seasonally scheduled service visits (applications).

Early season. The first visit of the year involves an application that will promote spring green-up and lawn recovery from winter stress. The application will also help control weeds and crabgrass.

Spring. This application is designed to give your lawn extra nutrients which will result in a greener and thicker lawn. Weed and crabgrass control will be applied, only if necessary.

Early summer. This fertilizer application gets your lawn ready for the possible stressful summer (heat and draught) ahead. The lawn will be checked for isolated weed and insect problems and treated accordingly.

Late summer. Like application 3, this is a fertilizer that will help promote color without pushing growth. Again, the lawn will be checked for isolated weed and insect problems and treated accordingly.

Early fall. This application is designed to help thicken the lawn and to promote new root growth. Since weeds and insects can be present in fall lawns, the technician will check for those problems and treat the lawn accordingly.

Late fall. This application consists of a special fertilizer that will promote root growth and food storage for the winter ahead. This application is critical for winter survival and will help bring about a healthier lawn for the following spring.

COMPETITIVE COMPARISONS

Many of the services offered by Evergreen are comparable in price and value to that of GreenThumb. However, there are four differences.

Evergreen will offer a free 14 point evaluation that will help the technician design an appropriate program and will give the homeowner a better understanding of his or her lawn's needs. The 14 point evaluation is in writing (in a checklist format) and examines the following:

- Grass type
- Turf density
- Color
- Thatch
- Diseases
- Soil type
- Weeds
- Mowing
- Insects
- Shade

- Watering
- Problem grasses
- Potential
- Present conditions

Another distinct difference between GreenThumb and Evergreen is that Evergreen will give the homeowner the option of using organic and environmentally safe fertilizers. The homeowner will be told, in writing, the pros and cons of organic versus non-organic fertilizers and the difference in cost between the two will be clearly disclosed.

The third competitive difference is that Evergreen will not charge an additional amount for grub control as is the case with GreenThumb.

Finally, another competitive advantage is Mr. Wentworth who is well known in the community and has already developed rapport with many of GreenThumb's customers. In addition to working with many homeowners in South County, Mr. Wentworth is a frequent guest on a local talk radio home and garden show. The benefits Evergreen can sell because of Mr. Wentworth's background, reputation, and experience include many intangibles: confidence, reliability, and answers to questions about lawn care.

COMPETITION COMPARISON

The following chart summarizes the key differences between GreenThumb and EverGreen Lawn Care:

FEATURE	EVERGREEN	GREENTHUMB
Seasonal Cost	$10.00 per 1,000 sq. ft.	$9.75 per 1,000 sq. ft.
Customer Satisfaction	Money Back Guarantee	Money Back Guarantee
Treatment	Organic	Toxic Chemicals
Child and Pet Safe	Yes	No
Grub Control	Included	Extra Charge
Effective Long Term Treatment	Yes	No (Requires more and more chemicals)

RESEARCH AND DEVELOPMENT

Evergreen has access to a regional argonomist who is employed by Grass Roots, Inc., Evergreen's fertilizer supplier. Grass Roots, Inc. spends in excess of $500,000 annually on R&D and freely shares its findings with its customers. Grass Roots, Inc. also conducts quarterly seminars on lawn care at its Montvale, New Jersey, headquarters. In his study of the organic treatments, Mr. Wentworth spent a lot of time with Grass Roots, Inc. and has a strong working relationship with its research team.

PATENTS AND TRADEMARKS

Evergreen does not own any patents or trademarks.

MARKETING PLAN

CREATING AND MAINTAINING CUSTOMERS

Evergreen will attract and maintain its customer base by competitively pricing the service and demonstrating, through hard work and a customer driven approach, that the company can take the time and hassle out of lawn care. Evergreen will position itself as the busy person's safe and natural way to a beautiful lawn. Customers will quickly recognize that the company's main "asset" is its founder, Mr. Nolan Wentworth. And as is often the case with service oriented businesses, new customers will be created as current customers begin to appreciate the skill, expertise, and knowledge of Mr. Wentworth. Those customers will recommend Evergreen to their family and friends and will help to broaden the customer base.

PRODUCT PRICING STRATEGY

Evergreen's service will be priced to be competitive with the marketplace. Mr. Wentworth understands the pricing strategy of the competitor and he will monitor its pricing to stay competitive. GreenThumb's basic price is $9.75 per 1,000 square feet (with discounts given, because of economies of scale, when total square footage is greater than 12,000 feet).

Evergreen's sales literature tells customers that Evergreen will meet the price or promotional appeals of any competitor, as long as the customer has documented proof — such as a competitor's bid sheet, program estimate, or coupon. Existing GreenThumb customers will be given a one year 10% discount enticement to convert their lawn care service to Evergreen. Mr. Wentworth is happy to give these discounts for the first year in order to establish the business base. He is confident that he will be able to retain the customer over a several year period.

PRODUCT POSITIONING

While Mr. Wentworth brings some clear skills to the business, the most important positioning of the business is its safe, natural and longer lasting approach. There have been many negative reports on the use of lawn chemicals. EverGreen has contracted with a local artist to design a truck that will communicate this message loud and clear to the customer. The company has also secured a local telephone number that spells NATURAL. Call NATURAL to find out more will be one of the messages on the truck.

The Evergreen service will be positioned as the professional/ executive solution to expert lawn care. Advertising will discuss how just about every homeowner could perform their own lawn care program but the time and hassle of the task are a barrier. Emphasis will also be placed on the value of expert service. Mr. Wentworth's background/reputation and the 14 point evaluation will help substantiate the expert claim.

SALES AND SERVICE DELIVERY

The sales cycle in this service business is very seasonal. Seventy-five percent of all purchase decisions are made between February 15th and April 15th. The service delivery begins on May 1st. There are three main ways to get a new client and the chances of success are in this order:

- Friend referral
- Article or other public relations opportunity
- Direct mail
- Newspaper advertisement
- Prospect notices truck in neighborhood

The promotional plan below is designed to complement this sales cycle and customer buying mentality.

Mr. Wentworth will perform much of the direct calls on sales prospects and lead the follow-up efforts. He will also use the services of freelancers in the area to perform telemarketing. Mr. Wentworth's wife, Jane, will handle the books, manage the billing and sign up customers from one year to the next.

The service will be delivered to the customer using a variety of equipment and tools. Evergreen will initially purchase a 1996 GMC small flat bed truck that will be retrofitted with a tank and pump system used to apply the fertilizer and weed control. The truck, tank, and pump system is the key equipment of the business. The estimated cost of the system is $65,000.

PROMOTIONAL STRATEGY

The promotional strategy will consist of telemarketing calls to existing GreenThumb customers who will be told about Mr. Wentworth's service and who will be offered the one year 10% discount. In addition, any customer who refers two customers to Evergreen will receive one of the applications free. On average, the free application represents a $60 value. A telemarketing service will also be utilized to set up appointments for the *14 Point Lawn Evaluation.* Homeowners will be contacted and informed that an Evergreen technician will be in the area conducting free, no obligation, lawn analysis. The calls will clearly differentiate the service from EverGreen's chemical unfriendly competitor.

Evergreen will also use a local bulk mail coupon service that will mail monthly coupon savers and offers for the *free 14 Point Lawn Evaluation* to households with median incomes of $60,000 or more. The mailing will include a special offer for 1,000 frequent flier miles on American or United, the two most frequently held affinity programs. Mr. Wentworth recently attended a convention that discussed the value of these programs when services of over $500 are offered to high income purchasers.

Newspaper advertising campaigns, both in traditional hometown papers and in the free "shopper papers," will be executed in late winter/early spring and in early fall.

The service truck for the company will bear the company logo and a brief listing of services offered, along with the NATURAL business telephone number.

A brochure will be given to each potential customer when the written estimate is completed. The brochure will describe Mr. Wentworth's skills and experience and the type of service the customer will receive. In addition, after a service is rendered, a brochure describing what the customer needs to do to maintain the grass will be given.

Special prices in the spring will be offered and discounts to regular customers who contract for year-long services.

Mr. Wentworth plans to spend a reasonable part of his time working with local newspapers and radio shows to place articles about the advantages of natural lawn care. He has enlisted the services of some local college journalism students to write some example articles that will be distributed to the media.

FINANCIAL PLAN AND ANALYSIS

INITIAL CAPITAL REQUIREMENTS

The initial start-up capital requirements of the business are expected to be about $110,000. A large portion of the initial capital (76%) is for the upfront costs for equipment and supplies. The remaining amount (24%) is for the monthly expenses needed to launch the business.

FINANCIAL HIGHLIGHTS

Key financial ratios have been calculated for the five year planning period and are shown below. Although the Debt/Equity ratio is a bit high at the end of year 1, it improves significantly during years 2 through 5. Please note that since this is a service business, the gross margin is 100% because there is no cost of sales, just operating expenses.

5-YEAR INCOME STATEMENT

The projected operating results for the five year planning period are shown below in the pro-forma income statements. Net profits range from $8,000 for the first full year of operation to $36,000 by the fifth year.

5-YEAR BALANCE SHEET

The projected financial position as of the end of each fiscal year in the planning period is shown below.

CASH BUDGETS

Cash budgets have been prepared using two formats: a 12 month cash budget for year one and annual budgets for each of the five planning periods. Both reports are shown below.

BREAK-EVEN ANALYSIS

The monthly break-even point of about $5,200 in sales translates to about $62,400 annually. According to income statement projections, the store will operate above the break-even point for all five years in the planning period.

Estimated Start-Up Capital

	Monthly Expenses	Cash Needed to Start	% of Total
MONTHLY			
Salary of owner-manager	$1,000	$3,000	2.7%
All other salaries and wages	833	2,499	2.3%
Rent		0	0.0%
Advertising	250	3,000	2.7%
Delivery expense		0	0.0%
Supplies	1,250	15,000	13.6%
Telephone		0	0.0%
Other utilities		0	0.0%
Insurance	250	3,000	2.7%
Taxes, including Social Security		0	0.0%
Interest		0	0.0%
Maintenance		0	0.0%
Legal and other professional fees		0	0.0%
Miscellaneous		0	0.0%
Subtotal		**$26,499**	**24%**
ONE-TIME COSTS			
Fixtures and Equipment		$65,000	59.1%
Decorating and remodeling			0.0%
Installation charges			0.0%
Starting inventory		10,000	9.1%
Deposits with public utilities			0.0%
Legal and other professional fees		1,000	0.9%
Licenses and permits		500	0.5%
Advertising and promotion for opening		2,000	1.8%
Cash		5,000	4.5%
Other			0.0%
Subtotal		**$83,500**	**76%**
TOTAL ESTIMATED START-UP CAPITAL		**$109,999**	

Financial Highlights

	1997	1998	1999	2000	2001
Liquidity					
Current Ratio	7.46	9.92	17.15	20.69	25.92
Acid-Test Ratio	5.92	7.62	14.08	16.85	21.31
Leverage					
Debt Ratio	34.43%	19.85%	12.18%	7.19%	3.89%
Debt/Equity Ratio	52.52%	24.77%	13.87%	7.75%	4.04%
Times Interest Earned	13.33	19.80	31.00	49.33	90.50
Efficiency					
Inventory Turnover	0.70	0.57	0.50	0.50	0.48
Average Collection Period	25.35	31.65	31.59	29.32	24.50
Total Asset Turnover	0.68	0.65	0.59	0.54	0.50
Profitability					
Gross Margin	90.28%	90.17%	90.38%	89.96%	90.27%
Return on Assets	34.91%	35.21%	33.99%	31.59%	30.24%
Return on Equity	53.24%	43.93%	38.71%	34.04%	31.46%

Income Statement

For the Years 1997 through 2001
(all numbers in $000)

REVENUE	1997	1998	1999	2000	2001
Gross sales	$144	$173	$208	$249	$298
Less returns and allowances	0	0	0	0	0
Net Sales	$144	$173	$208	$249	$298
COST OF SALES					
Total Cost of Goods Sold	$14	$17	$20	$25	$29
Gross Profit (Loss)	$130	$156	$188	$224	$269
OPERATING EXPENSES					
Selling					
Salaries and wages	$3	$3	$3	$3	$3
Commissions	0	0	0	0	0
Advertising	5	5	5	5	5
Depreciation					
Other	1	1	1	1	1
Total Selling Expenses	$9	$9	$9	$9	$9
General & Administrative					
Salaries and wages	$20	$25	$30	$40	$50
Employee benefits	3	4	5	6	7
Payroll taxes	3	4	5	6	7
Insurance	4	4	4	4	4
Rent	0	0	0	0	0
Utilities	2	2	2	2	2
Depreciation & amortization	5	5	5	5	5
Office supplies	1	1	1	1	1
Travel & entertainment	1	1	1	1	1
Postage	1	1	1	1	1
Interest	6	5	4	3	2
Furniture & equipment	1	1	1	1	1
Total G&A Expenses	$47	$53	$59	$70	$81
Total Operating Expenses	$56	$62	$68	$79	$90
Net Income Before Taxes	$74	$94	$120	$145	$179
Taxes on income	0	0	0	0	0
Net Income After Taxes	$74	$94	$120	$145	$179
Extraordinary gain or loss					
Income tax on extraordinary gain					
NET INCOME (LOSS)	$74	$94	$120	$145	$179

Balance Sheet

1997 through 2001
(all numbers in $000)

ASSETS	1997	1998	1999	2000	2001
Current Assets					
Cash	$53	$68	$148	$191	$237
Net accounts receivable	10	15	18	20	20
Inventory	20	30	40	50	60
Temporary investment	9	10	10	0	11
Prepaid expenses	5	6	7	8	9
Total Current Assets	$97	$129	$223	$269	$337
Fixed Assets					
Long-term investments	$25	$45	$45	$0	$65
Land	0	0	0	0	0
Buildings (net of depreciation)	0	0	0	100	100
Plant & equipment (net)	80	83	75	80	80
Furniture & fixtures (net)	10	10	10	10	10
Total Net Fixed Assets	$115	$138	$130	$190	$255
TOTAL ASSETS	$212	$267	$353	$459	$592
LIABILITIES					
Current Liabilities					
Accounts payable	$10	$10	$10	$10	$10
Short-term notes	0	0	0	0	0
Current portion of long-term notes	0	0	0	0	0
Accruals & other payables	3	3	3	3	3
Total Current Liabilities	$13	$13	$13	$13	$13
Long-term Liabilities					
Mortgage	$0	$0	$0	$0	$0
Other long-term liabilities	60	40	30	20	10
Total Long-term Liabilities	$60	$40	$30	$20	$10
Shareholders' Equity					
Capital stock	$80	$80	$80	$80	$80
Retained earnings	59	134	230	346	489
Total Shareholders'	$139	$214	$310	$426	$569
TOTAL LIABILITIES & EQUITY	$212	$267	$353	$459	$592

Cash Budget

For the Year 1997
(all numbers are in $000)

Cash Budget

For the Year 1997
(all numbers in $000)

	Jan	Feb	Mar	Apr	May	Jun	Jul	Aug	Sep	Oct	Nov	Dec
Beginning cash balance	$2	$22	$25	$26	$30	$34	$35	$39	$42	$45	$47	$51
Cash from operations	10	10	10	10	10	10	10	10	10	10	10	10
Total Available Cash	$12	$32	$35	$36	$40	$44	$45	$49	$52	$55	$57	$61
Less:												
Capital expenditures	$84											
Operating Expenses	$15	$6	$6	$5	$5	$6	$5	$6	$6	$5	$5	$5
Interest			2			2				2		2
Dividends												
Debt retirement	1	1	1	1	1	1	1	1	1	1	1	1
Other												
Total Disbursements	$100	$7	$9	$6	$6	$9	$6	$7	$7	$8	$6	$8
Cash Surplus (Deficit)	($88)	$25	$26	$30	$34	$35	$39	$42	$45	$47	$51	$53
Add:												
Short-term loans												
Long-term loans	75											
Capital stock issues	35											
Total Additions	$110	$0	$0	$0	$0	$0	$0	$0	$0	$0	$0	$0
Ending Cash Balance	$22	$25	$26	$30	$34	$35	$39	$42	$45	$47	$51	$53

Cash Budget Activity – First 12 Months

(all numbers in $000)

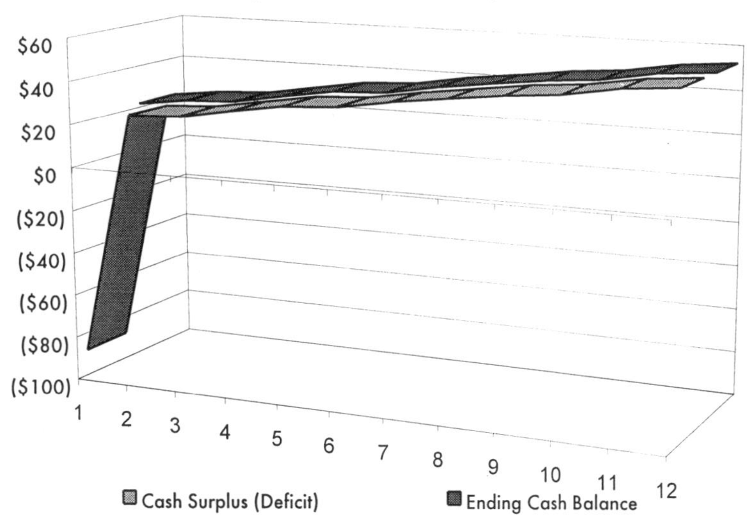

Cash Budget

For the Years 1997 through 2001
(all numbers in $000)

	1997	1998	1999	2000	2001
Beginning cash balance	$2	$53	$68	$148	$191
Cash from operations	120	112	185	190	190
Total Available Cash	$122	$165	$253	$338	$381
Less:					
Capital expenditures	$84				
Operating Expenses	75	80	89	132	130
Interest	8	5	4	3	2
Dividends	0				
Debt retirement	12	12	12	12	12
Other	0				
Total Disbursements	$179	$97	$105	$147	$144
Cash Surplus (Deficit)	($57)	$68	$148	$191	$237
Add:					
Short-term loans	$0				
Long-term loans	75				
Capital stock issues	35				
Total Additions	$110	$0	$0	$0	$0
Ending Cash Balance	$53	$68	$148	$191	$237

Cash Budget Activity – 5 Years

(all numbers in $000)

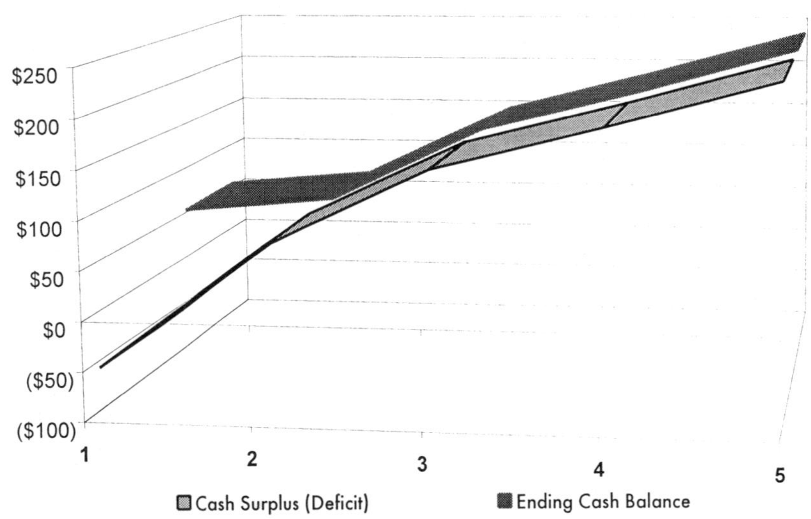

Break-Even Analysis

	Fixed Costs	Variable Costs
Product		
Average Cost of Product		$15.00
Monthly Selling		
Sales salaries & commissions	$1,000	
Advertising	$500	
Miscellaneous selling expense	$400	
Monthly General		
Office salaries	$0	
Supplies	$1,000	
Miscellaneous general expense	$1,000	
Totals	$3,900	$15.00
Average Selling price per unit		$60.00
Results:		
Contribution margin per unit		$45.00
Monthly unit sales at break-even point		87
Monthly Sales Dollars at break-even point		$5,200

Break-Even Analysis

(all numbrs in ($000)

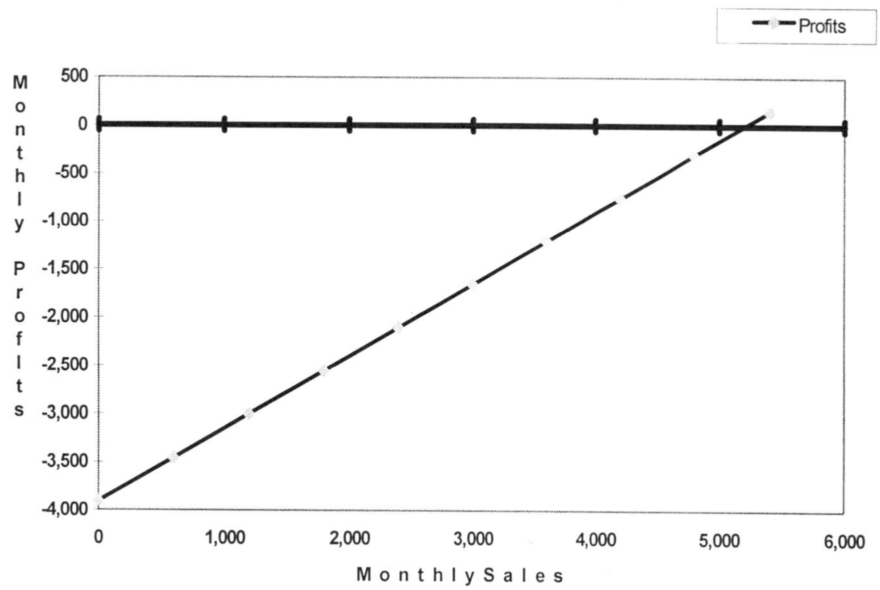

CHAPTER 8

Obtaining the Financing You Need

Business ownership can bring many new challenges to your life. Many of these challenges center around having enough money to help you stay afloat in down times and keep you riding high during times of profitability. As a startup, you will need to consider how you will obtain financing for many aspects of your venture. For instance, unless you are a home-based business, you will need to purchase a building or rent office space to operate your business. More than likely, you will need equipment or machinery — even if all you need is a computer and a fax machine. And, until your profits can carry your business, you will need working capital to sustain your business' life.

This chapter explores the world of financing and teaches you how to:

- Understand the basic types of funding and to learn which one might be best for you;
- Deal with your local bank;
- Approach the often elusive venture capital community; and
- Find out more about the numerous federal, state, and private loan programs available to today's small businesses.

You may be fortunate enough to have family members, friends, or local associates who can lend you money. You may even be able to rely completely on your personal savings. For the majority of both new and existing small business owners, however, obtaining financing from outside sources is a must.

SOME FACTORS A LENDER WILL CONSIDER

Obtaining financing for your small business will ultimately depend on two major factors:

- Your business' ability to repay the loan, and
- The ability of the principal owners, or management team, of the business.

Funding a new business venture from outside sources can be difficult to obtain for one overriding reason: A start-up business usually has no track record that will show its ability to repay a loan. The owners or managers may not have a proven track record either. Risks are very high for untested ideas and untested owners and managers. Just because you were a manager for a large corporation doesn't necessarily mean you can successfully run a small business. In fact, you may find it easier to obtain financing for an existing business than for one that you start from scratch.

The time to look for start-up or expansion funds from prospective lenders is when you have completed your business plan. As you read in the previous chapter, a business plan can make or break your business. And, in the case of securing financing, this is especially true.

BASIC TYPES OF FUNDING

Before you approach a lender, make sure you understand the basic types of funding. The two most common types of funding are:

- Debt financing, which usually centers around asset-based loans, and
- Venture, or equity financing.

Lenders will fund asset-based loans on the probability of obtaining repayment of the loan and the type and marketability of the collateral you have. Your collateral may be in the form of stocks or bonds, a home or automobile, or any other items that have a value and can be easily sold by the holder of the collateral if you fail to make your loan payments. Equity financing usually does not require collateral but the lender will probably put a performance requirement on your business. If your business does not meet the requirement(s), you may lose management say-so in the business and, in some cases, you may lose your stake in the venture.

Most equity funding is based on a participation in ownership of the business with the expectation of getting a multiple of the investment during a fixed period — usually five years. This compares to debt financing where the lender makes no provision for participation in your business. In this case, the lender simply expects a payback of the amount borrowed, plus interest (or rent on the money), for the period of the loan. The loan can normally be paid in installments or a lump sum or a combination of both.

Most debt lenders want to rent money to you at a rate that is higher than what they can get by investing in safer investments, such as treasuries, municipal bonds, or other businesses. Most lenders do not want to risk their money — it is to get a good interest return on it, with a reasonable risk. They do not want to own your collateral and collect their money by the sale of the collateral; they want to receive payment on the scheduled dates with both interest and principal. Most lenders will require you to guarantee the loan with other assets you may have other than the collateral that is pledged for the loan. Therefore, your entire net worth may be at risk if your business fails.

Keep in mind, asset-based loans are usually funded for long-term debt whereas equity financing is for short-term lending.

ALTERNATIVE TYPES OF FUNDING

In addition to the above traditional methods of funding, alternative types of financing exist, including:

- Lines of credit
- Letters of credit
- Factoring
- Floor planning

Take a moment to learn about these nontraditional financing forms to see if one might apply to your business situation.

LINE OF CREDIT

If your business is in need of a quick infusion of cash to maintain a positive cash flow, you may want to consider using a line of credit. Most commercial banks will give revolving lines of credit — where a fixed amount is available with the ability to draw down on funds under the line, repay the funds on receipt of invoiced sales, and redraw the funds again when you need them. This prearranged amount of credit can be used to meet expected increases in inventory and receivables that may be caused by seasonal fluctuations. Keep in mind, a line of credit needs to be paid to a zero balance as soon as you have an inflow of cash from collecting receivables. Lines of credit are not to be used for long-term capital purposes nor to fund a continuing operating deficit.

LETTER OF CREDIT

If you find yourself dealing with a new vendor who is not assured of your company's creditworthiness, you may want to look into a letter of credit. A letter of credit is a guarantee from a bank that a specific obligation will be honored by a bank if a borrower fails to pay. Because your bank knows you and your ability to pay — either from cash, cash collateral, or from some other prearranged credit facility — it will put its own credit standing in place of your credit standing. A bank will normally charge a fee to grant a letter of credit.

FACTORING

You can acquire cash based on the value of your receivables not in the form of a loan, but rather by selling your account to a lender. In this situation the lender is referred to as a factor and the factor is responsible (not you) for collecting on the account. As a result, your customers pay their bills directly to the factor, and the factor reduces the loan as money is collected. This way, the factor bases all credit decisions on the credit of your customer, not on your business' credit.

FLOOR PLANNING

Floor planning is a relatively new financing tool that uses an asset-based lending approach. In this situation, a company would finance its inventory and the purchased inventory would act as collateral until the sale is made. Floor planning is ideal for businesses that have large ticket retail items, such as furniture, appliances, and automobiles.

Floor planning allows these businesses to maintain a high level of inventory so their customers have many choices. As items are purchased, the business repays the inventory cost to the lender.

To learn more about what types of funding are available and how to find the best fit given your company's capital and cash flow needs, get a copy of *The Small Business Insider's Guide to Bankers* by Suzanne Caplan and Thomas M. Nunnally. To learn more about this helpful publication, see the Useful Resources section at the end of this chapter.

LENDING SOURCES

There are many sources of assistance for obtaining funding. Some possible sources of capital include banks, credit unions, loan companies, family, friends, credit cards, venture capitalists, private investors, small business loan consortiums, and even government loans and grants. Start with your bank or local small business development center (SBDC).

YOUR LOCAL BANK

Like all businesses, your venture will need banking services to maintain a checking account, conduct credit card transactions, and handle other specialized services. It is only natural to go to a local bank for business financing. Unfortunately, banks rarely finance new businesses because they haven't yet established an ability to repay, don't have much collateral, and the ownership or management is often inexperienced.

Frequently, banks will not finance you unless your business has been established for several years and shows a history of clear profitability. Even then, very small businesses may have difficulty obtaining conventional financing. Banks notoriously shy away from funding ongoing operations, and prefer giving loans for expansion or improvements where significant collateral and a large safety margin play a big role.

Not all banks cater to small businesses. Some banks specialize in handling consumer accounts and generally avoid small businesses. Fortunately, the reverse is also true and there is probably a bank in your area that is experienced in small business loans.

Select and Develop a Good Banking Relationship

To establish good banking relations, be honest and provide your banker with knowledge about your business and industry. A good banker will become interested in your business and keep abreast of your problems and successes. If you only see your banker when you need a loan, you are not developing a good relationship. Your banker is much like your attorney and accountant. He or she should be kept up-to-date about your business and is an integral part of helping you solve problems in your business.

It is extremely important that you understand your bank's lending philosophy. Most bankers require two sources of repayment. For instance, your bank may give you a loan as long as you agree to a lien on your accounts receivables, inventory, fixed assets, or real property. In addition to this, a bank will require your personal guaranty — a situation that fosters a psychological commitment to the success of your business. If you are not willing to personally sign and stand behind your business, your banker may hesitate to give you a loan.

Once you have established a relationship with your banker and have earned a reputation for fiscal responsibility, sound management, and trustworthiness, your banker will begin to consider you a valued customer. This distinction carries significant advantages to your small business, including easier financing in the future.

When you present your banker with a loan request and your business plan, your proposal undergoes an evaluation process. Your banker will look for the following information:

- The requested amount of the loan
- The purpose of the loan
- The source and ability of repayment
- Sources and type of collateral
- Management abilities

You can easily remember the loan evaluation process by learning the "five C method." Your bank will look at all five Cs, including:

Conditions. What is the current status of the economy and your business' industry?

Collateral. What will be your secondary source of repayment?

Capacity. Are you prepared for others to take a cold, hard look at your financial track record?

Capital. Do you or your business have any equity?

Character. A key to the lending process, do you have the ability to convey your trustworthiness and integrity?

If you've done your homework, your business plan will contain all of this information in a highly readable and readily understandable format.

Foster your banking relationship by avoiding some actions that will send red-flag danger signals. Don't request another loan after you have spent the money from your first loan. Don't change banks to get a better interest rate. Don't approach a bank if you are undercapitalized or have a history of bad management or serious profit losses. Above all, stay in close communication with your banker — presenting both the good and bad sides of your business.

VENTURE CAPITALISTS

Whereas banks use past performance as primary criteria when evaluating a loan proposal, venture capitalists focus mainly on the future prospects of a company. Venture capital is a major source of funding for high-tech companies that have the potential of going public or being sold to another company at a large profit in a relatively short period of time. It is no big surprise that the information technology and health care industries attracted more than two-thirds of venture capital dollars disbursed in 1993.

If your business is part of an industry segment that is poised for rapid growth and exceptional profits then you may want to pursue venture capital funding. Venture investors seek to earn between five to ten times their initial investment within a five- to eight-year investment horizon. Looking at it another way, venture capitalists seek markets that are sufficiently large to achieve $100 million or greater in value. The primary goal of the venture capitalists is rapid capital appreciation. This goal is usually achieved through a sale of a company to a strategic buyer or through an initial public stock offering (IPO). Keep in mind, sustained growth and profitability beyond a five-year horizon are essential for creating top value when the venture capitalist takes your company public or sells it.

Most companies will not qualify for venture capital funding. As a rule, over one hundred investment proposals are reviewed for every one company that receives venture funding. But if you think your idea has potential for funding, you should seek help in developing your plan to make presentations to venture capitalists.

If you do decide to seek venture capital funding, be prepared to give up a portion of your ownership in your company's equity. Equity ownership will have a direct relationship to the amount a venture capitalist invests in your business and the risk that firm assumes if your company fails. As an example, suppose you want to start a business and only have ten percent of the $100,000 you need to start the business. A venture capitalist may fund the other 90 percent but that also means you may lose 90 percent ownership in your company. This percentage ownership varies depending on the business type, business plan, competition, your management expertise, projected profits, and the overall investment risk. If this issue scares you, look into obtaining venture capital through small business investment companies (SBICs) — investors that use long-term debt guaranteed by the Small Business Administration (SBA) to supplement their private capital. A detailed discussion of SBICs is located later in this chapter.

Finding a venture capitalist that may be interested in your business takes a lot of effort on your part. You will need to identify a list of venture capitalists whose investment preferences match your needs and business profile. Look for firms that are looking for businesses like yours — relative to investment size, development stage, and industry and geographic location. Then, narrow your search to a manageable number of investor candidates, preferably six or less.

After you have narrowed your search, you will need to write a well-documented financing proposal. There are several types of proposals you can use to raise venture capital and loans, including a private placement circular, a prospectus, and a limited partnership offering. To understand which proposal works best for your situation, make sure you have picked up a copy of *Raising Capital: How to Write a Financing Proposal* by Lawrence Flanagan. This helpful book describes the essential components of a winning proposal — and helps you save thousands of dollars in professional writing fees. See the Useful Resources section at the end of this chapter for more details.

For sources of venture capital, check your library, ask your banker, and discuss your project with your local SBDC or business department at a college near you. Seek out resource guides that list venture capitalists. One helpful book is *Pratt's Guide to Venture Capital Sources.* This guide lists each firm's location, investment preferences, contact persons, and available capital pools. Also, you may want to get quick reference to prospective venture capitalists through *The Money Connection: Where and How to Apply for Business Loans and Venture Capital* by Lawrence Flanagan. To learn more about this comprehensive resource manual, see the Useful Resources section at the end of this chapter.

If you have access to the Internet, you may want to check out the Angel Capital Electronic Network (ACE). This Internet-based listing service provides information to angel investors on small businesses that are seeking to raise $250,000 to $5 million in equity financing. Using ACE, an enrolled investor can anonymously view, via the Internet, executive summaries and additional investment information provided by participating entrepreneurs. Thus, an investor in California and an entrepreneur in Maine, can seem as close to each other as next door. To find out more, contact ACE via email at *acenet@sba.gov.*

PRIVATE LOAN COMPANIES

In the past, most small businesses steered away from private loan companies because they were known for high interest rates and were the lender of last resort. This situation has changed during the 1970s. Thanks to the SBA, private loan companies, working as small business lending companies (SBLCs), have become one of the most important SBA loan sources today. AT&T Small Business Lending Corporation, a wholly owned subsidiary of AT&T Capital Corporation, is one of the largest lenders to small businesses nationwide.

There are some advantages to using an SBLC rather than a traditional bank lender. First, an SBLC is regulated only by the SBA whereas other lenders must report to other regulatory authorities as well. Second, SBLCs specialize in SBA-guaranteed loans. Therefore, your loan request is processed in an expeditious and professional manner.

FEDERAL GOVERNMENT PROGRAMS

Although most small businesses are funded from private sources, there are numerous sources of state and federal help.

Most federal loan programs are processed by the Small Business Administration (SBA). In fact, up to one-third of all small business loans are guaranteed through the SBA. The SBA does not fund the loan but guarantees it through a bank or other institution. If a borrower defaults on a loan, then the SBA will reimburse the bank for a percentage of the loan loss. Thus, banks are more apt to make loans with the SBA's guarantee then on terms it would otherwise not be able to make available.

To be eligible for an SBA loan, your business must meet the size standards established by the SBA regarding your industry type. Further, there are other loans for specific purposes, such as to assist the disabled or for minority or economically disadvantaged individuals, provide incentives for energy savings, pollution control, or doing business in a specific location.

Loan Guaranty

The 7(a) loan guaranty program is the SBA's primary business loan program. It provides loans to small businesses that are unable to secure financing on reasonable terms through normal lending channels. The program operates through private-sector lenders that provide loans that are guaranteed by the SBA. The lenders, not the SBA, approve and service the loans and request the SBA guaranties. Lenders look favorably on the 7(a) loan guaranty program. The guaranties reduce the risks to the lenders, thus expanding their abilities to make small business loans.

For most SBA loans there is no legislated limit to the total amount of a loan that you may request from a lender. Generally, the SBA will guarantee up to $750,000. Under the program, the SBA can guarantee as much as 75 percent of a commercial loan. For instance, on a $50,000 loan, the SBA guarantees to repay the lender up to 75 percent of the unpaid balance if the borrower defaults. The lender's liability, then, is 25 percent, or $12,500. For its guaranty, the SBA will charge the lender a one-time guaranty fee of two percent of the guaranteed portion of the loan.

The interest rate on loans of more than seven years may not exceed 2.75 percent of the prime lending rate and may not exceed 2.25 percent for loans under seven years.

The maximum SBA loan maturity is 25 years. However, your loan's maturity will be based on the cash flow and ability of your business to repay it without hardship. Generally, the maturity will vary according to the purpose of the loan and can be up to 7 years for working capital and 25 years for fixed assets, the purchase of machinery or equipment, or the purchase or construction of plant facilities.

You can use the proceeds of an SBA loan for most business purposes including:

- To purchase real estate to house your business operations,
- To fund construction, renovation, or leasehold improvements,
- To acquire furniture, fixtures, machinery and equipment,
- To purchase inventory, or
- For working capital.

You cannot use the proceeds of an SBA loan for any of the following:

- To finance floor plan needs;
- To purchase real estate where the participant has issued a forward commitment to the builder/developer, or where the real estate will be held primarily for investment purposes;
- To make payments to owners or pay delinquent withholding taxes; or
- To pay an existing debt unless you can show that the refinancing will benefit your business and that the need to refinance is not a sign of bad management on your part.

Several loan programs under the 7(a) program address specific needs and include:

Low Documentation Loan (LowDoc). If your business needs a loan of $100,000 or less, applying for the loan under LowDoc could be as easy as completing a one-page SBA application.

CAPLines. Under this program, loan proceeds generally will be advanced against a borrower's existing or anticipated inventory or accounts receivable to meet the cyclical working capital needs of small business.

Women's and Minority Prequalification. If you are a woman or minority owned business, you could meet with an SBA-designated intermediary, such as an SBDC counselor, to obtain prequalification from the SBA before approaching a lender.

504 Certified Development Company Program. This program could allow you to get long-term, fixed-asset financing through certified development companies.

Small Business Investment Company (SBIC)

Licensed and regulated by the SBA, SBICs are privately owned and managed investment firms that make capital investment in small businesses. They use their own funds plus funds obtained at favorable rates with an SBA guaranty or by selling their preferred stock to the SBA. This vital partnership between government and the private sector economy has resulted in more than $9 billion in loans to more than 65,000 small business throughout the United States.

The SBIC program provides funding to all types of manufacturing and service industries. Some investment companies specialize in certain fields, while others seek out small businesses with new products or services because of the strong growth potential. Your business is qualified for SBIC financing if it has a net worth of less than $18 million and average after-tax earnings of less than $6 million during the past two years. If your business does not meet this test, it may still qualify as a small business under either an employment standard or amount-of-annual-sales standard. Both of these standards vary from industry to industry. Keep in mind, SBICs differ in size and investment philosophy. Each SBIC has a policy on the type of financing it prefers, size preferences, industry preferences, and geographic requirements.

If your business qualifies under the SBIC program, you may be able to receive equity capital, long-term loans, and expert management assistance. SBICs may invest only in qualifying small business concerns. SBICs may not invest in:

- Other SBICs;
- Finance and investment companies or finance-type leasing companies;
- Unimproved real estate;

- Companies with less than one-half of their assets and operation in the United States;
- Passive or casual businesses (those not engaged in a regular and continuous business operation); or
- Companies that will use the proceeds to acquire farm land.

You should understand the differences between the two types of SBICs. You may encounter a "regular" SBIC, or a firm that is known as a "specialized" small business investment company (SSBIC). SSBICs are specifically targeted toward the needs of entrepreneurs who have been denied the opportunity to own and operate a business because of social or economic disadvantage. To qualify, your business must be 51 percent owned by socially or economically disadvantaged persons. More than 100 SSBICs operate in the United States. For a complete list of SBICs and SSBICs, contact the National Association of Small Business Investment Companies (NASBIC). The address and phone number of this agency is listed in Appendix C. A nationwide listing is also included in *The Insider's Guide to Small Business Loans* by Dan M. Koehler. See the end of the chapter for information on this guide.

Microloan Program

One of the most difficult types of loans to obtain are for small amounts of debt. It has been very difficult to get loans of a few thousand dollars because they are not profitable to most lenders and generally are of a higher risk. In response to this issue, the SBA created the Microloan Program. Under this program, the SBA makes funds available to nonprofit intermediaries who in turn make loans to eligible borrowers. The amounts of the microloans can range anywhere from $100 to a maximum of $25,000. The average microloan is for $10,000.

Another advantage of the microloan is that a completed application can be processed by a nonprofit intermediary in less than one week. Although each lending organization has its own loan requirements, an intermediary is required to take as collateral any assets that you bought with the microloan. Further, your personal guaranty will be required.

Recently microloans have become more available through entrepreneur associations and some state agencies. Check with your chamber of commerce or small business development center if you are considering a business that needs a small amount of capital to get started. Often you will be required to have a mentor who is in business and possibly attend classes that discuss developing a plan and managing your prospective business.

Small Business Innovation Research (SBIR) Program

Since 1982, the SBA has used the Small Business Innovation Research (SBIR) program to:

- Stimulate technological innovation;
- Fund projects initiated by high-tech small business to help meet federal research and development needs;
- Foster and encourage participation by minority and disadvantaged persons in technological innovation; and
- Increase the commercialization of innovations from federal research and development.

Eleven federal agencies — from the Department of Agriculture to the Nuclear Regulatory Commission — participate in the SBIR program. Under the program, these federal agencies request highly competitive proposals from small businesses in response to solicitations outlining their research and development needs. Awards are granted after an evaluation of the technical feasibility of the research and development concept. For more information, contact the Office of Technology as listed in Appendix B.

Certified and Preferred Lenders

The SBA recently streamlined its guarantee program, expediting loans through its Certified and Preferred Lending program. Only the most active and expert lenders qualify for this program.

Certified lenders make up nearly one-third of all SBA business loan guaranties. Certified lenders are those who have been heavily involved in regular SBA loan guaranty processing and have met certain other criteria. The SBA delegates partial authority to certified lenders and processes loan applications with a three-day turnaround. Preferred lenders are the SBA's best lenders and have been given full lending authority in exchange for a lower rate of guaranty.

Check with your bank to be sure it is a certified or preferred lender to make the approval process faster. A list of certified and preferred lenders is included in the comprehensive guide, *The Insider's Guide to Small Business Loans.*

Tips for Obtaining an SBA Loan

The most important thing you can do in your attempts at getting an SBA loan is to be prepared. Your second most important task is to find the right lender. You must know your needs and have a ready explanation for how you arrived at the amount you are requesting. Ideally, you will use your business plan to show the past, present, and future condition of your business. As a reminder, make sure you include the financial history, management background, and monthly cash flow projections of your business. You will probably be required to submit personal financial statement and tax returns also.

STATE GOVERNMENT PROGRAMS

Most states have economic development agencies that encourage the development of new businesses. The loans may be to encourage starting a business in a target area or expanding a business by building new facilities or adding equipment. Often the amount of the loan is tied to the number of new jobs to be created in the area.

Check Appendix D for a list of some state sources of funding. Funding of the programs often is insufficient to respond to a large percentage of applicants. However, it is well worth your time to check to see if there are loans for which your business qualifies.

CAUTION: You may hear of loans offered at very low rates of interest through federal or state agencies. If this is information is available by buying a tape or video or going to a seminar, beware. You will find that there are no such loans: the lending requirements are similar for all businesses. You may also be directed to companies that charge much higher rates of interest than banks charge if you have a high risk venture. Beware of such loans because you must repay a much larger share of your business income to repay the loan, and you will increase the chances of failure of your business.

CHAPTER WRAP-UP

One of the worst situations you can get into as a business owner is not having enough money to run your business. Top on your priority list should be a clear picture of your business and personal financial needs before you make your first sale.

To assist you, first estimate the money you will need to set up your business — from office set up expenses to production equipment needs; from utilities deposits to insurance; from withholding taxes to licensing fees. Review chapters 2, 3, and 4 and make a list of the fees for which you will be responsible — both in the short-term as well as the long-term.

Next, establish a business bank account. The key here is to find the right banker for your business' needs. Compare fees and credit card arrangements. Inquire about floor planning, factoring, lines of credit, and accounts receivable financing. Gain a thorough understanding of a bank's policies, procedures, and personalities of the major players before you choose to do business with it.

Last, but certainly not least, know which lenders to approach and which ones to avoid. Stay informed about the federal and state loan programs available to your small business. Lenders will notice how educated you are and respond with a greater respect and appreciation. Keep your financial records up-to-date. Be ready to show proforma (projected) financial statements for at least the next three years. Maintain easy access to your business' cash flow projections, balance sheets, and profit and loss (P&L) statements. (These and other critical finance and accounting terms are fully covered in the next chapter.) Show your prospective lenders that you mean business — be prepared with a completed business plan before you approach a lender. Make sure you use the tips for creating a smart business plan from the previous chapter.

USEFUL RESOURCES

The Small Business Insider's Guide to Bankers by Suzanne Caplan and Thomas Nunnally. A useful guide for both new and existing small business owners, this book will help you understand how to develop a business relationship with your banker.

Raising Capital: How to Write a Financing Proposal by Lawrence Flanagan. This book gives a tried-and-proven method for getting the capital you need. It describes and gives examples of different types of offerings to raise capital and the legal requirements for each type.

The Money Connection: Where and How to Apply for Business Loans and Venture Capital by Lawrence Flanagan. This comprehensive text provides a listing of hundreds of sources for debt and venture financing.

The Insider's Guide to Small Business Loans by Dan M. Koehler. Gets into the nitty gritty of applying for an SBA guaranteed loan. It provides documentation and listings of certified and preferred lenders, microloan lenders, and small business investment companies. Includes two sample business plans that show the necessary data for gaining the attention of a lender.

Financing Your Small Business: Techniques for Planning, Acquiring and Managing Debt by Art DeThomas. Helps you evaluate different types of loan sources and determine which is the best for you.

CHAPTER 9

Essential Finance and Accounting Methods

Every business owner will benefit from a better understanding of finance and accounting. Admittedly, these tasks are the last things most business owners care to spend time working with on a regular basis. In fact, many feel that a once-a-year accounting at tax time provides sufficient financial information to guide them through the year. Unfortunately, this is unlikely to be true except for the smallest businesses.

Approximately one million new businesses are started every year in the United States. Many of them will fail, leaving the owners and investors poorer, but wiser, about how to operate a business successfully. One of the primary reasons for any business failure is insufficient financial resources.

Some start-up companies have enough money to operate for years without making a profit from the business. Most businesses are not that fortunate. They must generate enough revenue from the business to pay creditors, employees (including themselves), and vendors. Some businesses are even so successful that they grow faster than they can afford to and go out of business because of too much success.

The secret to remaining in business is being able to monitor the lifeblood of the business — the cash flow. There are many indicators of the health of a business. They include the income statement, the balance sheet, the cash flow analysis, and a multitude of ratios and other indicators that monitor the daily, weekly, monthly, and annual success of a business.

Having a full understanding of basic finance and accounting could mean the difference between the success or failure of your business. Even if you hire an accountant or bookkeeper to maintain your business accounts, you still need to understand the significance of the numbers they generate in order to manage your business.

This chapter will introduce you to the main types of accounting methods, including:

- Cash based accounting
- Accrual based accounting
- Tax accounting
- Financial accounting
- Management accounting

You should understand each of these to get a full picture of your company's financial position. Also, you will learn some basic accounting documentation procedures and payment acceptance methods.

CASH BASED ACCOUNTING

Cash based accounting is the easiest and most popular method for sole proprietorships. Cash enters and leaves an account as income and expense.

Cash based accounting in its simplest form is similar to a checkbook ledger with a running balance. The balance gives you a snapshot view of the health of your business — the larger the balance at any given moment, the healthier your state of affairs. However, a snapshot view such as this clearly has a limited value. A healthy balance now means nothing if you have to pay an expense tomorrow that is three times that amount. In addition, the ledger cannot show the value vested in inventory, equipment, or accounts receivable.

Cash based accounting is used by the smallest of businesses — and usually best utilized by service type businesses. Keep in mind, the method you use for income tax purposes may be different than what you use for your own internal accounting. For the most accurate picture of your business' cash flow, you may want to use accrual based accounting.

ACCRUAL BASED ACCOUNTING

Accrual based accounting gives a more accurate picture of the state of your business' financial health and more closely conforms to generally accepted accounting practices. Suppose you have a grounds maintenance business and you charge a flat fee of $600 for six month's worth of work. Even though you collect and deposit your fee in April, a more accurate picture of your business is produced by amortizing — taking the monthly value of the fee and applying it to monthly income and expenses — rather than showing it as income in the month it was collected. For example, if you collect the fee in April and apply it to your account at the rate of $100 per month, you will amortize the fee over six months. If you make a sale in December and don't receive the cash for it until the following year, the sale is recorded as occurring in the year it was recorded — not the year the cash was received. This can seriously affect your income tax if a large sale at the end of the year will create a larger profit than you would without the sale.

The effects of accrual accounting may cause an expense to be booked in one year, but paid for in the following year. Be aware of the accrual accounting rules — as well as the cash based accounting rules — especially at the end of a year when you can dramatically affect your profit by delaying or accelerating a sale or expense.

TAX ACCOUNTING

The IRS has developed its own set of rules for accounting, and the information required to compile and pay your taxes differs from the information you need to manage your business. Further, the IRS rules you must follow may be different from the rules you choose to follow for your banker. While you may keep two sets of books — one for tax purposes and one for business operations — most small business owners simply maintain one set of books and comply with the IRS' requirements. For example, you may have a piece of equipment that you can depreciate according to IRS rules in five years. But the actual useful life of the equipment may be ten years. For tax purposes you would depreciate it as rapidly as the law allows, but for your own accounting you would know that it would not have to be replaced for 20 years. Thus, you would depreciate it over a longer period for your internal calculations.

Most new business owners are confused by the rules and meaning of depreciation. If a machine is purchased with cash or a loan, it is paid for and most business owners would expect that they could deduct the cost of the machine from the current year's expenses. This is not the case when it comes to IRS requirements. Since there is a useful life to the machine, the IRS requires that you write it off over a period of years. IRS groups different equipment into different categories for depreciation purposes. It is wise to consult with an accountant to be sure you select the correct depreciation period for equipment you purchase.

There are many rules regarding how you account for expenses or income. Do not use your judgment as to what you think is fair or reasonable about the IRS' rules. Fair and reasonable have nothing to do with IRS rules.

To help you use the tax accounting method, you may want to look into using a software program to get you started. Some popular tax software comes close to achieving expert level advice and works directly with files from your bookkeeping or existing accounting software. These programs often include interactive video clips and sound files from top tax advisors, can generate completed IRS forms for filing, and have the capability of filing your taxes electronically. If you decide to use these tools, shop the market carefully. The software should meet these following minimum requirements:

- It should be updated annually;
- It should be able to use your existing accounting program files; and
- It should be endorsed by one of the "Big Six" accounting firms.

Be cautious in relying on your computer and your wits in computing your taxes. While you are likely to file a return that meets the IRS' requirements and expectations by using these methods, you are just as likely to end up paying too much.

GET EXPERT HELP

As your business grows in both size and revenue, you will benefit more and more from the advice of a knowledgeable tax accountant. Tax law is complicated and changes on a yearly basis. Without expert help, you could end up paying thousands of dollars in excess taxes or be penalized for not paying sufficient taxes or taking deductions that are not acceptable to the IRS.

To help you survive in today's tax-reformed environment, check out the numerous tax tips in *Top Tax Saving Ideas for Today's Small Business* by Thomas J. Stemmy. The Useful Resources section at the end of the chapter will give you more information on this publication. Another valuable source of timely information that offers hints on avoiding a tax crunch is *Small Business Computing.* This monthly magazine — and its cousin *Home Office Computing* — provides current information on a variety of business topics via its Internet Web site. To learn more about this helpful resource, log on at *http://www.smalloffice.com.* Even the IRS has its own user-friendly publication. As a new business owner you can get IRS *Publication 1558* — a series of twelve newsletters that contains tax tips and explanations of new tax legislation. The address and phone number of the nearest IRS services office is listed in Appendix B.

FINANCIAL ACCOUNTING

Financial accounting is the basis for all entry level accounting classes and textbooks. It is used to prepare financial reports, such as income statements, balance sheets, and cash flow statements. Most often, these reports are generated using accrual based methods so that income is recorded as it is earned instead of as it is collected and expenses are recorded as they occur instead of as payment is made for them. To better understand financial accounting, take a moment to become familiar with three essential financial reports. Samples of each of the statements are included in Appendix A.

INCOME STATEMENT

An income statement is sometimes called a profit and loss (P&L) statement. It is used to determine current profitability and is based on the most current information available. It is the basis for determining income tax obligations and levels of supportable debt by lending institutions.

An income statement provides detailed information about your expenses broken down into as many categories as you feel are necessary. For example, you may choose to list a single utilities expense or you may choose to break utilities down into gas for heat, electricity for lighting, and water. The more information available to you, the more able you are to make informed decisions about expenses in the future. Don't collect more information than you will use, however.

Income statements may also be used to track expenses against a budget. By comparing actual costs against projections, you can decide where you need to place more controls or where unexpected expenses occurred. This process will allow you to better plan your operating budget for the following year.

It is not unusual for your income statement to show that you have a profit for a given period, but you wonder where the profit is because your bank account is much lower than the income statement indicates. This situation occurs because you show depreciation of equipment which adds to the income but does not produce an equivalent amount of cash. You may also be building inventory, using available cash, but the income statement will reflect the cost of what you sold during the period, but will not add the additional inventory to the profit or loss situation.

You can see that while your income statement is useful to explain how much profit you made relative to your cost of goods and other expenses, it does not describe accurately the state of your business. If you want a snapshot view of your business regarding its overall condition on a specific day, use a balance sheet.

BALANCE SHEET

Balance sheets are prepared periodically, usually on a monthly, quarterly, or yearly basis. They are used to summarize your business' net worth, taking into account all assets, liabilities, and equity at a given moment in time. Assets include everything the business owns — cash, accounts receivable, fixed assets, and inventory. Liabilities are everything the business owes — such as accounts payable, payroll, and tax liabilities. Total equity is equal to the sum of all assets minus the sum of all liabilities. If you operate your business as a corporation, then equity is the current value of all capital stock as well as the total profit or loss since the start of your corporation.

Balance sheets provide a numerical bottom line that is useful in evaluating business growth or decline and creditworthiness. By comparing a current period with previous periods, you can observe trends. While the income statement and balance sheet are the typical indicators of the condition of a business, the cash flow statement will explain why you do not have the cash in your bank account that you might expect. When projected for the following months or years, it will help you plan for critical cash need periods if your business is seasonal or cyclical.

CASH FLOW STATEMENT

A cash flow statement will help you understand where cash has been used and where and why cash is short or in abundance. A cash flow statement is basically an accounting of available cash, plus cash income minus cash disbursements, for each period forecast.

As you become more experienced in looking at your historical cash flow, you should project your cash flow for at least a year in advance. A projection will provide a clear picture of your ability to meet expenses over the forecast period. If you will need a loan in the future, start before the need is upon you; most lenders are suspicious of a business owner who suddenly realizes that there will be a cash shortage and must obtain a loan within the next week or two.

Once established, use your cash flow statement to compare against actual performance during a forecast period. This comparison provides crucial feedback that will allow you to predict potential cash shortfalls and prevent them before they occur. Comparing predicted performance with actual performance also allows you to adjust basic assumptions and thereby more accurately prepare future cash flow forecasts.

MANAGEMENT ACCOUNTING

Management accounting, also called cost accounting, is a specialized form of internal accounting that provides managers and owners detailed operating information about production processes. This type of reporting is particularly useful in manufacturing businesses and may include such information as unit production cost, product line profitability breakdowns, and sales performance by region or by store.

The information produced by management accounting will give you timely, detailed feedback about your operations. This feedback will allow you to draw conclusions about efficiency, cost, inventory valuation, quality control, product turnover, return or repair rates, warranty issues, and the cost effectiveness of design changes. Anything that can be measured will provide potential fodder for management accounting. Management accounting can be complex and labor-intensive depending on the amount and type of information gathered. So, it is important to place controls on how much and how often management accounting is needed to adequately control your business.

TRACK KEY INDICATORS

Your business may benefit from simply tracking a few key indicators instead of a wide array of information. Economy analysts, for instance, often rely on key economic indicators to predict how the economy is reacting to world events. They rely on these indicators instead of the numerous other factors that affect the economy. If they were to analyze all factors, their reports would be out-of-date and completely useless. Similarly, your business can rely on key indicators to predict its performance.

For instance, suppose you have a small retail business and are concerned about losses to shoplifting. So you start to collect information about profit versus sales and inventory data on a monthly basis to determine the rate of losses incurred and to test the effectiveness of the control methods you employ to deter shoplifters. This same concept can be applied to other types of businesses. A manufacturer will measure quality control reject ratios to evaluate the effectiveness of their job training program. And a service station will compare storage tank inventory data to sales to determine whether its underground tanks are leaking.

ACCOUNTING DOCUMENTATION

All businesses need to develop ways to process and account for their purchases and sales. When you start your business you may be able to remember what you have ordered and how much cash it will take when it is received. As your business grows and you hire employees, you will need to develop procedures that track income and expenses. In addition, the IRS demands that you have documentation relating to what you report in your income tax return for the business. A paper trail of sales and expenses will help you better understand the true cost of doing business and your profit. It can make an IRS auditor happier, if you have the unpleasant experience of having an audit. The two simplest methods for documenting income and expenses involve using purchase orders and invoices.

PURCHASE ORDERS

Regardless of which method of accounting you use, you will need to have a means to collect data. As a small business owner, you need to know how to use standardized forms to document sales transactions. One of these standard forms is the purchase order.

A purchase order is used to place an order with a supplier or a manufacturer. It acts as official authorization for the supplier to ship the merchandise being ordered. Since it functions as a permanent record of a transaction, prepare a purchase order even when placing orders by telephone or by letter.

A purchase order is traditionally designed as a three-part form — that is, an original and two copies. The original is sent to the supplier as the transaction approval document. The first copy is forwarded to the accounting department for payment processing once an invoice is received. The second copy is retained by the purchasing department as a record that the required merchandise was ordered. An optional third copy, used in larger companies, is returned to the requisitioning department as documentation that purchasing action was taken. Very small businesses — fewer than five employees — may require only the original and a single file copy.

If your business ships merchandise, you will receive purchase orders from customers as a normal part of business. These purchase orders will contain the same information as the purchase orders that you prepare. These purchase orders are a promise to pay for goods shipped. They also provide the shipping department with an accurate location address, phone number, and mailing address. A well-designed purchase order is essential to accurate recordkeeping. At a minimum, the purchase orders you use should include the following information:

- Your company's name, address, phone number, fax number and email address, if available;
- A purchase order number to allow future tracking and filing of the purchase;
- The supplier's address and a "ship to" address (keep in mind, this may be different from the actual physical address of the business);
- The date the purchase order was prepared;

- The quantity, product code number, description, unit price, and extended price of the merchandise (unit price multiplied by quantity less any discounts) being ordered;
- A column listing the line item costs, applicable sales tax, shipping and handling costs, and final total for the purchase order;
- Your internal accounting information that identifies which account the purchase is to be charged against;
- An authorization signature line; and
- Any other information you may require as well as special instructions to the supplier.

Your purchase orders should project the same degree of professionalism as any other paperwork that leaves your company.

Beyond the value of the tracking and internal control, purchase orders are important legal documents. If you disagree with a supplier as to what was supplied or the terms under which the item was shipped or produced, a purchase order which spells out the exact details of the expected purchase can provide you with a legal document and probably will help resolve an issue before it gets to the lawyer level.

INVOICES

Another business form that you will use to collect accounting data is an invoice. An invoice is an itemized list of the merchandise shipped to you and an accounting of the costs associated with it. It is used to document merchandise shipped to you. As delivery is made, you will use the invoice to inventory what you receive and verify that everything that was shipped to you arrived in good condition. The invoice is then forwarded to the accounting department for approval and filing. The accounting department will routinely compare the invoice to the originating purchase order to verify that no errors were made, and that actual costs were in line with expected costs.

As a supplier, you will prepare a shipping invoice or packing list to send with the merchandise that you ship out to your customers.

Like a purchase order, an invoice will contain specific information about your company such as your company name, address, and phone number. An invoice will reference a specific purchase order or purchase agreement and will contain an itemized listing of goods shipped and may contain information about costs of the items and the aggregate costs.

A copy of an invoice is sent to your customer as a billing invoice. Additionally, a copy of the outgoing invoice is forwarded to the accounting department where it is verified and filed. An outgoing invoice is filed as an account receivable, while an incoming invoice is filed as an account payable.

Standardized forms — like purchase orders and invoices — are available through mail order business supply companies, from your local printer, or from office supply stores. Another helpful resource is the *Complete Book of Business Forms* by Richard G. Stuart, which contains sample purchase orders that you can copy and adapt to your business. See the Useful Resources section at the end of this chapter for information on this invaluable resource. Finally, most of the popular business software includes standardized templates that you can use in your business. Merely fill in the blanks on your computer screen and the program will prepare completed purchase orders for you. For your convenience, a sample purchase order and an invoice are included in Appendix A.

PAYMENT METHODS

Every business needs cash to operate. How you collect the cash will differ greatly between the type of business and custom within your industry. If you are in an industry that traditionally gives credit for 30 or 60 days, you will be at a disadvantage if you can't provide the same to your potential customers. If you don't offer to take checks or credit cards, but your competitors do, you can bet that many customers will buy your product or use your service only once. However, there are downside risks on all types of payment options except cash, and even with cash, there is a greater chance that you will be robbed or that employees can siphon off some of the receipts.

You need to develop payment acceptance policies and procedures. If you sell with the expectation of receiving payment within 30 days after billing, you will need to have a cash reserve to help you get through your initial months of business. Some companies do not pay from invoices — they expect to receive a statement at the end of the month that summarizes their account and will pay at the end of the month or sometime during the following month.

If you do accept checks, you run the risk of receiving bad checks for which there is little chance you will collect at a later time. Take some time now to familiarize yourself with the various methods of payment. Then, make a decision on what will work best for your business' situation.

PAYING BY CHECK

One of the first financial actions you should take after deciding to get into business is to open a checking account under your business name. Many banks will not open an account unless you have documentation that a business has been legally formed.

Although you can operate a sole proprietorship from your personal checking account, it is advisable to have a separate checking account for all business transactions. If you form a corporation it is imperative that you do not mix your personal funds with your business funds. Nothing raises a red flag quicker than lack of responsibility with your business finances and your personal finances. Having separate bank accounts will help you avoid future accounting and accountability problems. Banks will probably demand some proof that you operate as a corporation and will expect to see documentation from a state authority that the corporation operates legally in your state.

Once an incoming invoice is received, verified, routed and filed, all that remains is to pay for the transaction. By convention, most invoices are paid by check, allowing you to easily track expenditures and simplify bookkeeping tasks. However, you will want to establish a petty cash account that will enable you to purchase some items with cash. It is important to keep track of the use of petty cash purchases. If you can't show they were used for business purposes, you will not be able to deduct the expenses and may pay additional taxes because of a higher profit. Billing invoices generally indicate a specific due date, and you will prepare payments based on that date. A check provides you with a record of payment, and it should reference the purchase order number or invoice number on the memo line. Send the check to the supplier along with a copy of the invoice so as to arrive on or just before the payment due date.

Accepting Checks

Accepting checks as payment for goods or services is a generally accepted practice, but it is unwise to accept checks indiscriminately, particularly from new or potentially unreliable customers. A check can be thought of as a promise to pay, and it is only as good as the word of the person or entity issuing it. Some problems that can occur when accepting a check include fraud, insufficient funds, and stop payments.

Fraud. This occurs when a check is intentionally written against a dormant, empty, or closed account or against an account that the customer does not own. Frequently, the checks have been stolen or illegally reproduced, but in all cases the customer has no intention of ever making the check good.

Nonsufficient funds (NSF). When a customer's check is returned marked NSF, you should immediately call the issuing bank to see if conditions have changed and the funds now exist to cover the check. If so, immediately send the check through again or take the check directly to the bank and cash it. If there are still insufficient funds, you will have to take steps to collect from the customer directly.

Stop payments. By law, your customers can put a stop payment on their checks if they have good reason to do so, such as dissatisfaction with the product or the service. Having an adjustment and returns policy in place will help you collect on the account if it comes into dispute.

You can protect yourself against bad checks through local and national services that verify checks as you accept them. They may also guarantee reimbursement if the check is bad. However, you may find that the cost of such a service is greater than the potential or real loss you will incur if you take a few precautions.

Verifying Checks

A few basic precautions will reduce the chances of getting stuck with a bad check. The effort expended to verify a check before you accept it will pay dividends in the long run.

Proper identification. Make sure the check is properly signed and that the signature matches the signature on the driver's license or other identification. The check should be made out to your business.

Check the amount. The amount of the check should be written legibly in two places. The amount in both places should match exactly.

No "starter" checks. The check should have a preprinted address and phone number. Do not accept "starter" checks.

No two-person checks. Checks that are written by someone else to your customer are usually not accepted by a business. You cannot obtain information about the originator of the check, only the person to whom the check is written.

Verification. If the sale is especially large or the customer is unknown to you, call the bank to verify the check before providing the service or merchandise.

Check guarantees. Require your customer to present a check verification card when writing a check or subscribe to an electronic check verification service accessed during the point of sale.

Waiting periods. If your business is a mailorder business, you may decide to hold some checks before shipping an item ordered. You will need to determine how long it will take for a check to reach the bank on which it was written and be returned if the check is bad.

CREDIT CARDS

Accepting credit cards for your business transactions represents a significant advantage to potential customers. But the practice has a downside in addition to the expense and paperwork.

You need to go through several basic steps before you can accept credit cards from customers. You must establish merchant discount agreements with each major credit card you decide to accept. You must establish a working agreement with your bank to handle the transactions. And you must learn how to process credit vouchers.

Some private companies handle all parts of the credit card transaction for you by establishing agreements with the appropriate credit card companies, conducting the credit transactions, and verifying available credit electronically before completing the sale. However, the one-step convenience comes at the cost of considerably higher processing fees. As electronic transactions become more commonplace, fees for these services will drop considerably.

Credit card transactions are subject to much of the same problems that check transactions present. Credit card fraud is a growing concern. If you accept a card that has been lost, stolen, altered, or counterfeited, you will lose any income from that sale as well as the cost of the merchandise.

Even if the sale and the card are valid, a customer could return merchandise or dispute a charge, resulting in a chargeback to your account and lost income for your business. You have rights regarding chargeback but you should clearly understand how the credit card company handles complaints and be certain to respond to the credit card company's inquiry about the chargeback within the time indicated by the credit card company.

You can avoid many of the problems associated with accepting credit card transactions by taking a few extra precautions at the time of the sale. Take the necessary precautions and:

- Check the card against an invalid card list provided by the credit card company.
- Certify the card electronically through a card verification service.
- Verify the signature on the card against the signature on the driver's license or other valid identification.
- Record additional information on the credit card invoice, such as address, phone number and driver's license number.
- Have the customer sign an adjustment and returns agreement to help you collect on the account if a chargeback is made to your account.

DEBIT CARDS

Many banks are turning to a debit card as a means of controlling overdraft on checking accounts. The debit card is similar to a credit card in appearance and operation, but operates on an entirely different principle. Instead of drawing funds for the transaction against a line of credit the way a credit card does, the debit card draws funds directly from the customer's checking or savings account.

This system provides significant advantages to the retailer. Funds are verified as being available at the point of sale, eliminating bounced checks and failed transactions. Also, a personal code, which must be entered electronically by the customer, virtually eliminates fraudulent use of the debit card. Since no cash changes hands, the opportunity for theft is reduced as well as the impact on the business if theft does occur. Finally, funds are frequently transferred from the customer's account to your business account within one working day.

CHAPTER WRAP-UP

Now that you are familiar with the basic accounting methods, you may even be more convinced of your desire to steer clear of the books and let an accountant manage your finances. Hiring a financial professional is a wise management decision. However, controlling your business' financial health is the difference between success and failure.

Work toward a personal involvement with your business' finances and educate yourself as much as possible so you can better understand the cash flow needs of your business. Establish internal controls — like purchase orders and invoices to help track income and expenses. In addition, establish procedures that apply to all customers across-the-board. You may change your procedures as you learn more about your customers and customs within your industry. Also, it is essential to have procedures if you hire employees because they cannot guess what your procedures may be from customer to customer or from day to day.

Finally, get a firm grasp on which collection techniques your business will employ. Collecting the cash that is owed you, either immediately upon culmination of the sale or within 30 or 60 days, is what will make your business work successfully. You may feel uneasy about calling customers to remind them that a bill has not been paid. You will find customers who will take advantage of your unwillingness to call and ask for payment if it is overdue. If you want to stay in business you must be able to collect on your accounts receivable.

USEFUL RESOURCES

Business Owners Guide to Accounting and Bookkeeping by Jose Placencia, Bruce Welge, and Don Oliver. Will give you step-by-step instructions for generating accounting statements and, more important, it will teach you how to spot errors and recognize warning signs.

Financial Management Techniques by Art DeThomas. Book and computer disk package will help you project income and cash flow and show you how to pinpoint your financial standing using the indicators that are used by major financial institutions.

Complete Book of Business Forms by Richard G. Stuart. This all-in-one resource book contains more than 200 reproducible forms for every business need imaginable. Use these standardized forms to save you time and money.

Bottom Line Basics by Robert J. Low. Provides immediate solutions for improving your cash flow and reducing your business' costs, and gives you a clear idea of what drives your business.

Collection Techniques for Small Business by Gini Graham Scott and John J. Harrison. Tells you the quick and easy way to turn your receivables into cash. Also, gives business owners tips on establishing credit policies, tracking accounts, and knowing when to bring in a collection agency.

Top Tax Saving Ideas for Today's Small Business by Thomas J. Stemmy. Will give you year-round strategies for lowering your taxes and avoiding common pitfalls. Discusses tax deductions, fringe benefits, and tax deferrals.

Information Breakthrough: How to Turn Mountains of Confusing Data into Gems of Useful Information by Charles J. Bodenstab. Gives business owners and managers a new way to look at their financial information. Shows non-number crunchers how to turn numbers data into practical knowledge for any small- to medium-sized business.

NOTES FOR FINANCE AND ACCOUNTING:

CHAPTER 10

Effective Human Resources Management

As federal, state, and local governments focus more on the rights of employees, no employer can afford to be unaware of the laws affecting selection, hiring, and dismissal. In Chapter 4 you were introduced to the various duties of an employer, including fair employment, minimum wage, reporting wages, and anti-discrimination practices. This chapter gets into the nitty gritty of managing your personnel program and establishing and enforcing company policies. In short, this chapter tells you the basics of managing your human resources. From writing a job description to interviewing prospective applicants; from conducting performance reviews to dealing with disciplinary issues; from establishing a benefits package for your small business to developing a company policy handbook — this chapter gives you a beginner's look at the oftentimes elusive subject of human resources management. Even if you don't plan on hiring employees right away, make sure you know what laws pertain to you when and if you do decide to post that first job opening.

HIRING

Eventually you will face the task of hiring new employees. This important process will have an enormous impact on the success of your business. Your employees are a representation of your business and it is natural to want to select the best candidate possible for each position in your company. Select well and you will add an effective team member to your organization. Select poorly and you will lose valuable time and money attempting to correct your mistake.

The most common method of recruitment is to first clearly define the job position by writing a job description and then take applications. If you have done your homework, you will end up selecting the best candidate. Even this simple scenario contains hidden pitfalls. As a small business owner, you must strictly base the decision to hire one applicant over another on the individual's relative qualifications and suitability for the position. Failure to be aware of the various laws regulating hiring practices leaves you open to litigation. The Americans with Disabilities Act of 1990 (ADA) and the Civil Rights Act of 1964 (CRA) contain specific guidance in hiring individuals. Both acts prohibit discrimination in hiring based on race, sex, national origin, color, religion, age, marital status, sexual preference, or physical or mental disabilities. Both apply to employers having 15 or more employees for 20 weeks or more per year.

As guidance for complying with the requirements of the ADA and the CRA, the Equal Employment Opportunity Commission (EEOC) and other federal agencies adopted the *1978 Guidelines on Uniform Employee Selection Procedures.* To learn more about these guidelines, contact your state's employment agency.

WRITING A JOB DESCRIPTION

The key to selecting well-qualified people for your employees is to clearly spell out their job positions. Make sure your job descriptions include job qualifications, assigned duties, responsibilities, knowledge, coordination, reporting requirements, and physical working conditions. Good position descriptions will help your employees understand what their jobs entail and what your company expects from them. Good job descriptions will also help your company's organization and serve as a blueprint for a well-structured operation. For an example of a well-written job description, see Appendix A.

ADVERTISING A JOB POSITION

Advertising a job position is the first step in the recruitment process. A well-thought-out ad will draw a diverse group of applicants who meet the qualifications of the position. Before writing the ad copy, consider the requirements of the position you are filling. Will the position require interaction with the public, your customers, or both? Will your new employee require a valid driver's license to fulfill his or her duties? Does the job require any special skills or abilities? What experience level are you seeking?

Review your ad for discriminatory language. Make sure the wording of your ad does not unintentionally exclude a segment of the population. Place your ad in as many places as necessary to ensure that everyone has the same opportunity to see it and apply for the position. Include a phone number and physical address in each ad to avoid discriminating against hearing or visually impaired applicants. Consider listing the position with the unemployment agency in your state as a means to ensure that all potential applicants are aware of the opening in your business. Select a closing date and time for the position. Require that all applications be submitted before that time expires, or specifically state in your ad that you will accept applications until the position fills.

THE JOB APPLICATION

A well-prepared application form is your first line of defense in preventing hiring discrimination lawsuits. It is also your best tool for reducing a large pool of applicants to a group of the best qualified. Use a standardized application form for your company, ensuring that you collect the same information for each applicant. Because it must conform to the requirements of the ADA and the CRA, it serves as a guide to prevent collecting data that might become the basis for discrimination.

The application package should include a company statement of equal opportunity, a privacy act statement, and a release allowing your business to investigate the accuracy of the application. Appendix A contains a sample application. You must ensure that all applicants understand these special provisions of the application, and that the wording or layout of the application is not discriminatory. Extra fine print, for instance, discriminates against someone with weak or impaired vision.

You may optionally elect to have applicants provide you with a resume along with a completed application. Other sources of information may include letters of recommendation and copies of awards, transcripts, and professional citations. While these documents can be helpful in deciding between two equally qualified candidates, they are no substitute for a completed application form in protecting you against claims of hiring discrimination.

THE SCREENING PROCESS

Review application packages as you receive them. Place those that do not meet the advertised qualifications in a separate pile from those that do meet the selection criteria. Record which qualifications the applicant did not meet. When the closing date has passed, review the qualified applicants objectively. Select the five or six best qualified applicants to schedule for interviews. Record the reasons why you didn't select the other applicants. Ensure that your reasoning is as objective as possible and based solely on selecting the best qualified applicant for the job. For example, do not discriminate against applicants who are from a town that rivals your high school's football team.

Once you have selected which applicants to interview, contact each of them to verify their continued interest in the position, and to set a date and time for their interviews. While one or more applicants may withdraw for various reasons, try to interview at least three to allow an objective comparison of each person's qualifications.

HOW TO CONDUCT AN INTERVIEW

Interview each applicant under the same conditions and in the same way. Conduct the interviews in a place where there will be no interruptions or distractions. Make sure the atmosphere is nonthreatening to allow a free flow of communication. It is a good idea to have a third party present during the interview to prevent accusations of sexual harassment or misconduct. Use the job description to direct you through the interview process as you become familiar with the qualifications and strengths of each applicant in relation to the specific job.

Prepare for the interviews by deciding what questions to ask and what types of information to elicit from the applicant. Determine exactly what you need to know and avoid asking forbidden questions that could become the basis for hiring discrimination. Use a checklist, if necessary, to ensure that you stay in focus during the interview. Ask each applicant the same general questions. You can use one of four basic types of interview — the structured, informal, stress, or panel interview.

A structured interview relies on preselected questions asked of each applicant. It is quick and consistent, but lacks flexibility. It is suitable as an initial screening interview.

An informal interview occurs in a far more relaxed atmosphere and can be nearly conversational in manner. This type of interview requires more skill and usually takes a great deal more time than a structured interview. By asking open-ended, nonjudgmental questions, you can establish a flow of information from your applicants about their expectations, qualifications, and abilities. In this type of interview, you can gain information from applicants that you cannot legally request.

Use a stress interview to screen applicants for jobs where calmness under pressure is particularly desirable. Such an interview may be useful in eliminating candidates from consideration. The questions asked in a stress interview require the applicants to respond to hypothetical situations, describe past experiences, or discuss their relative strengths or weaknesses. Successful applicants usually require a follow-up interview to further determine their qualifications.

A panel interview is efficient when a group or committee is responsible for filling a position. The panel is headed by a single individual who keeps the panel focused. Appearing before a panel allows all hiring members to see each applicant under similar conditions.

After you have finished an interview, take the time to record what happened. Using notes you took during the interview as a guide, record the applicant's responses to your questions as well as your observations about the applicant's demeanor and characteristics. Include an appraisal of that individual's qualifications for the position and suitability for employment with your company. Also make note of negative characteristics, if any.

HANDLING THE BACKGROUND CHECK

After the interview, you will want to do a background check. Obtain permission to contact past employers, educators, family members, and references from the applicant early in the selection process. Most employers include an authorization statement in the application form. Refusal to grant permission for the employer to investigate can be reason to reject an application for employment.

The best approach in verifying application information and checking references is to call past employers and references directly.

Speaking to a person on the telephone usually results in more detailed information with less likelihood of misunderstanding. Restrict your questions to verifying information given on the application and to gaining impressions of the applicant's work habits and qualifications. Collect information only from sources authorized by the applicant, and take care to avoid questions relating to the applicant's physical or mental health.

Generally, references provided by past employers, educators, and coworkers are more useful than those obtained from friends, neighbors, and relatives. The former are more likely to have observed the applicant's work habits while the latter may simply be doing the applicant a favor rather than providing an objective appraisal.

Keep in mind, you assume liability for information that your receive during the background checks. Therefore, avoid basing your hiring decision solely on information given during the verification process.

WHEN TESTING A JOB APPLICANT

Occasionally, it may be appropriate to include testing as a part of the applicant screening process. When using testing as part of the recruitment process, all applicants must take the same test under the same conditions. Some types of testing may include aptitude, achievement, situational, personality, drug, polygraph, and honesty testing. You must carefully consider which types of testing you will conduct, if any. It is not always appropriate to test applicants.

Testing is sometimes useful in filling certain positions. For instance, you may wish to test an applicant's typing speed if a specific typing proficiency is a job requirement. Drug testing is allowable provided the test cannot detect prescribed medication. If it can, you must make an offer of employment before conducted the testing. You may require a test for HIV only when there is reasonable risk of an exchange of bodily fluids between employees. Remember that it is illegal to discriminate against persons with HIV. You may use "paper-and-pencil honesty" testing when prospective employees will handle money or have access to pilferable equipment. Testing is always inappropriate when it results in hiring discrimination. You must always administer it fairly and apply it correctly and appropriately. Only allow qualified professionals to conduct testing. Ensure all testing conforms to the *1978 Guidelines on Uniform Employment Selection Procedures* as adopted by the Equal Employment Opportunity Commission.

ALTERNATIVES TO HIRING EMPLOYEES

There are alternatives to hiring through applications and interviews, including contracting to independent agents, hiring temporaries from an agency, or leasing employees. Each method offers advantages over conventional methods, including handling less paperwork and lower employee costs.

USING INDEPENDENT CONTRACTORS

If the work you need done can be accomplished away from your business or outside normal business hours, an independent contractor may work best for you. For instance, suppose you need standard bookkeeping accomplished each week. A private bookkeeper can complete this work at his or her place of business on a weekly basis — usually for a set fee. You save the expense of providing the bookkeeper with office space and equipment. The fee you pay is your only expense. All overhead employee costs such as federal, state, and Social Security taxes as well as the paperwork required to collect and deposit those taxes are borne by the contractor. You need only file IRS *Form MISC-1099* as required by the IRS.

The Fair Labor Standards Act (FLSA) defines employer-employee relationships. The distinction between employee and contractor is important and you are required to properly classify such workers. For instance, if you provide office space or equipment and set specific work hours, the IRS may consider the contractor to be an employee. You must then collect and file taxes for that person. A rule of thumb is that a contractor provides a service or a product while an employee provides labor in a structured way. Refer back to Chapter 4 for more information on dealing with independent contractors in your state.

TEMPORARY AGENCIES TO THE RESCUE

Temporary agencies rent employees, typically for periods from half a day to several years. A temporary employee frequently possesses characteristics not found in a regular employee. They possess qualifications beyond their job description. They possess a wide range of experience. They can be available on very short notice.

Situations that warrant hiring temporary employees include conducting inventory for tax purposes, sudden increases in business production, or the temporary loss of a permanent employee due to illness, pregnancy, or military recall. The temporary agency will normally bill you on a weekly basis. The fee you pay to an agency usually covers all employee expenses.

EMPLOYEE LEASING AS AN OPTION

Employee leasing, also called contract staffing, is a relatively new idea in business. An agency provides your business with all employees and handles all personnel management concerns from hiring to firing. You start to realize savings over the normal hiring process when you lease more than five employees. The benefit to the employee is that the leasing agency typically manages a much larger workforce than your business will and, therefore, is able to provide a better, more diverse benefits package.

Keep in mind, when you hire an employee, provide a federal *Form W-4, Employee Withholding Allowance Certificate* for the employee to complete and return to you prior to paying the first payroll for the employee. You may obtain forms from your IRS district office. You will receive copies of the forms and tax withholding tables and instructions from the IRS when you register with your state's employment office. A copy of *Form W-4* is located in Appendix A. Refer to Appendix B for the address and phone number of the IRS district office nearest you.

YOUR COMPANY'S POLICY AND PROCEDURES

Policy and procedures are predetermined responses to employee-related problems. Important advantages are gained by setting and writing company policies before a problem occurs that requires policy response. A policy and procedures handbook will help you:

- Provide written guidance for handling employees;
- Communicate your business rules and expectations to your employees;
- Communicate your business approach and philosophy;
- Protect your business from litigation; and
- Ensure all problems are handled consistently.

The process of developing a cohesive set of policies and procedures for your business will lead you to firmly review your goals and business philosophy. This process will be particularly helpful if you haven't yet considered a set of policies. Some policies will be required by law. Others will be extensions of your personal approach to business. In either case, you will want to be certain that each policy is accurate, complete, and reflects the best interests of you and your company.

While nearly any issue can be addressed as a matter of policy, there are a few that are basic to any policy manual or handbook. In most cases, these policies were developed in response to federal regulations, so it is prudent to use them as the foundation of your policy manual. Some of these "hot" policies include:

- Equal employment opportunity,
- Equal pay,
- Sexual harassment,
- Substance abuse,
- Smoking,
- Safety,
- Termination,
- Leaves of absence, and
- Use of company time, equipment, or resources.

EQUAL EMPLOYMENT OPPORTUNITY

Equal employment opportunity is mandated by federal law under the Civil Rights Act of 1964 (CRA) and the Americans with Disabilities Act of 1990 (ADA), as well as other clarifying legislation. These laws prohibit employment discrimination based on race, religion, color, national origin, age, gender or sexual orientation, and physical or mental disability. Your company policy should address these issues directly and prohibit discriminatory practices in hiring, promoting, demoting, or firing employees. Additionally, this policy should prohibit discrimination in pay, compensation, working conditions, and working assignments.

EQUAL PAY

The Equal Pay Act of 1963 is an amendment to the Fair Labor Standards Act of 1938 (FLSA). It prohibits unequal pay for equal work to members of the opposite sex. For instance, paying a male supervisor a higher wage than a female supervisor when both possess similar skills, tenure, experience, and performance levels constitutes wage or sexual discrimination under this act. This is equally true of the reverse scenario.

When preparing company policy statements regarding equal pay and equal opportunity, seek the advice from professional sources to ensure that you are complying with all federal, state, and local guidelines. An extremely helpful resource in developing company policy is *A Company Policy and Personnel Workbook* by Carl R. J. Sniffen and Ardella Ramey. For more information on this helpful guidebook, see the Useful Resources section at the end of this chapter.

SEXUAL HARASSMENT

There are two types of sexual harassment, quid pro quo and hostile environment. In a quid pro quo sexual harassment case, employment conditions are based on the individual submitting to sexual harassment, abuse or conditions. Employment conditions include promotions, demotions, hiring, firing, and preferential treatment in job assignments, opportunities, and perks.

On the other hand, hostile environment sexual harassment includes behavior that is unwelcome to the recipient which includes requests for sexual favors, exposure to sexually explicit jokes, innuendoes, telephone calls, faxes, email or other forms of visual, aural or written communication. When these conditions are so prevalent they produce an uncomfortable working environment for the recipient, sexual harassment exists.

Sexual harassment is not gender specific as dramatized by the book and movie "*Disclosure*" by Michael Crichton. Both men and women can be victimized by sexual harassment, usually by members of the opposite sex, but also by same-sex coworkers. In the case of quid pro quo sexual harassment, the employer is liable regardless of whether or not he or she knew what was happening. Employers are usually free of liability for hostile environment sexual harassment unless it can be shown they knew or should have known that a hostile environment existed.

Your company policy should clearly state a zero-tolerance for sexual harassment. You may want to address punitive and corrective measures in the event a claim of sexual harassment occurs. Make a clear channel for reporting abuses to the appropriate management resource. Consider formal training for your employees during orientation and on a periodic basis thereafter.

Office romances and flirtations do not constitute sexual harassment provided the following conditions are met:

- The romance is consensual,
- The romance does not spill over into the work environment, or
- No quid pro quo condition can be inferred or implied.

Even meeting these conditions is not a guarantee that accusations of sexual harassment will not be made if the relationship ends poorly. As an employer, any interference in the personal lives of your employees may be considered an invasion of privacy. Thus, word your policy to insist on professionalism and decorum in the workplace.

For more information on sexual harassment in the workplace, get a copy of *Draw the Line: A Sexual Harassment-Free Workplace* by Frances Lynch.

SUBSTANCE ABUSE

Drug or alcohol impairment on the job results in lowered performance levels, production losses, and higher rates of absenteeism. Employees who engage in substance abuse are four times more likely to have accidents and five times more likely to file workers' compensation claims.

If an employee is impaired while on the job, he or she represents a safety risk to themselves as well as to other employees. In addition, if they represent your company to the public or to customers, your business is not being presented in the best light. Your company's personal liability insurance may not protect in the case of the former, and no insurance coverage exists to protect you from the latter.

Company-sponsored events, such as picnics, dinners, and outings, may invite abuse, particularly if alcohol is served. Your policy must address these issues to protect your company from litigation. In addition, your policy must clearly define behavior that is unacceptable, such as:

- Drug or alcohol impairment while on the job;
- Possession or use of drugs or alcohol on the job; or
- Sale of drugs or alcohol on business property during business hours.

Clearly explain disciplinary actions for violations of substance abuse policy. Be careful not to discipline an employee for addiction. Addiction is a medical condition beyond the employee's control that requires outside, professional assistance to correct.

Consider drug and alcohol awareness training for managers or for all employees as a method to prevent substance abuse. Require managers to be aware of substance abuse indicators and to intervene when appropriate, even if substance abuse is not specifically suspected. You may even require that employees inform you when they are taking prescribed medication that may cause drowsiness or interfere with the operation of machinery.

SMOKING

Smoking reform laws have dramatically changed the way America works. Where smoking on the job was once the norm, most companies now prohibit smoking on the job and require smokers to either go outside or retire to a specially ventilated area to smoke.

These policies were largely enacted in response to legislation, despite vigorous opposition from smokers. The majority of legislation has been based on clinical studies linking second-hand smoke to health risks for nonsmokers. But smoking also presents risks to the smoker in the workplace beyond the health risk of smoking itself.

Smokers have a higher absentee rate and get sick more often than nonsmokers. Smoking on the job diverts attention from the task at hand, increasing the risk of accidents. Smoking takes time, resulting in a lower productivity rate when compared to nonsmokers. Smokers statistically file more workers' compensation and health insurance claims than nonsmokers. Taken in aggregate, smokers represent a significantly higher expense than nonsmokers. Yet many states specifically prohibit discrimination against smokers.

In your company policy handbook, address smoking as a health risk that violates the rights of nonsmokers while preserving smokers' rights. Use company policy to define the rights of each group. Ensure that designated smoking areas are adequately ventilated. Designate specific areas and times for smoking which do not interfere with productivity. Ensure that nonsmokers receive a comparable amount of time away from their workstations so smoking is not perceived to be a privilege.

SAFETY

As an employer, you have a duty to provide a safe working environment for your employees. This duty has both an ethical and a legal basis. As discussed in Chapter 4, the Occupational Safety and Health Act (OSHA) as well as similar laws at the federal, state, and local level regulate many aspects of business safety and require reporting of workplace accidents and illnesses.

Your business may present specific risks to your employees that may result in physical dangers, hazardous or toxic materials, or environmental conditions such as excessive heat or noise. You must provide protective equipment and training to employees exposed to these risks.

Most risks can be identified through careful evaluation of the workplace by an objective individual. Professional evaluations are available at little or no cost. Your insurance carrier, state department of labor office, or even local OSHA office can provide assistance. Further, the local office of the U.S. Small Business Administration (SBA) or small business development center (SBDC) can provide you with referrals to safety professionals. Finally, professional safety consultants can be found in most metropolitan areas. Keep in mind, however, that hiring a consultant can be expensive. Refer to Appendix B and Appendix C to learn how you can contact your local SBA office or nearest SBDC.

You can word your safety policy so that unsafe practices by any employee are strictly prohibited. Accident report forms should be readily available to all employees and filled out promptly after each on-the-job accident. Your policy should also define disciplinary actions as well as provide a means for reporting unsafe conditions or practices.

Many companies have formed active safety committees whose duties include safety monitoring, accident investigation, and recommendations for handling unsafe practices or conditions. Further, large companies are incorporating wellness topics into the training programs that address such issues as alcoholism, smoking cessation, and stress reduction.

TERMINATION

A well-written termination policy may save you from unnecessary litigation at the hands of a former, disgruntled employee. Sadly, not all employees are models of perfection and, sooner or later, you will encounter an employee who is a frequent discipline problem.

Your termination policy should specifically define which behaviors will result in immediate termination such as:

- Theft of company property
- Crime on company property
- Violence against another employee

You may also desire that your company policy include an employment-at-will clause. Employment-at-will means employment can be terminated at any time by either the employer or the employee for any reason.

Your termination policy should also address lesser infractions that could lead to termination if a behavior isn't corrected. This part of the policy must define procedures to be followed to correct inadequate or errant behavior. Then, strictly follow these procedures to protect your company from litigation.

Ironically, there is a longer list of unlawful reasons for terminating employment, most of which have developed from legal precedents. These include, but are not limited to retaliatory discharge, breach of contract, discrimination, and bad faith. The National Labor Relations Act (NLRA), as well as numerous other pieces of legislation, are increasingly protecting employees from wrongful discharge. You should consult with an attorney prior to terminating an employee whenever legal precedents are unclear.

Certain laws apply to terminated employees with some minor variations from state to state. You should pay a terminated employee up-to-date at the time of termination, including all money owed for accrued vacation time or sick time. This is a good time to collect keys, identification cards, and company property.

LEAVES OF ABSENCE

Employees may encounter various reasons for requiring extended leaves of absence. Keep in mind, brief absences of ten days or less should be considered personal leave rather than a leave of absence.

Family Leave

The Family and Medical Leave Act of 1993 (FMLA) permits employees to take up to twelve weeks of unpaid leave each year for the birth or adoption of a child; to attend to a seriously ill child, spouse, or parent; or for serious personal illness. As an employer you must guarantee that your employees can return to their same jobs or a comparable job and must continue health care coverage, if provided, during the leave period. This law is regulated by the Equal Employment Opportunity Commission (EEOC) and applies to employers with 50 or more employees within a 75-mile radius. The law does not apply to employees with less than one year on the job or who have not worked at least 1,250 hours or at least 25 hours per week in the past year. Workers who are on family leave are not eligible for unemployment benefits or other government compensation. To learn how your state handles family and medical leaves, refer to Chapter 4.

Military Leave

The Uniformed Services Employment and Re-employment Rights Act of 1994 requires that military leave must be granted for up to five years. The employer must rehire the employee if that person was inducted into or voluntarily enlisted in the armed forces of the United States. The law also protects reservists who are called to active duty.

USE OF COMPANY TIME, EQUIPMENT, OR RESOURCES

The temptation to use company property or equipment for personal benefit is fairly understandable. Your business is likely to be able to afford equipment that is bigger, faster, stronger, or better than home equipment. The employee who types a garage sale flyer and makes 50 copies during his or her lunch hour has still imposed some degree of wear and tear on company equipment. Similarly, sending or receiving personal faxes, using the company phone for personal business, or borrowing a tool set to work on the family car all constitute misuse of company property for personal gain.

You may decide to take a no-harm-done approach to some of these abuses, but small abuses invite larger ones, and a thousand minor expenses add up to a significant loss over the course of a year. Conversely, you don't want to impose a harsh, prohibitive atmosphere that makes employees feel uncomfortable working for you.

Your policy should make it clear that all equipment, supplies, and services were purchased for the benefit of the company and that minor theft of services or supplies is not in the company's best interest. At your discretion, you may allow provision for employees to check equipment out over night for personal use. However, such practices invite theft and make tax depreciation of eligible equipment difficult to determine.

EMPLOYEE ORIENTATION

Now that you have a good idea of the major issues to include in your company policy manual, you will want to ensure that your employees understand the importance of adhering to these procedures. One way to open up a clear line of communication is to formally acquaint each new employee on the day the employee joins your business. As part of your employee orientation make sure you discuss:

- The driving force — overall vision and spirit — of your business;
- The structure and organization of your business, identifying the key players and major divisions;
- The various employee policies, with a focus on essentials like starting and quitting times, breaks, meal times, sick days, vacation days, and timecards; and
- The benefits package your business offers and its participation eligibility dates.

By establishing this open line of communication upfront, your employees will feel more valued and will get a clear picture of where they fit in.

MONITORING YOUR EMPLOYEES' PERFORMANCE

A performance review and improvement plan are valuable tools to ensure that employees stay on the job and remain a productive and viable part of your workforce. Firing employees is costly to your business. Your losses include the time and effort expended in training, making them a part of your workforce, and attempting to assist them in overcoming deficiencies. Finally, the time you spend when terminating an employee represents a significant loss.

THE IMPORTANCE OF PERFORMANCE REVIEWS

A performance review is a process used by business managers or owners to evaluate and document an employee's job performance. To be effective, performance reviews must be fair and impartial. Administer them following the schedule set forth in your employee handbook or other company policy document.

Effective performance reviews, based on job requirements, provide a systematic record of an employee's job performance. This continuous record gives the employee valuable feedback and encourages improvement. It provides fair documentation of strengths and weaknesses, simplifies management decisions regarding raises, promotions, transfers, demotions, and terminations. Complete records may even protect a company in the event of legal actions initiated by a discontented or former employee.

It is important to use standardized methods and formats for all performance reviews. You will want to rate all employees according to a set of consistent standards. The *1978 Guidelines on Uniform Employee Selection Procedures* prohibits basing performance reviews on discriminatory practices or biases concerning racial, ethnic, religious, or gender preferences.

Most employers conduct performance reviews annually, usually during the anniversary month of the employee's start date, while a few prefer scheduling them semiannually. Schedule several reviews during, and one at the end of, the employee's initial probationary period. These reviews provide feedback to the new employee on his or her conformance with job requirements as well as company policy, and serve to identify problem areas early in the employer-employee relationship. They also provide information on which to base a decision to terminate a new employee, if necessary, at the end of a probationary period.

PREVENTING PERFORMANCE REVIEW PROBLEMS

When properly and fairly administered, performance reviews are a valuable management tool. However, even a well-designed program is subject to problems resulting from human error. An awareness of these potential problems will allow you to take steps to prevent them, and will help maintain the consistency and fairness of your program.

Managers Rate Employees Differently

Managers will not rate employees in the same way. Some tend to see all employees in the most positive light, while others take a more negative approach. Ideally, you want everyone involved in rating employees to do so in a balanced, even-handed way that uniformly recognizes strengths as well as weaknesses. Periodic discussion of the review process with your managers is the best method of ensuring fairness and objectivity in the performance review process. Some employers use a dual review method. The employee's supervisor and a supervisor from another area who is familiar with the employee's work each evaluate the employee separately.

Unclear Rating Standards

Unclear rating standards result in an inconsistent performance review program. Poorly defined standards result in a situation where one manager defines good attendance as zero absenteeism, and another manager defines good attendance as no more than three absences. Performance standards must be clear to supervisors and workers alike. Define all terms and avoid vague generalities when defining standards.

Last In, First Out

It is natural for reviewers to remember recent events best; therefore, rating an employee's performance based on work accomplished during recent months rather than during the entire evaluation period. A significant improvement in performance as evaluation time approaches is a good indication that this problem exists in your review process.

To prevent that from happening, encourage supervisors to frequently notice performance trends and to collect performance data throughout the evaluation period. Examples of pertinent information include letters of recommendation or congratulation, voluntary participation on committees, taking on new leadership positions, and completing additional training. Also, make note of minor infractions, tardiness, and informal counseling.

The Halo Effect

An employee who is neat, well-mannered, and cheerful seems to be brighter and more capable than a casually dressed, introverted employee. This "halo effect" is a hindrance to objective performance appraisal. Reviewers must be alert to this and ensure that they are evaluating real performance rather than perceived performance. Train your reviewers to be aware of the halo effect and provide them with clear-cut standards to use in appraising performance.

THE DOCUMENTATION PROCESS

Document all performance reviews consistently using a standardized performance review report. The performance review report provides a permanent record of the performance review, its timeliness, and its fairness. It is best to use a standardized form when conducting performance reviews. The report form should be general enough to be applicable to all employees, yet specific enough to provide a clear appraisal that generates useful management information. Most forms combine a scaled rating system with space for amplifying comments. A sample performance review is located in Appendix A for your use. For other formats consider getting a copy of *The Complete Book of Business Forms* by Richard G. Stuart.

The employee and the supervisor fill out the performance review report through cooperative effort. The employee should sign the report to indicate that he or she has read it and understands its content. Keep in mind, signing does not necessarily indicate that the employee agrees with the report. After completing and signing the report, the supervisor forwards it to upper management for review, if applicable. After review, file the report in the employee's personnel record.

In cases where the employee disagrees with the content of the performance appraisal, you should have a procedure in place that allows fair rebuttal. Typically, an employee can rebut in written form to an upper manager. After review, the rebuttal becomes a part of the employee's personnel file.

COUNSELING – AN OPPORTUNITY TO IMPROVE

Counseling is similar to the performance review, but differs in that it occurs as a result of a change in performance. Generally, employees view counseling as being negative because it most often occurs as a result of poor job performance. Management's role when this happens is to help the employee understand how his or her performance is inadequate. Then, you can work with that individual to identify the source of the problem and recommend ways to correct it.

Ideally, both management and the employee will approach counseling as an opportunity to improve rather than as a punitive measure. It is important to state the goal of the counseling at the beginning of the meeting. Remember that your employee is a valued asset who has contributed time and effort to your business. Your goal is to keep all your employees productive and motivated.

Poor performance may be job related as a result of poorly defined policy, personality conflict, politics, or environment. An employee suffering from eye strain from his or her computer terminal may perceive that management is uncaring, particularly if the condition has persisted over time. Timely counseling in an open and supportive atmosphere will allow you to identify these problems and correct them.

Management will rarely intervene directly when degraded performance is the result of external problems, such as family difficulties, substance abuse, or financial woes. In these cases, refer the employee to an outside professional agency. A referral gives the employee the clear message that he or she is a valued asset. Arrange for a follow-up meeting to inquire about the employee's progress in coping with the problem and provide feedback on performance issues.

YOUR DISCIPLINARY ACTION POLICY

The time to decide how to handle a discipline problem comes long before it occurs. Disciplinary actions must follow a prescribed format in accordance with your company policy manual. This is a case where preparation will save you a great deal of trouble in the long run. Decide which behaviors you will consider as minor infractions and which ones you will consider to be grounds for immediate suspension or termination. Develop a policy for dealing with each of these two types of infraction.

Typical minor infractions include tardiness, waste of supplies, arguing with coworkers, or violating company policy. While your company policy manual is the basis for determining infractions, leave room in your discipline policy for supervisors to use good judgment in determining when violations have occurred.

Your disciplinary action policy is a series of specific steps. Those steps include, but are not limited to a verbal warning, counseling with a written warning, an improvement plan, review, suspension, and termination. The process takes time, but when compared to the cost of training and nurturing a new employee, it is worth the effort to save an otherwise good employee.

GIVING WARNINGS

As part of your disciplinary action policy, you will need to decide the basis and process of giving warnings. Warnings can come in a verbal or written form. A verbal warning given when an infraction occurs will send a clear message to your employee that the specified behavior is inappropriate and unacceptable. Give verbal warnings in a friendly, yet firm manner. Most people want to do well and will respond immediately to friendly guidance. When a behavior ends with a verbal warning, place a note to that effect in the employee's personnel file.

A written warning is the next step in the process. It is a formal counseling session with the employee, documented on a standardized company form. The form will include a detailed explanation of the infraction and the expected behavior. It will provide space for the employee to explain extenuating or mitigating circumstances. It will suggest methods for the employee to correct the deficiency, set a time limit for improvement, and explain the consequences for failure to improve. As a supervisor or manager, you will discuss the written warning with your employee and clearly explain each portion. At the conclusion of the counseling session, the employee should sign the warning to indicate that he or she completely understands it. Then, forward the warning to upper management for review, if applicable, and file it in the employee's personnel record.

HANDLING SUSPENSIONS

When an employee does not respond to warnings, suspension should follow. Suspension of an employee is a serious matter and is reserved for only the most serious disciplinary problems. Suspension without pay is a clear message to the employee that he or she must change problem behavior or risk termination. Your goal is to retain otherwise valuable employees by giving them every opportunity to change.

As with counseling and written warnings, it is important to keep detailed records of your personnel actions. Remember, you are attempting to correct a performance problem, not a personality problem. Detailed records will clearly show that you acted appropriately and dealt with the problem fairly and professionally. Use a formal suspension notice to record this action.

A suspension notice is a standardized form that should be completed, dated, and signed by an employee's supervisor. A notice should include:

- A description of the suspension action,
- A statement of the reason for the suspension, and
- A list of the corrective actions required.

The form should include space for the employee to sign to acknowledge understanding and receipt of the suspension notice. File the original in the employee's personnel folder and provide copies to the employee and the employee's supervisor.

A suspension is not a substitute for termination. You cannot suspend an employee indefinitely. So be certain that you include a specific ending point for the suspension in the description of the suspension action, usually a period lasting from several days to several weeks. After the employee returns to work following suspension, any further infractions normally lead to termination.

TAKE CAUTION WITH DISCIPLINARY TERMINATIONS

The practice of employment-at-will and the right to terminate an employee for good or just cause are being increasingly challenged in the courts. There is a growing list of legal precedents for wrongful discharge of an employee. The list includes such concepts as retaliatory discharge, breach of written contract, breach of implied contract, and discrimination based on sex, age, or disability.

As an employer, your best defense is to ensure that your employee handbook and company policies make the employment at will doctrine perfectly clear. Further, ensure that the wording of these documents does not imply permanent employment.

Observe the following guidelines when terminating an employee:

- Only terminate an employee based on documented substandard performance or misconduct and only in accordance with established equal opportunity doctrine.
- Handle terminations discreetly, privately, and professionally.
- Ensure the employee receives all pay earned to date.
- Make sure that all company policies, including performance review, counseling, grievance, and appeal policies are followed, when applicable.

Use a standardized company form to document the termination. Make sure the form includes the reason for termination and refers to supporting records and documents. Provide a checklist on the form to ensure that correct termination procedures are followed and that the employee's rights are observed. Following these recommendations does not guarantee protection from a wrongful discharge suit. The law is changing continuously and your best insurance is to consult with your attorney when you prepare your company policy manual. Stay abreast of changes in the law and keep your manual current with legislation.

Write a separate policy in your personnel manual for handling termination due to misconduct, such as theft or destruction of company property, fighting, criminal activity, or continuous unexcused absence. Carefully define those conditions that will result in either immediate termination or termination following suspension. When you terminate someone for misconduct, take care to observe all the precautions and requirements of normal termination procedures. Fully document the termination decision and process, including a description of the type of misconduct that occurred. Include documentation that proves or supports the determination of misconduct.

OTHER TYPES OF TERMINATIONS

Termination also results from other actions such as resignation and layoff due to restructuring or the elimination of a position. These terminations follow the same basic procedures as other types of termination. Fully document the circumstances of the termination, treat the departing employee with dignity and professionalism, and provide the employee with all earned pay before his or her departure.

Require resigning employees to give notice of their intent to resign whenever possible. Sufficient notice allows you time to complete all administrative paperwork, verify pay and benefit requirements, conduct an exit interview, and start looking for a replacement employee. Generally, two weeks or ten working days is sufficient notice. A departing employee frequently feels more free to express dissatisfaction with working conditions, and an exit interview is a valuable means of getting feedback about the company, the working environment, and management practices.

Layoffs result from a reduction in the workforce and the elimination of a position through restructuring. Notify employees of an impending layoff and the reasons for it as far in advance as possible. Carefully consider which employees will be laid off, following established policy guidelines. Consider company needs, seniority issues, and the abilities of individual employees. When possible, consider reassigning individuals to other areas for which they are qualified.

For an in-depth look at hiring, firing, and disciplining your employees, refer to *People Investment: How to Make Your Hiring Decisions Pay Off for Everyone* by E. R. Worthington and Anita Worthington. To find out more about this book, see the Useful Resources section at the end of this chapter.

BENEFITS PACKAGES

Benefits fall into two categories: those that are legally required and those at the discretion of the employer. Legally required benefits include payment of Social Security taxes, workers' compensation insurance, and unemployment insurance. Discretionary benefits include anything from medical insurance to free tickets to sporting events. Virtually anything of value that you provide or make available to your workforce qualifies as a discretionary benefit. The only limitation is your imagination.

Keep in mind, in today's job market, employees expect a benefits package along with their salary or hourly wage. Typical benefits include medical insurance coverage, accidental death and disability coverage, and some form of retirement plan. The cost of these benefits increases each year, but you can generally expect to pay approximately 25 to 35 percent of the wage expenses for each employee. This means that an employee who earns $7.50 per hour will represent an hourly expense of as much as $10.15. Generally, employees are not aware of the costs associated with providing benefits.

You may decide that the nature of your business does not support the cost of providing employee benefits. This is particularly true under the following conditions:

- Your workforce is largely unskilled;
- All or most of your employees are part-time or temporary; or
- Your nearest competitors are not providing a benefits package.

However, as your business grows and you require a larger, more skilled workforce, a comprehensive benefits package will help to attract the best qualified employees to your business.

If you decide to include a retirement plan as part of your employee benefits package, make sure it is in sync with the Employee Retirement Income Security Act (ERISA). This act governs how certain pension plans and welfare plans are administered. Pension plans include certain retirement plans, profit sharing, stock option plans, and individual retirement accounts (IRAs). Welfare plans include most types of employee insurance such as health, disability, life, and accidental death coverage.

Recent shifts in cultural values are subtly changing the way today's workforce views benefits. Tomorrow's employees are likely to value a clean and pleasant working environment, state-of-the-art equipment, and a four-day workweek over tickets to the next big game. So before planning a benefits package, take the time to survey the needs and desires of your employees.

One way to learn what your employees think about your company is to use *The Survey Genie* — an easy-to-use software program that allows you to evaluate how your business is perceived by your employees. You can also learn what your customers think about your business by using the customer version of *The Survey Genie*. To learn more about this insightful tool for your business, see below.

CHAPTER WRAP-UP

If your business will have employees, you will need to carefully manage the people you hire. Just like other critical investments for your business, the time you take to hire and retain top-quality employees is an investment that can pay huge dividends or seriously affect your ability to make a profit.

Effective human resources management is a multi-faceted process. This process will require you to:

- Keep thorough job descriptions before you announce a job opening.
- Understand anti-discrimination laws so you know which questions to avoid on written applications and during interviews.
- Know how to screen job applicants and track your evaluations after both formal and informal interviews.
- Properly acquaint and train new employees so they know exactly what your business expects of them.
- Review and monitor your employees' performance and help foster existing skills and develop new skills.

A good human resources package means having well-defined company policies and procedures. In short, create a company policy and procedures manual or an employee handbook and make sure each employee gets a copy. Document that employees have read your handbook by having them sign a paper indicating they understand all the policies and procedures outlined in the manual. As a general rule, make sure your company policy manual covers:

- Benefits
- Career opportunities
- Company background
- Employee evaluation procedures

- Employee grievance procedures
- Employee safety
- Employee/Management relations
- General policies and procedures
- Pay rates and schedules

Remember, the people who will work for you will communicate the character and quality of your business and its product or service. Build a team that will help you and your employees make the most of your enterprise. For specific state and federal government regulations related to your business, refer back to Chapter 4.

USEFUL RESOURCES

A Company Policy and Personnel Workbook by Carl R. J. Sniffen and Ardella Ramey. This manual can help save costly consultant or staff hours in creating company personnel policies. Gives model policy text for such topics as employee safety, leaves of absence, flex time, smoking, substance abuse, sexual harassment, and performance improvement.

Draw the Line: A Sexual Harassment-Free Workplace by Frances Lynch. In the wake of controversy and legal proceedings regarding sexual harassment in the workplace, business owners and managers need to educate themselves on how to set up an environment that discourages any form of harassment. This easy-to-read manual helps owners communicate policy to employees and spells out the procedures that are most effective if a lawsuit is filed.

People Investment: How to Make Your Hiring Decisions Pay Off for Everyone by E. R. Worthington and Anita Worthington. Most business owners don't specialize in personnel management. However, effective human resources management calls for a solid grasp of knowing how to hire and retain qualified employees. This book gives tips on how to hire the best people for your business.

The Survey Genie. Use this software to gain valuable feedback from your employees. Contains 200 pre-developed questions that will help you produce a comprehensive, yet easy-to-use survey.

NOTES FOR HUMAN RESOURCES:

CHAPTER 11

Insurance Matters

Getting into business is inherently a risk. There is no guarantee of success. However, you can reduce risks by making informed decisions which can reduce the possibility of loss due to the risk, eliminate the chance of a particular risk, or insure against loss due to a risk. The most common way to guard against many risks is by obtaining insurance.

Insurance is a necessary business expense. You need insurance to protect you and your business from hazards, such as fire or other disasters, crime, general liability, or an interruption of business. As an employer, you are required to purchase workers' compensation insurance and may additionally choose to provide health, life, or disability benefits for your employees. This chapter introduces you to the numerous type of insurance coverage to help you make an informed decision.

Not all risks are insurable and, in some cases, the cost of insuring is too great. You will assume the risk and hope that you do not have a loss that is not covered by insurance. Your first step in evaluating your need for insurance is to assess the risks to your business.

WHAT IS RISK ASSESSMENT?

Risk assessment is the process of determining the risks your business has and what you should do about them. You will have to strike a balance between the expense of being covered against every eventuality and the risks associated with having insufficient insurance coverage. By critically evaluating each aspect of your business and considering its relative importance to your business, you will lay the groundwork for determining your insurance needs. This will save you a great deal of time and money as you shop for the best coverage at the best price.

To assess risk you must determine where losses can occur by reviewing every aspect of your business to identify which people, property, or conditions you need to continue to operate. Evaluate safety issues and concerns, your crime risk, and the potential for fire or other disaster. Evaluate the financial condition of your business and decide how much loss your business can absorb without risking failure. Consider temporary closures, downtime, inventory, cash flow, borrowing power, and other pertinent variables. Prioritize and categorize each potential loss based on its severity and potential frequency.

FOUR WAYS TO HANDLE RISKS

You will handle risks in one of four ways: elimination, reduction, retention, and transference.

Elimination. This means that you decide to drop a product or service that exposed you to a particular risk. For example, you would eliminate the potential for a delivery van accident with potential damage to your vehicle, driver, another driver and other property if you no longer delivered your product or only provided service for items that would be brought to your place of business by a customer.

Reduction. This entails modifying a potential loss by continuing to assume the risk. However, you change an element of the risk that would reduce the likelihood or the severity of a loss.

Retention. You understand the potentials for the risk, but because the likelihood of a loss or because the cost of insuring against the loss or changing your business are higher than you can afford or want to pay, you assume the full consequences of the potential loss.

Transference. When you obtain insurance to cover a risk, you transfer the risk to the insurance company. The company is insuring many risks and thus spreads the cost of the consequences of a loss across many insured companies or individuals.

Each alternative imposes different levels of cost or potential cost. Your task is to weigh the cost of each method against the potential risk to your business. The example below, while simplistic, clearly demonstrates the application of each method.

For example, suppose your business is a feed and grain store. You determine that one of your risks is loss of inventory due to spoilage from mice. So, you choose to eliminate a frequent and severe mouse problem by periodically hiring an exterminator. If mice are frequent visitors, but don't spoil much inventory, you may choose to reduce the risk instead by investing in one or more cats. When infestation is infrequent and does not result in much spoilage, you will probably retain the risk and absorb the losses as part of the cost of doing business. A rare, devastating invasion resulting in complete loss of your inventory will lead you to transfer the risk to an insurance carrier. To better understand the four methods of handling risks, consider the following scenario.

You own a food processing company with over 100 products. One of the products requires much more care in preparation than the others because of past problems with a fungus in the food. The food item accounts for only one percent of the total sales and less than one percent of the profit of the company. You can:

Eliminate the risk. Discontinue the product; thus, you eliminate the extra care that is required to offer a product that is marginal in profit.

Reduce the risk. Install new equipment that is easier to maintain and monitor and is more reliable than your other equipment.

Retain the risk. Assume that with constant vigilance you will not have a problem with the food item.

Transfer the risk. Purchase a liability insurance policy that will cover the consequences of bad food being purchased and making people sick as well as a recall of the product if such a problem should occur.

The above scenario assumes you have all four options regarding how to handle risks. In many cases, you may have risks that are not insurable. For example, You may be at the end of a road where a flood may cause the road to be impassable during certain times of the year. Although you may obtain flood insurance, the risk is not that you are flooded, only that you can't reach your business because of a flood. Although you may be able to obtain special insurance for such an eventuality, most insurance will not cover this risk.

You may also find that although you can obtain insurance for certain risks, the costs associated with insuring certain risks may be more than the potential loss over a given period. For example, if you want to insure against theft and you believe that the greatest loss you would incur due to theft would be $10,000 you may have to pay $2,000 in premiums per year if you were insuring all items that could be stolen. If you have a loss more than every five years, you would be financially ahead to insure the loss. However, if a loss might occur only once in ten years, you can cover the loss with what you would pay in insurance premiums. Of course, you don't know how often a loss will occur. Be certain that if your business is prone to losses often, either your insurance will be canceled or the premium will be increased.

Insurance is very cost effective if you can obtain low premiums for potentially high losses as in liability insurance. However, the insurance companies will determine if your business has a high potential for liability claims and will charge on the basis of the industry experience for such claims and may even refuse to write insurance because of the potential of high losses.

Other risks normally associated with running your business are not insurable, such as losing a major customer or the cost of raw materials increasing after you have made a bid or set a price for an item you produce. In such cases, you need to determine the potential risks and include solutions into contracts or pricing policies.

TYPES OF INSURANCE

To start, understand the unique characteristics involved with the two broad classes of insurance — property-casualty insurance and life insurance.

Property-casualty insurance. This type includes property insurance for fire and other hazards and casualty insurance. Workers' compensation is a casualty insurance but also covered under this type of insurance is auto liability, general liability, credit insurance, bonds, boiler and machinery, crime and other miscellaneous casualty.

Life insurance. Both term and whole life policies are available. These types of insurance are used in business where two partners take insurance out for the other partner so each can buy the other partner's share in case of his or her death.

PROPERTY INSURANCE

As a new business owner, the chances are high that you will need some form of property insurance. If you lease an office or warehouse the lease will probably require you to obtain some type of fire policy. If your product is transported ship via truck or marine vessel you may want a policy to cover potential loss.

Fire insurance is generally thought of as property insurance. There are many types of property insurance. Some are for a direct loss such as the loss due to a fire; others are for consequential losses such as being out of business for a couple of months due to a fire.

There are many ways policies can be written and interpreted, but you should determine whether your policy is for:

- Replacement cost (replacing an old item with a new one with no deductions for depreciation);
- A stated loss amount; or
- Actual cash value (what you paid less an amount for depreciation).

There is also a provision in some insurance policies called coinsurance. If you do not insure for at least 80% (sometimes 90% or 100%) of your potential loss, the insurance will only pay the percentage of loss that you have insured of the total potential loss. For example, you may insure a building that has a value of $1,000,000 for $500,000 (thinking that you would not suffer a complete loss of the building and would be willing to take the chance that it would not be a complete loss. If a fire occurred which caused $50,000 damage, the insurer would only pay 50% of the $50,000 loss ($500,000 divided by $1,000,000).

In addition, if your building increased in value while you occupied it, and the value at the time of loss was considerably more than when you took out the insurance, the insurer may invoke the coinsurance provision based on the value of the building at the time of loss, not when you became insured. Therefore, you should review your policies regarding the values you insure on an annual basis when the policy is renewed.

If you operate your business out of your home your coverage for losses to your business will be limited with usual homeowners insurance. In addition, if you conduct part of your business from buildings other than the home, but on the same property as your home, the other buildings and contents will probably not be covered unless you have a separate business policy for them.

CASUALTY INSURANCE

Insurance that is not life insurance or property insurance is normally considered casualty insurance. Workers' compensation is a form of casualty insurance and was described above. Other casualty insurance includes automobile and liability insurance.

Automobile Insurance

If you own or lease a vehicle for your business you should be aware that there are different rules for a business policy than for your personally owned vehicles. As an individual, automobile insurance covers the individual (the named insured) for whatever vehicle the person drives, including rental vehicles. For business insurance, the vehicle is covered for drivers who have permission to use the vehicle. There is also coverage called Drive Other Car Endorsement (B.F.D.O.C.) — which you can get on your company policy to cover you when you are driving a noncompany vehicle if you do not have other personal insurance. As a part of automobile insurance, liability insurance pays for bodily injury or property damage to others due to the use of the automobile.

Physical damage insurance is composed of two types of classifications: comprehensive and collision. Comprehensive covers most losses except those caused by collision. It includes vandalism, theft, and broken windshields. Collision covers a loss due to collision of the vehicle with another object.

A third element of automobile insurance is for medical payments. It includes the occupants of either or both vehicles and normally covers medical, dental, surgical, ambulance, and funeral services.

In many states you can obtain uninsured motorist coverage to protect the company against loss due to the lack of insurance of another driver.

A type of insurance called employers nonowned auto and hired auto coverage will protect your company in the event an employee, while on company business, has an accident and may be held liable.

Liability Insurance

Liability for a situation occurs in one of three ways:

- Negligence
- Statutory law
- Assumption by contract

There are legal requirements for acts to be defined as negligent and a discussion of the requirements is not in the scope of this book. Virtually every business has a potential for being sued for a negligent act. Therefore, you should carefully determine your potential exposure in this area and locate an insurance company that can insure what might be devastating loss to your company. As an employer you can be held responsible for the actions of one of your employees even though you have taken steps to prevent a situation from occurring.

Statutory law liability occurs when a law has been enacted that creates a legal obligation, such as the requirement to carry workers' compensation insurance or liability regarding products that may be inherently dangerous.

Assumption by contract refers to a hold-harmless agreement in a contract. For example, your lease agreement probably will contain a hold-harmless agreement that requires you to maintain liability insurance and hold the landlord harmless for any accident that may occur on the premises.

There are several forms of liability insurance coverage but many can be combined into one policy or insured individually. Check with your agent regarding potential liability that your company may have and see if the cost of insurance is reasonable for the level of coverage you will receive. If you have a home office and have a homeowners policy with liability coverage, the policy may not cover liability for anyone hurt at your place of business. Check with your agent to see if you need a separate policy for your home office.

Crime Coverage

Crime is a real threat to many businesses. Virtually all businesses must be aware of employee dishonesty, theft, bad checks, vandalism and personal injury as daily occurrences. Some businesses have a higher potential for one type of loss rather than another so there are different types of coverage that meet individual needs.

One of the most frequently used coverage for loss of money by employees or others handling cash or accounts in business is through the use of bonds. There are various types of bonds available that protect against theft, embezzlement, loss of money on or off the premises, counterfeit money, and forging. The cost of coverage for such problems may exceed the value of the coverage or you may decide to implement company policies that protect you from such loss. For example, some retail establishments do not accept checks without the customer having a check guarantee card, or they may not accept checks at all.

Even if you have a policy for theft, you many not be able to collect the amount of loss. The policies will generally limit the types of theft for which you can claim against the policy. For example, you probably will not be able to collect on a theft policy if you find that your inventory is actually $10,000 lower than you expected according to your computerized inventory. You may suspect a theft, but there is little likelihood that the insurance company will pay for the loss.

Theft policies also have coinsurance provisions, described previously, so be careful that you are aware of the potential payoff if there is a claim.

LIFE INSURANCE

Life insurance is probably the best known of all insurance policies. There are two major types of life insurance: term and whole life. There are variations of the policies but basically they insure against a person's life rather than against other hazards.

Term insurance pays a benefit if an insured person dies during the term of the policy. If the person does not die, there is no remainder value of the policy. It is similar to other casualty policies that expire with no payment made if no claim arises. Term insurance is less expensive and the most widely used form of life insurance.

Whole life policies are designed to pay the beneficiary the face amount of the policy in case of death. If the insured decides to terminate the policy there may be some cash value to the policy.

There are many variations of both types of policies. Their applications in business generally are designed for retirement, purchase of partners' shares of the business or in some cases, the cash value of the whole life policy can be borrowed from the insurance company or used as collateral to make a loan to the business.

WHEN YOU HAVE EMPLOYEES

In addition to property-casualty and life insurance choices, you will need to explore other types of insurance should you have employees. Some of these employer insurance considerations include:

- State mandated workers' compensation, and
- Optional health, disability, and accidental death insurance.

If you offer insurance as part of your employee compensation package, be aware of certain recent legislation that affects how you administer that insurance.

WORKERS' COMPENSATION INSURANCE

As an employer you are required to purchase workers' compensation insurance if you have a certain number of employees. The requirements vary from state to state. Make sure you read Chapter 4 to understand the workers' compensation laws applicable to your state. Workers' compensation coverage pays benefits for job-related illnesses, injuries, and death. Paid benefits may include medical expenses, death benefits, lost wages, and vocational rehabilitation. Failure to carry coverage for your employees could leave you liable for payment of all benefits and subject to fines.

To better understand your role in carrying workers' compensation insurance, make sure you know how your premium is calculated. Premiums are calculated by dividing an employee's annual payroll by 100 and multiplying the result by a factor based on the employee's classification rating. Classification ratings vary from occupation to occupation and from state to state. The insurance industry in your state has classified hundreds of occupations according to the risk of injury suggested by the occupations' loss histories. For instance, cashiers experience lower job-related injury risks than mill workers, and thus have a much lower rating factor. Accordingly, workers' compensation insurance coverage for a cashier is much less expensive than for a mill worker.

Premiums are further modified by an experience factor based on a business' claim history. For example, a business with a good workers' compensation claim history will have a lower experience modification factor — resulting in lower premiums. The reverse is also true. Thus, as a purchaser of workers' compensation insurance, you must ensure that all your employees are correctly classified and their claim histories have been considered in the final premium calculations. These simple checks could save you a considerable amount of money each year.

You can reduce your insurance costs in other ways. Purchase a type of policy called a participating policy, which pays dividends to companies with low loss records. Another good service to look for is loss control assistance. Your insurance company's loss control department can help you prevent or reduce claims by providing free published materials and guidance as well as evaluation and troubleshooting. Work environment and safety program evaluations are expensive to purchase independently, but may be provided as a free service by your insurance company.

Investing in safety will usually produce a positive return on your investment. You can lower your compensation payments if claims are low. It usually takes three years to develop a rate, called experience modification. This rating can be higher or lower than the standard rate, based on claims. Remember, if the rate goes up, you pay the increase on all employees based on their payroll for the entire year. Thus, a small increase or decrease in a rate can mean a substantial savings or additional payment at the end of the year.

Some states require companies to have employee committees that review safety issues in the workplace. Even if your state does not require it, it is a good idea to obtain ideas from employees regarding workplace safety. You can have a formal policy or a suggestion box. Employees are good at anticipating safety problems because of their close proximity to potentially dangerous situations. Not all industrial accidents involve heavy machinery. Individuals may slip on the floor or over wires or obstacles. Lighting or seating can cause long term problems that will cost you much more money than correcting the problem would cost. In addition, accidents cost you in terms of time due to an employee's absence. If an employee has an accident you either must do without his or her services or get a temporary who is not as familiar with your business as the employee who is off, and spend time training the new employee.

If you are a home-based business, you will find it helpful to obtain information from your workers' compensation company regarding how it handles injuries when workers are at your home. Your insurance company's policies may affect your policies regarding working at home.

For a comprehensive study of workers' compensation, get a copy of *CompControl: The Secrets of Reducing Workers' Compensation Costs* by Edward J. Priz. For more information on this business guidebook, see the Useful Resources section at the end of this chapter.

HEALTH INSURANCE

Recent national debate concerning health insurance has made businesses the major provider of health insurance for most workers in the United States. There are two basic types of health insurance: disability insurance and medical insurance.

Disability Insurance

Disability insurance can be used in a business to assist an owner to hire a manager in the case of the owner's disability. It may also be used to pay off a partner if the person who is disabled is unlikely to be able to return to work.

Whatever kind of disability insurance you obtain, be certain to get the following information:

- The income per month that the policy will pay;
- The number of months payments will be made; and
- The period of time you are disabled and other conditions necessary for payment to be made.

Medical Insurance

Most people will identify their primary source of medical insurance as the place where they are employed. Whether you are the owner of a business or an employee, medical insurance will likely be one of the first and most sought after benefits derived from the business.

If you incorporate, your corporation will be able to deduct the full cost of medical insurance premiums as a business expense. If you are a sole proprietor or partner, only a portion of the expense will be deductible. If your business is not a corporation, be sure to check the changing percentages with your accountant.

There are two major elements of medical insurance: major medical and comprehensive coverage. Major medical is coverage for hospital and recuperation expenses. Comprehensive is used for hospital and outpatient treatment, office visits, testing, and other health treatment.

There are many ways to purchase medical insurance that reflect higher or lower costs and benefits. The amount of deductible is one of the major sources of price differential in plans. By having a higher deductible, thus insuring for major medical problems, you will be able to keep the cost per employee lower than with higher deductible amounts.

Check with your industry association to see if insurance is offered as part of its benefit plan. You should also check with your insurance agent regarding the coverage period for a policy. If you change insurance companies and a claim is filed for the period when you were with the previous company, you may not be covered. It is best to know how you are covered especially if there is a chance that a claim can occur after you change your insurance company.

FOLLOW ERISA GUIDELINES

If you provide employees with insurance other than workers' compensation or if you give other benefits such as a profit sharing or retirement plans, you will need to comply with the Employment Retirement Income Security Act of 1974 (ERISA). ERISA requires that you have a summary plan description (SPD) for each welfare plan in effect. Then, you must distribute a copy of each SPD to all covered employees. Each SPD must include specific information as well as an ERISA rights statement as specified by U.S. Department of Labor regulations. Insurance companies will often supply you with an SPD for each plan as a part of their service.

When your company grows to 100 or more employees, ERISA requirements become much more complex, involving several annual reports to the U.S. Department of Labor and an annual report to all employees. You should consult an expert in these regulations. Most insurance or investment companies have experts available to help you.

COBRA

Recent legislation applies to businesses with 20 or more employees. This legislation, the Consolidated Omnibus Reconciliation Act (COBRA), requires you to offer the same group health benefits as you offer regular eligible employees to:

- Employees who have been terminated (for reasons other than gross misconduct), laid off, or resigned;
- Employees whose hours have been reduced;
- The widowed or divorced spouses of employees;
- Employees eligible for Medicare; and
- The children of employees who have lost dependent status.

Eligibility for this coverage begins as soon as a sponsoring employee becomes eligible for coverage under the group health plan. Then, that employee and his or her dependents are eligible for continued benefits for up to 36 months thereafter. Your company can charge the employee up to 100 percent of the coverage cost plus a 2 percent surcharge.

If you fail to comply with the requirements of this act, your company cannot deduct health plan contributions from its taxes. Further, COBRA does not prevent your company from terminating your group health care plan.

Should you have employees, make sure you understand your responsibilities under COBRA. Consult with a knowledgeable insurance specialist; most insurance companies can provide up-to-date information about COBRA.

SHOPPING FOR COVERAGE

Becoming an expert on insurance matters is probably the last thing on your mind as you attempt to start your business. However, high on your priority list during startup should be finding the best coverage for the best price. Your best option is to find a reputable agent or broker you can trust. Finding an agent may not be as difficult as it sounds. Ask for referrals from friends, your lawyer, your accountant, or friendly competitors.

Once you have several referrals, your next step is to narrow your search by selecting agents who have earned Chartered Life Underwriter (CLU) or Chartered Property/Casualty Underwriter (CPCU) designations. These professionals are generally more experienced and capable than agents without one of these designations. The Certified Insurance Counselor (CID) agent is a professional designation very popular among agents and keeps the agent up to date on a current basis.

If you are unable to locate a suitable agent, you can choose to hire an insurance consultant instead. An insurance consultant is an expert in insurance matters and will provide an objective analysis of your risk management and insurance needs. Hiring an insurance consultant is similar to seeing a doctor or an attorney. Follow your consultant's advice carefully when selecting coverage from your agent or broker. The hourly fees for consultants are usually quite high but can result in significant savings in annual premiums. Billing is usually broken down into quarter-hour segments. Be wary of consultants who attempt to pad their fees by offering extended services that you may not need or that you can get elsewhere at a far less expensive cost.

If you hire a consultant, make sure he or she is a member of the Society of Risk Management Consultants. To be a member of this society, a consultant cannot be an insurance broker. This stipulation prevents potential conflicts of interest and reduces the risk of unethical behavior. To contact the society, use the address and phone number listed in Appendix C.

You can get to know the insurance process and learn easy methods for getting the best coverage at the best price by reading *The Buyer's Guide to Business Insurance* by Don Bury and Larry Heischman. For more information, see the Useful Resources section below.

CHAPTER WRAP-UP

A smartstart for new entrepreneurs involves a close look at their business insurance needs. It might seem unusual to plan for a major loss or potential disaster while at the same time you are planning to open your doors for business. However, countless business owners — even relatively new businesses — have benefited from a solid insurance package.

The tasks of getting insurance quotes and making contacts with agents, brokers, and insurance companies are not high on anyone's list of favorite things to do. You can simplify the process by informing yourself of the various types of insurance available. Then, look at your business as a whole and assess the potential risks. Know how you want to handle these risks — whether you will transfer, reduce, retain, or eliminate — before you approach an insurance agent.

To be able to get the best quote, you will need to decide which types of coverage are necessary for your type of business. If crime is a real threat, then you will need to consider some form of crime coverage. If potential negligence as a result of using your product or service is likely, then you will want to explore liability coverage. Of course, as an employer you will have to comply with workers' compensation issues for the state in which you will operate. Also, you must evaluate the need to include disability and medical insurance as part of your employee benefits package.

One thing you can be sure of as you start your business: problems will surface on a regular basis. The way you problemsolve includes being prepared for emergencies. Risk assessment and insurance will protect your assets and help you stay in business.

USEFUL RESOURCES

CompControl: The Secrets of Reducing Workers' Compensation Costs by Edward J. Priz. Shows you how to reduce the cost of your workers' compensation insurance without the typical accident prevention or claims minimization lectures.

The Buyer's Guide to Business Insurance by Don Bury and Larry Heischman. Gives expert advice on shopping for insurance and will help you understand the various types of coverage and compare proposals and premium rates.

NOTES FOR INSURANCE:

CHAPTER 12

Setting Up Your Office

New business owners tend to view office work as something to be handled later, when they get the time. This is generally a mistake. The adage that "no job is finished until the paperwork is done" has been presented humorously, yet it is based on a fundamental truth. Somewhere amid the excitement of producing and selling a new product hides the simple fact that you are engaged in a business. Businesses are managed from an office setting.

To lessen the pain of dealing with records and paperwork, it is vital to be as organized as possible. This chapter will help you:

- Get organized with your incoming mail;
- Improve your telephone answering techniques;
- Establish a home-based office;
- Choose the right furniture and equipment for your operation; and
- Select the best location for your business.

The effort put forth in becoming organized will pay off a hundredfold as your business grows and demands more of your time and energy. Luckily, there are well-established tools to help you handle these chores until such time as you can hire someone to handle them for you.

MANAGING YOUR INCOMING MAIL

Handling mail and other correspondence is the nuts and bolts of office management. Mail procedures are fairly simple to put into place. It takes a little self-discipline to follow these procedures, but the payoff is a headache-free office.

The easiest way to handle incoming mail is by using the one-touch approach. With the one-touch approach you only handle each piece of mail once as you go through your incoming mailbox. You may handle some of it again later as you respond to it, but only once as it comes in. Incoming mail goes to one of three places after you have screened it:

- The wastebasket
- The interesting mail basket
- The action mail basket

WASTEBASKET MAIL

When handling incoming mail, the wastebasket is your friend. By throwing away the mail that you don't need as soon as possible, you eliminate time lost in rereading junk mail and your desk stays clean and uncluttered. One small business owner automatically throws bulk mail away without even opening it. Her feeling is that no important material will be sent out bulk rate. She may be right. Her business is thriving. On the other hand, junk mail is fun to read and can be a source of marketplace intelligence unavailable anywhere else. Either way, unless you find that you can't live without the touted product, throw it out.

INTERESTING MAIL

Occasionally, mail will arrive that has the potential for being useful at some future point. Some possibilities include equipment catalogs for your type of business, trade magazines, and business propositions. Place this type of mail in the interesting mail basket. Interesting mail always does one of two things with time: it becomes junk mail or it becomes invaluable. Sort through it every week or so as you get the time to find the valuable parts. Keep your wastebasket at hand for the rest of it.

ACTION MAIL

Action mail requires a response of some sort on your part. Your action mail box should be kept as empty as possible. Write the type of response required and a due date on the outside of the envelope. Make a similar notation on your calendar or in your computer. Computerized personal information managers (PIMs) can help you stay organized. To learn more about PIMs, see the discussion later in this chapter. Respond to this type of mail as soon as possible, preferably long before the due date and definitely not after it. As a general rule, do not take more than one week to respond to action mail.

Set aside a time in your workweek to handle action mail. Use this time to pay bills, respond to inquiries, and schedule appointments. As you respond to each piece of action mail, try to handle each item only once. Mail that is handled many times before acted upon can waste huge amounts of office time.

AVOIDING THE TELEPHONE TRAFFIC JAM

The telephone has been called the lifeline of business. With it, you can reach the world, and the world can reach you. But as anyone starting out in business can tell you, the phone will always ring at the worst possible time and you can become so busy handling telephone calls that you never get anything done. But the telephone is basic to business. One popular policy manual workbook makes sixteen different references to the use of the telephone.

Telephone technology has continued to advance rapidly in the wake of personal computer technology. Today's "smart phones" and associated phone company services perform a wide variety of functions such as:

- Call waiting
- Call forwarding
- Conference calls
- Voice mail
- Data and voice differentiation
- Full duplex speakerphone technology

These features combined will allow today's small business owner unprecedented flexibility in handling telephone traffic. Recent innovations in computer technology allow you to handle many of these functions directly from your computer terminal.

With the help of a personal computer, you can eliminate most of the hassles associated with business phones, while preserving many of the advantages. The technology to do this has been getting steadily less costly and more accessible to the average person starting out in business. Many people are beginning to place telephone handling features above word processing and bookkeeping convenience as the number one reason for purchasing a business computer.

ANSWERING MACHINES AND VOICE MAIL

If you have decided that a computer is not in your start-up budget, technology is still on your side. Today's telephones incorporate some of the features of computer-based phone technology — such as answering machines and voice mail — at a fraction of the cost. Spend your phone dollars on the quality of features rather than quantity, and test telephones and answering machines in the store before you buy. A bargain buy is not a bargain if it makes your voice sound odd or unintelligible.

You may be tempted to record a cute or humorous message on your answering machine. Resist the urge to do so unless you know your customers and potential customers very well. Your message should be short and straightforward; avoid extraneous or superfluous information. A good message includes a greeting, the name of your company, the hours you are available, and how to leave a message. Avoid saying that you are unable to answer the phone right now. The caller will have already figured that out. Including the hours you are open is especially effective for a retail business where fully half of the incoming callers want to know how late the store is open. An appropriate message might sound something like this:

> "Hello. Thank you for calling ABC Mousetraps. Our hours are from 8:00 a.m. to 5:00 p.m., Monday through Friday. Please leave a message after the tone."

Many people use their answering machine to screen calls to pick up only those that require an immediate response. This approach is far more appropriate in a private setting. Your personal telephone is in place largely for your convenience. In a business setting, the tables become partially turned. You probably installed your business phone for the convenience of your customers, as well as for your own convenience. When customers take the time to call you, they generally deserve some of your time in return. So, in a business setting, take care to screen out only those calls that don't have the potential to result in a sale.

Similarly, make sure your system is as efficient and professional as possible. Give the same basic information and briefly describe the options available to the caller. Avoid, if at all possible, forcing the caller through a maze of multilayered menu options. Most customers will not be pleased at the prospect of having a lot of their time wasted just to leave a message. The basic elements of a good voice mail message are included in this example:

> "Thank you for calling. This is the ABC Mousetraps' voice mail messaging system. You may enter the extension you wish to contact now, or leave a message for the marketing department by pressing one, a message for the production department by pressing two, or a message for management systems by pressing three. Press four to listen to a general information message about ABC Mousetraps. Press zero to speak to an operator."

The last sentence would be deleted for the after-hours version of the message. This message format is effective even when you are the only employee. Many single employee businesses appear to be much larger through the clever use of voice mail and technology. There are even special audio tapes available to simulate the background noise of a large office while you are on the phone.

For those times when you are not available by phone, an answering machine or voice mail allows your customers to leave messages for you. Your job, then, is to check your machine frequently for important calls and return them as soon as possible. Make note of who called you, when they placed the call, and from where they placed the call.

THE HOME-BASED OFFICE

A home-based office presents many difficulties that you may have never considered in a structured work environment. The greatest risk is a complete loss of organization as paperwork slowly spreads from your home office desk to the floor and out into the next room, or even throughout the house. Before you decide to go out and lease space in a new office, learn how you can easily keep track of the growing mounds of paperwork. Keep in mind, the suggestions that follow apply to a business office as well as a home office.

When setting up their home office, many people take a haphazard approach when selecting furniture, equipment, and location. If successful in business, these people end up rebuilding their home office at great trouble and expense, or they end up entering *Home Office Computing* magazine's annual contest for a makeover of the most disorganized office.

The best time to set up your home office is before you hang out your shingle. The slightest care at this point will pay dividends later. The most obvious benefit to careful setup is avoiding the back pain and muscle aches associated with improperly fitted furniture. Careless placement of keyboards, monitors, tables, and chairs can lead to a whole series of repetitive stress injuries, including the dreaded Carpal Tunnel Syndrome and bursitis as the most well-known. There are dozens of these disorders. Some are permanently debilitating; all are painful and preventable.

Setting up your home office need not be an expensive proposition. Unless you will be receiving customers in your office, try using used furniture and fixtures for your office. Create an environment that is cheerful and motivates you to produce. An office composed of gray metal desks, files, and cabinets from a military surplus depot, while undeniably cheap, may have a withering effect on your productivity.

BASEMENT, GARAGE, OR SPARE ROOM?

Where you decide to locate your office in your home may be dictated by available space. Hopefully, your home office isn't relegated to a corner of the dining room, even though some successful home businesses are operated from that very location. It is more common, however, to have use of a separate room such as a spare bedroom, the corner of a basement, a converted porch, or an attic loft or garret. Some home business owners convert a section of the garage or build an office over the garage. And a very few make their office from a garden cottage or gazebo.

If you have a choice of locations, there are a number of factors that you may want to consider before choosing one over the other. Some of these factors are practical, some are environmental, some merely a matter of personal taste.

Practical Considerations

A primary influence on choosing the location of your home office is accessibility. If customers or clients will be regularly coming to your office, a location with or near a separate outside entrance is desirable. However, that is not always possible. When clients must travel through your home to get to your office, it is important that this part of your house is neat and orderly. Keeping areas of the home orderly can be especially difficult when there are very young or teenage children living there.

If at all possible, your home office should not be located in your bedroom. As many new business owners will attest, a start-up business demands a great deal of time, and rest comes dearly enough as it is without unfinished details calling to you in the middle of the night. Conversely, it is probably not a good idea to have your bed just a few steps away as your energy levels wane in the afternoon or as you face the dreaded tedium of bookkeeping or routine correspondence.

Locating your office away from the living area of your home provides specific psychological benefits. A basement, attic, or garage office allows you the illusion of working away from home, helping you to tune out the distraction of waiting chores, visiting neighbors, and personal calls. In addition, having a remote office helps to maintain your home as a refuge from the demands of your business.

Environmental Concerns

Environmental concerns, in this case, refer to the office environment rather than where rabbits and coyotes play. Creating a good working environment is a challenge to any home worker, but choosing the wrong office location can make that challenge far more difficult.

Consider the vivid images invoked by the following descriptive phrases of the following home office locations:

- A dark, damp basement;
- A hot, dusty attic;
- A cold garage; or
- A cramped loft.

These locations require special treatment to be effective workplaces. You will need to pay more attention to extra lighting and heating, cooling, and ventilation. More than other places in the home, these will benefit from the installation of natural light sources.

An attic or over-the-garage office will benefit greatly from the installation of skylights or large gable windows. They will need extra cooling and ventilation during summer heat and a source of heat when it is cool. Basement offices will require improved ventilation and extra light to make up for the lack of natural light.

Noise is another environmental consideration. A typical home office is much quieter than its corporate counterpart, and many corporate refugees find the change disconcerting at first. Soft music in the background may help ease the transition. If music is a distraction in itself, consider buying a noise machine, an electronic device that produces white noises, such as static, ocean waves, running water, rustling leaves, or rainfall. Other noise producers include aquariums, small tabletop fountains or burbles, and wooden or bamboo wind chimes.

Some home office workers have complained of the opposite effect. Playing children, running lawn mowers, and the general hubbub of today's busy world seem to filter more easily through the walls of your home than through the walls of the office building you may leave behind. Simple fixes for this problem include installing acoustical tile ceilings, sound absorbing materials on walls and floors, and double or triple glazed windows.

Other Office Location Considerations

Everything else considered, the decision on where to locate your home office may boil down to personal considerations. Consider the following:

- Will office work conflict with children watching television or vice versa?
- Is your office so close to the refrigerator that you will indulge in excessive or frequent snacking?
- Do doorbells and telephone calls from the house intrude into the office?

In short, consider those things unique to your home and personality that will distract you the most and prevent you from accomplishing the work you need to get done. Conversely, consider those things about working at home that you value the most, such as being in regular contact with your family and integrating your work life and your home life. Then select the location of your office with these factors in mind.

You will learn about setting up your home and a slew of other home business concerns by reading *Home Business Made Easy: How to Select & Start a Home Business that Fits Your Interest, Lifestyle & Pocketbook* by David Hanania. To find out more about this guidebook, see the Useful Resources section at the end of this chapter.

OFFICE ON A BUDGET

Many start-up businesses are concerned with trimming costs wherever possible, and balk at equipping a home office with expensive equipment and furnishings. A few are successful at creating a functional work environment that is efficient, productive, and inexpensive. In general, setting up an office on a budget requires more room and more work. Important ergonomic, comfort, and lighting characteristics can be short-changed only at the expense of productivity, health, or well-being.

SETTING UP BASIC FURNITURE, EQUIPMENT, AND FIXTURES

Now that you have chosen the right location for your home office, take the time to choose its furnishings. To begin with, consider the basic office furniture complement of desk, chair, and filing cabinet. Then, evaluate your needs for equipment, lighting, and location. Arguably, the most important piece of office furniture is the office chair. But, even the most perfectly fitted chair will be of little benefit if the desk is at the wrong height. So, when setting up your home office, be particularly sensitive to the various dimensions suggested, and make fine adjustments as necessary to suit your particular size and configuration.

The Office Chair

If your tendency is to either use whatever you have on hand, such as a spare kitchen chair or to buy a used swivel chair, you may want to think twice. Many people even splurge on a new office chair. The decision to purchase office chairs is far more important than for mere convenience. When you consider that up to three-quarters of your workday will be spent sitting in your office chair, your personal comfort and efficiency take on meaningful proportions.

The best approach to selecting the proper chair for your office is to sit in it with a "Goldilocks" mindset. The chair cannot be too big, too small, too soft, or too hard. It must be just right. Often this feeling of being just right is the result of an intangible set of conditions, but there are characteristics that you can look for while sitting in the prospective chair.

Height of the seat. Make sure your thighs are parallel to the floor and your feet rest flat on the floor. If the chair isn't naturally at this height, it should be fully adjustable and, ideally, should be fully height adjustable from a sitting position so that you can easily change it to accomplish different tasks. You may require an ergonomic footrest if your legs are too short to rest comfortably on the floor.

Choose a comfortable chair seat. Your chair should have a firm cushion and be contoured so as not to cut into your legs. The chair back should extend from the lumbar region of your lower back to mid-shoulder blade, providing firm, adjustable support to your entire back while in a normal sitting position. The armrests, if any, should be positioned at or just below the point of your elbow.

Make sure it's accident proofed. The base of the chair should extend beyond the dimensions of the seat for stability and, if on casters, should be designed with five points to prevent the chance of an accidental tipping.

To meet these requirements, you can spend up to $1,000 or more for a fully adjustable, designer, ergonomic chair. Or, as one home office worker did, slightly modify a wooden kitchen chair for less than $20. In either case, be certain that the chair fits you and that you can spend six to ten or more hours each day sitting in it. Remember, even a perfect chair will become uncomfortable with time, so make sure your daily routine includes occasional breaks away from your chair to prevent stiffness and fatigue.

Your Desk

Different office tasks demand different working surface heights relative to your chair height. For instance, the ideal writing surface height may be 30 inches, while the ideal height for a keyboard (typewriter or computer) may be 26 inches. Actual heights will, of course, vary from individual to individual. Luckily, there are ready solutions to this varying height problem in most workstations available on the market today.

Your best strategy in purchasing a workstation or desk is to test it out in the showroom first. This requires no small effort on your part as you must first locate a suitable chair and get it properly adjusted. Sit at the workstation and test the writing table height, the typing height, and the reading height for comfort. Ideally, each of these surfaces will be slightly adjustable to allow for variations in your body proportions from national averages. Many higher quality workstations today offer several work surfaces with adjustable heights and positions. Some workstations will even alert you if you have worked from one position too long for comfort!

Other considerations besides working height include depth and width of the desk. Obviously, it must fit in your available office space without overpowering it or making the remaining space awkward or cramped in either function or appearance. Many mass-marketed manufacturers are cutting costs by making the desktop shorter and narrower. Frequently, the result is a computer monitor positioned so closely that eyestrain is inevitable with the remaining desktop space orphaned to the sides where it becomes unusable for reading and writing tasks.

Finally, in selecting your desk or workstations, consider the ease of shifting from one task to another. You should be able to easily shift from typing correspondence to answering the phone to checking your calendar; to writing a short memo; to pulling a file and back again without making a series of trips about your office. The transition from task to task should be smooth and seamless and accomplishable with the least effort possible.

Filing Cabinets

Surprisingly, you will find that you can't stay in business for long without a filing system. Your system may be as simple as having stacks of paperwork organized into piles around your office, or as complex as banks of filing cabinets lining the wall or anywhere in between. If you are like most people, however, you are likely to end up with at least one filing cabinet to hold the paperwork you will accumulate as your business grows.

New, well-made filing cabinets are expensive. However, it pays to seek quality in this purchase. Inexpensive, poorly made filing cabinets constructed of lightweight materials will inevitably become inadequate for your business needs. The drawer guides on cheaper filing cabinets can break or jam under heavy loads or repeated usage. A full file drawer can weigh as much as 100 pounds or more. Inexpensive cabinets are not designed to handle these loads safely.

There are many variations on the standard filing cabinet design. The drawers can be of standard width, or wide enough to accommodate legal-sized files. Lateral filing cabinets on wheels are growing in popularity, but don't make as efficient use of floorspace as vertical cabinets. Finally, the number of drawers in each cabinet can vary from two to six. Most quality filing cabinets are lockable.

EQUIPMENT

Office automation has had a profound and positive impact on the feasibility of working from a home office. Tasks such as routine correspondence and bookkeeping, which used to require a new business to hire at least a part-time office assistant, may now be accomplished by a sole proprietor as a part of the daily routine.

Fax machines, answering machines, copiers, and printers are being replaced by business computers with special features to handle faxes, voice mail, and routine paperwork tasks. While not yet inexpensive, the costs of these computer systems are rapidly falling and have already dropped well below the cost of purchasing individual office equipment components.

Just a few years ago it cost upwards from $6,000 to equip an office with a copier, fax machine, answering machine, and basic desktop computer for word processing and bookkeeping purposes. In today's business environment, a single business computer workstation can accomplish the same tasks for approximately half the expense, and do them simultaneously. Indeed, the personal computer has begun to fulfill early industry predictions as being an all-encompassing single tool office machine.

PERSONAL INFORMATION MANAGERS

If you have and use a personal computer in managing your business, there are dozens of programs on the market that will help you organize your time and efforts. These programs — called personal information managers (PIMs) — track business contacts, suppliers, customers, phone numbers, appointments, action items, and "to-do" lists. Many of these programs perform additional functions that may or may not be useful to you. Several good PIMs are available as shareware — that allows you to try the program before buying it. Choose one that is easy to use and you will come to depend upon it.

A personal computer will automate many tasks and help you to produce consistently high-quality correspondence. When it comes to handling stock and production records, payroll, and general ledger bookkeeping, a desktop computer shines. However, in-baskets, out-baskets, paperweights, and rotary card files are still basic office tools that will do much to handle the initial paper glut.

Surprisingly, today's office automated technology is easy to use. Hardware components require little maintenance, and recent advances allow the user to simply plug most components in and turn them on. The computer does the rest automatically, prompting you on what to do and how to do it. Much software has become similarly user-friendly and features automatic installation programs, interactive tutorials to teach you the ropes. There are even special deinstallation routines if you want to remove the software from your computer at some future date. Perhaps more importantly, most of the software marketed today features a look-alike appearance to other programs on the market. Drop-down menus, toolbars, and mouse-driven pointers allow new users to rapidly learn the ins and outs of new programs.

One downside of all-in-one technology is the risk, however remote, of equipment failure. While a complete loss of function is rare, it is important to purchase warranty plans and to have a qualified repair technician available should the need arise. Make sure you consider this as part of your risk assessment plans. Refer back to Chapter 11 to get up-to-date information on insurance issues. Many insurance companies will provide a rider to your policy that covers your hardware and software against theft, fire, and accidental damage.

You can do other things to reduce the impact of equipment failure:

Keep paper copies of all documents on file. The paperless office predicted about ten years ago is not yet a reality for most businesses. Relying on a single storage method for important business documents invites disaster.

Save work in progress frequently. At least once every ten minutes is a good rule of thumb. Most quality software incorporates an autosave feature, which can be customized as to the number of minutes between saves. The best approach, however, remains disciplining yourself to manually save your work. One unexpected power outage just as you reach the end of two hours of unsaved work will make a believer of you.

Make daily or weekly back-up copies. Include all data files on your computer in your backups. Computer operating systems incorporate a back-up function that can be invoked manually or sometimes on a specified schedule. Options include backing up to floppy disk, magnetic tape cartridge, or recordable CD-ROM.

Safety-proof your backups. Keep backups of vital information in fireproof safes or in an off-site location. Safes are available at office and business supply stores. Most safes provide protection to vital documents from temperatures of up to several thousand degrees Fahrenheit as well as some security against theft.

Get assistance. Subscribe to a service that stores electronic files for your company off site. This is a relatively new service which is available in most metropolitan areas. Check your phone directory for services near you.

Perform preventive maintenance. Your equipment should be checked and cleaned on a regular basis. Dirt and dust are the primary causes of electronic equipment failure. Excessive heat is the second most common culprit.

Plan for contingincies. Purchase an older computer for emergency use if your primary system fails. You will retain minimum capabilities during down time at about ten percent of the cost of a new system. You will also develop a new respect for the speed and versatility of your primary computer system should it become necessary to use the older system.

LIGHTING

Providing adequate lighting for your office space is an important consideration. The quantity, quality, and efficiency of various light sources will affect your decisions. Also, different tasks require different qualities and intensities of light. Finally, your age is a determining factor. Older workers require as much as 50 percent more light than younger workers for the same task.

Choosing the correct lighting is vital to preventing eyestrain and promoting maximum efficiency. The best source of light for all tasks is daylight. An open, airy office featuring lots of natural light is ideal for many businesses. Ready sources of daylight include windows, conventional skylights, and special tube type skylights that reflect light gathered from a hemispherical collector on the roof.

Not all offices have the advantage of access to natural light, nor is daylight always available. The solution, then, is to use artificial light from incandescent, fluorescent, or halogen sources. These light sources each possess differing characteristics.

Incandescent light is the most common. Bulbs are inexpensive and produce a soft, pale yellow light that is warm and localized. The localized nature of incandescent light bulbs makes them most suitable as tasklights providing spot illumination for paperwork, reading, or other close, detailed work. Incandescent lights are energy-inefficient, however, producing a great deal of heat as a byproduct. The bulbs wear out after as little as several hundred hours of use.

Halogen light bulbs are similar to incandescent light bulbs, but produce a whiter light. Halogen bulbs cost several times more than incandescent bulbs, but use about ten percent less electricity and last four to six times longer. They have the advantage of fitting into existing incandescent fixtures without modification. Also, you can easily adjust the output of both incandescent and halogen fixtures by installing a dimmer switch in the circuit.

Fluorescent fixtures are the most energy-efficient, producing the same amount of light as incandescent fixtures for approximately half the electricity. Fluorescent light is also diffuse, making it suitable for lighting large areas, but unsuitable for illuminating tasks. Fixtures are expensive, can have a noticeable flicker, and cannot be easily dimmed. However, numerous types of tubes are available, producing remarkably different qualities of light that are suitable for different purposes. If yours is a home-based business, a full-spectrum daylight tube will probably serve you best in your home office. Fluorescent lighting has the added advantage of being long lasting. Tubes are rated from 3,000 to 7,000 hours between failure.

The best lighting conditions for your office will depend on the tasks that you perform there. However, the following general guidelines apply to most workspaces:

Consistency. Prevent eyestrain resulting from adjusting to varying light levels by maintaining all lighting in the room at or near the same intensity.

Flourescent bulbs. Illuminate the room with indirect fluorescent lighting. Illuminate tasks with direct light from an incandescent or halogen source.

Glare. Eliminate glare and reflections from shiny objects. Position fixtures so that the light doesn't shine directly in your eyes.

Shadows. Illuminate computer workstations by reflecting light from the ceiling and walls. Reflected light is more diffuse and produces fewer shadows and reflections from computer monitor screens.

SELECT THE BEST LOCATION

Location! Location! Location! You have probably heard this phrase when discussing real estate issues. But did you know that location, location, location applies even more so when it comes to selecting a place from which to operate your business?

Location is the most important ingredient for success for any business that depends on customers finding it. You might have the highest-quality product or the most reliable service in your area. But the truth is: if you don't locate your business appropriately, you will lose potential customers traveling on foot or by car.

The reasons to locate in a certain place vary depending on your type of business. For example, if you are going to open a restaurant or retail business, you want to locate ideally in an area where there is a lot of available parking, a good flow of walk-in and drive-by traffic, and little competition. If you are a manufacturer or wholesaler, you will be more interested in a site that is close to major transportation services, has a large pool of skilled labor available, and has sufficient access to water, sewer, and other vital services. Lastly, if you are going to be one of the millions of people who are starting their businesses out of their homes, then your location considerations are basically concerned with knowing zoning and land use restrictions in your neighborhood. You will need to know what you can and cannot do in terms of shipping and receiving, signage, business activity, and remodeling in your particular residential area.

To select the best site for your business involves taking a serious look at four factors that will ultimately influence your business.

KNOW THE CITY

First, understand the dynamics of the city in which you wish to locate. This knowledge entails familiarizing yourself with the relationship of the surrounding cities, the road system and configurations within the city, the traffic patterns of the people who live, work, play, and travel in the city, and what causes people to travel in specific routes. In short, you must understand the traffic patterns of your potential customers and what generates these traffic patterns.

IDENTIFY YOUR TRADING AREA

Decide whether your product or service is suited for the type of city you want to locate in — whether it be downtown, urban, suburban, or rural. Study the ways the parts of the city connect with each other and how these connections or lack thereof affect the size, shape, and density of your trading area. Believe it or not: you will learn a lot about your trading area — and the people who make up your trading area — by studying the grocery stores in the area in which you want to serve.

ESSENTIAL CHARACTERISTICS

Consider the top location characteristics — accessibility, visibility, convenience, and high density. How visible, accessible, and convenient is your site? The flow of traffic or lack of flow will affect your customers' decisions to visit your business. Also, your customers' perceptions of safety and whether or not they have adequate parking will influence their decisions to return to your business place. How dense is the population? High density of the population in the area you want to serve is an ideal situation. The law of numbers will work in your favor.

KNOW YOUR MARKET POSITION

You have probably already done most of this research for your sales and marketing plan. However, the point cannot be overemphasized: have a thorough knowledge of your industry and your product or service, your customers, and your competitors. The first three location suggestions are worth nothing if you haven't clearly identified your market position.

To learn more about choosing the best spot for your business, check out *Location, Location, Location: How to Select the Best Site for Your Business* by Luigi Salvaneschi. For more information, see below.

CHAPTER WRAP-UP

Whether you start your business out of your home or purchase land to build a new office suite or production center, you will need to set up your business for maximum efficiency. This entails a thorough evaluation of your operations to find out what you need to maintain your business — both on the administrative and production ends. Seriously consider things like:

How to handle incoming mail and incoming phone calls. What type of phone system will you need for the services you offer?

How to arrange your workspace and your employees' workspaces. How many chairs and desks will you require? What type of lighting will best suite your operation? Are there any special equipment requirements?

Which city or road is the best area in which to locate your business. Which areas will provide maximum accessibility and visibility while at the same time be within a short distance from your target market?

The key to setting up your operation is organization. The more organized you are in the planning phase, the better you will be once your business is up and running.

USEFUL RESOURCES

Home Business Made Easy: How to Select & Start a Home Business that Fits Your Interests, Lifestyle & Pocketbook by David Hanania. This resource guide gives a road map for starting a home business that you could operate full-time or part-time. Identifies 175 different business ideas and gives suggestions on breaking into a specific field.

Location, Location, Location: How to Select the Best Site for Your Business by Luigi Salvaneschi. Whether you rent, build, or lease, this book is a must-have for retail business owners. Chockfull of insider tips and illustrations for selecting the best site for your business, you will gain a bigger picture understanding of the phrase "location, location, location."

CHAPTER 13

Welcome to Maryland

Maryland is a state divided — and yet, perhaps because of its many physical and sociological obstacles — one that is also strongly united, seeming to find strength in its very diversity. First, it is divided by water. From where the Susquehanna River pours into it at the north end, to where the shoreline becomes Virginia at the bay's southern end, Chesapeake Bay completely splits the state in two. And the split is more than physical. Urban and military centers (Baltimore, the suburban counties north of Washington, D.C., Annapolis, and the Aberdeen Proving Ground) dominate the western shore, while small towns, salt marshes, farms, the Atlantic Ocean, and national wildlife preserves characterize the Eastern Shore.

Second, the early state boundaries were reshaped several times due to border disputes with Pennsylvania to the north and Virginia to the south. More than 3 million acres were ceded to these states in 1732. Maryland was finally divided, officially, from Pennsylvania by the Mason-Dixon Line (1769), which also conceptually established the dividing line between the North and the South. Maryland even voluntarily divided itself when it ceded the land — about 70 square miles — for the District of Columbia. This gesture has, of course, proven an economic boon, as the employment and service opportunities afforded by the federal military and government complex in and around the nation's capital has assured the state relative prosperity even in the depths of the Great Depression.

Maryland also has a history of being ideologically divided. In the early days of this country's history, Maryland was divided on the issue of slavery — declaring itself first a slave state (slaves were used to plant and harvest the economically important tobacco crops), then a free state. State loyalties were so divided that the first fighting of the Civil War occurred when Baltimorians attacked Union troops in 1861; Lincoln ordered Baltimore occupied to ensure it remained loyal to the Union. And it did; in fact, one of the bloodiest battles of the Civil War — the Battle of Antietam — was fought on Maryland soil. Maryland residents again found themselves on both sides of the tracks, so to speak, when the state that built the first railway system in the nation (the Baltimore and Ohio Railroad in 1828) was also the origin of a crippling national railway strike not 50 years later.

The state motto — "Manly deeds, womanly words" — hints at the two sides of Maryland and how they work together. Maryland even has two nicknames: "Free State" and "Old Line State," and the state flag displays two family crests.

Today, however, there is nothing divided about Maryland's approach to business. Currently, Maryland is pulling itself together on all fronts to tackle the problems of a shrinking market sector and reduced employment in a state that has traditionally led the nation in industry and economics. Task forces have been appointed and funds allocated to take on this problem with all the energy of a full-blown war (what did you expect from a state that names "jousting" as its official sport?), and you and your business are well situated to reap the benefits of the initial skirmishes.

Welcome to Maryland, a land of great diversity, historical economic preeminence, and surprising resources. A state with its gaze fixed on the future and both feet firmly set upon the road ahead. So grab your rucksack and explore the advantages and disadvantages of smartstarting your business in this great state.

GET TO KNOW THE DEMOGRAPHICS OF MARYLAND

Demographics, or the vital statistics of human populations, should be of great interest to any prospective or existing small business owner. Variables such as size, growth, density, and distribution of the populations of the major counties and cities in Maryland will affect the way you do business — from your marketing strategy to how you will obtain financing.

The major source of demographic data for the United States is the U.S. Census Bureau. The major source of Maryland-specific data, including that from the U.S. Census Bureau, is the Maryland State Data Center (see below). The center will help you find and interpret demographic data such as the starter information provided below. Take a moment to understand the influence of the demographic makeup of Maryland on your proposed business. Start with a look at three main factors: population, major industries, and income and consumption rates.

POPULATION STATISTICS

Maryland has a relatively large population for its size, it is the 8th smallest of the 50 states by area. More than five million people coexist on 10,460 square miles, a statistical density of 482 persons per square mile. Nearly 93% of Maryland's residents live in sprawling metropolitan areas, mostly west of Chesapeake Bay, leaving 7% (or about 363,000 people) to scatter across farmlands on the Eastern Shore or the rugged Appalachian Plateaus of the far western region.

Table 1 – Population Totals and Projections

Resident population	Maryland	Rank	U.S.
1990	4,781,000	19	248,718,000
1995	5,042,000	19	262,755,000
Percent living inside metro area	**Maryland**	**Rank**	**U.S.**
1990	92.8%	7	79.6%
1994	92.8%	7	79.8%
Percent under 18 yrs old	**Maryland**	**Rank**	**U.S.**
1990	24.4%	41	25.7%
1995	25.2%	35	26.2%
Percent 65 yrs or older	**Maryland**	**Rank**	**U.S.**
1990	10.8%	40	12.5%
1995	11.3%	41	12.8%
Population projections	**Maryland**	**Rank**	**U.S.**
2000	5,275,000	19	274,635,000
2025	6,274,000	18	335,048,000

Source: U.S. Census Bureau

As you can see from the population projections, Maryland is expected to maintain its population ranking through 2025, which will be no mean feat, given the speed at which many western states are growing. Generally, growth has been very steady in Maryland, thus the state has avoided the problems that come with radical population swings. In fact, the slight increase in rank predicted by 2025, from 19th largest to 18th, may reflect expected growth in the state's economy as well, since jobs support (and often drive) population growth.

Another interesting statistical point to ponder is the low percentage of people in Maryland at either end of the employment spectrum. While nearby Pennsylvania ranks 2nd in the nation for the percentage of population 65 or older, Maryland ranks 41st. Why the discrepancy? Taking into account that the proportion of the population under 18 is also relatively small, you might conjecture that the type of employment in Maryland's larger population centers — Baltimore and the Washington D.C. area, in particular — draws work-aged people, and relatively few stay when the work is done. The large number of colleges, universities, and research institutions may also be a factor.

DOMINANT INDUSTRIES AND WAGES

Agriculture has always been important to Maryland. In colonial times, tobacco was the principal crop, and by the late 1700s the agricultural emphasis shifted to wheat and attendant industries, including milling, warehousing, and shipping. Currently, however, agriculture (including tobacco, greenhouse and nursery products, corn, soybeans, livestock, dairy, forestry, and shellfish) accounts for only 1.73% of employment in the state.

During the 1800s, the economic trend was toward processing (in particular, flour mills), manufacturing (including primary metals and equipment), and transportation industries (rail and ship building and freighting). In 1828, construction began on a significant trade artery — the Baltimore and Ohio (B&O) Railroad — which would link the east to the interior states and, most importantly, would establish a link to the west. The next year, the Chesapeake and Delaware Canal opened, linking Chesapeake Bay with Delaware Bay and the Atlantic Ocean. The B&O was the first railway system in the United States, and it boosted Baltimore to an enviable trade center. This early foothold on trade and manufacturing kept Maryland rich and growing through two world wars, and the Great Depression.

Steel, however, is not the king it used to be, and many of the products of the information age do not require ships and trains to freight them. But, Maryland's economy has traditionally been diverse enough to weather any shift in the world economy, and that is as true now as it was in the late 1800s, when Baltimore faded as a flour milling center, but flourished as a garment center, shipping center, banking center, and steel town. These days, the shift is away from steel and machinery, but food processing is still strong. The shipping and closely related banking industries have expanded to even more trade and services; and heavy industry is being replaced by chemical products, electrical/electronic equipment manufacturing, fiberoptics, and high technologies.

Currently, the service industry is the largest and fastest growing employment sector in the state. As can be seen in Table 2, which shows the number of jobs per industry for the standardized industry sectors, the services industry is one of the few industries to continue to grow between 1990 and 1995. The other growth industry is the transportation, communication, and public utilities cluster, a primarily high-tech industry sector. Fortunately, Maryland has a long-standing aerospace industry that is easily transitioning from federal work to commercial applications, particularly in its satellite communications services, which are in demand because of the rapid growth of business and personal communication technologies.

Table 2 – Nonfarm Employment by Industry

Industry sector	1970	1980	1990	1995
Mining	2,500	3,000	3,700	3,000
Construction	104,700	123,800	195,500	167,200
Manufacturing	273,400	241,100	212,900	179,900
Transportation, communication, and public utilities	90,400	95,900	118,200	119,000
Wholesale trade	63,300	92,300	117,400	112,900
Retail trade	279,500	355,400	475,700	472,300
Finance, insurance, and real estate	111,100	148,300	229,600	226,600
Services	322,300	489,700	831,400	958,600
Government	415,000	475,300	508,000	505,700

Source: Maryland Office of Planning, 1997

You can see from Table 2 that manufacturing has been steadily declining for years. This is one of the trends that Maryland would like to turn around in the near future, preferably with a shift to more light industry and high technology. Wholesale trade is also targeted for increases and expansion, although the downswings in these industries are fairly recent. According to Table 2, wholesale trade lost 4,500 positions in the five years between 1990 and 1995; that is a significant loss.

On the whole, Maryland's civilian employment/civilian population ratio has exhibited a downward trend in recent years. While still far ahead of its neighbors to the north and southwest (Pennsylvania ranks 45th, and West Virginia ranks 50th, the country's lowest), Maryland has fallen from the 9th to the 16th ranking in the nation, putting it on par with its southern neighbor, Virginia, which is ranked 17th. The employment losses in manufacturing are shockingly apparent in Table 3.

Table 3 – Employment and Wages

Percent of civilian population employed	Maryland	Rank	U.S.
1990	67.4%	9	62.8%
1995	67.1%	16	62.9%
Nonfarm employment percent in manufacturing	**Maryland**	**Rank**	**U.S.**
1990	9.5%	43	17.4%
1995	8.1%	42	15.8%
Average annual pay	**Maryland**	**Rank**	**U.S.**
1990	$27,730	9	$23,602
1994	$28,416	9	$26,939

Source: U.S. Census Bureau

It is unlikely that losses in the employment sectors are due to a lack of workforce to support the jobs, particularly since the average wages in this state are well above the national average. A more likely explanation is that industry demand has shifted, and Maryland is now scrambling to catch up with the new economic leaders — that is, technology firms in all their forms: particularly service, telecommunications, and manufacturing.

INCOME AND CONSUMPTION RATES

Not too surprisingly, given the relatively high average pay noted in Table 3, Maryland residents have high personal and household incomes. What is somewhat surprising is the low homeownership rate (Table 4). While the percentage of residents who own homes is higher than the national average, Maryland still ranks 36th in the nation. The low ownership rate could reflect any number of factors — the relative youth of the residents (see Table 1); the transience of the labor force (why buy if you will only be there a few years?); or the dense urban setting in which much of the population lives (that is, more apartments and townhouses than single-family dwellings, and a high number of rental properties) — or all of the above. If you are selling home improvement products or services, you will have to choose your target population carefully in this state. Renters aren't likely to be interested.

Table 4 – Income and Consumption Statistics

Personal income per capita	Maryland	Rank	U.S.
1990	$23,776	5	$20,090
1995	$24,107	5	$21,188
Median household income	**Maryland**	**Rank**	**U.S.**
1990	$44,060	5	$33,952
1994	$39,198	6	$32,264
Energy consumption per capita (BTUs)	**Maryland**	**Rank**	**U.S.**
1990	254,000,000	41	326,000,000
1993	245,000,000	43	322,000,000
Homeownership rates	**Maryland**	**Rank**	**U.S.**
1990	63.8%	39	64.1%
1995	65.8%	36	64.7%
Retail sales per household	**Maryland**	**Rank**	**U.S.**
1990	$21,065	11	$19,655
1994	$24,157	23	$23,363

Source: U.S. Census Bureau

Statistics on the energy consumption and retail sales habits of your target population may also be useful to your business decisions. Energy use is very low in this state, and retail sales are suddenly down in the average range. Do these consumption figures reflect tightened budgets (unemployment has been on the rise since 1990), or do the higher sales figures in 1990 reflect the costs of everyone trading over to energy-efficient appliances? Clearly, the information presented here is just enough to send up a few caution flags. To really explore the implications these data have for your business, you will need to gather more detailed information, such as that provided by your state data center.

MARYLAND STATE DATA CENTER

To break much of this census data down into manageable pieces, the Census Bureau created the State Data Center (SDC) Program. Since 1978, state data centers have provided training and technical assistance in accessing and using census data for research, administration, planning, and decisionmaking. Users of this information have ranged from state, county, and local governments to the business community and university researchers. Further, in 1988, the SDC expanded its services through its Business and Industry Data Center (BIDC) Program. The BIDC Program directly serves businesses through a variety of government, academic, and nonprofit organizations.

The Maryland State Data Center, operated under the auspices of the Maryland Office of Planning, is a federal-state cooperative program between the U.S. Census Bureau and the state of Maryland. It is the state's official source of population and economic statistics and projections. Your business can receive timely and accurate statistics, maps of recent trends, and resource directories data in either a published or electronic format. For a listing and description of the publications and data series available, contact the office of planning as listed in Appendix C. Also, the Maryland SDC Web site offers basic data tables and graphs for instant viewing and will connect you with region-specific statistical output. See *http://www.inform.umd.edu/UMS+State/MD_Resources/MSDC.*

You can learn more about the federal SDC program by contacting the Customer Liaison Office of the U.S. Census Bureau. Refer to Appendix B for the address and phone number of this agency.

INCENTIVES FOR DOING BUSINESS IN MARYLAND

The first telegraph line in the world was built between Baltimore and Washington, D.C. in 1844, and Maryland has been tied into the country's political and financial mainstream ever since. It is a position the state would like to maintain, but as its government has had to acknowledge in recent years, Maryland's economic position has been slipping. Maryland has, however, taken some key steps to reverse its decline and rebuild its business sectors, as the next few sections demonstrate.

OVERALL BUSINESS CLIMATE

Since 1996, when the Maryland Economic Development Commission conducted a strategic appraisal of the state's business policies, Maryland's leaders have focused on enhancing statewide economic growth, including specific programs aimed at increasing tourism and the state's presence in the international business community. The state has two broad objectives: 1) to make Maryland business friendly, and 2) to create, retain, and attract jobs.

To support the first objective, Maryland is streamlining its permit process and redrafting its regulations to eliminate those that essentially restate federal mandates. It is also trying to reorient its regulatory and enforcement agencies to make them more customer-focused, and to work with businesses to help them achieve compliance, instead of taking the more adversarial approach common in the past. The state is also reducing tax rates and offering more tax incentives.

One step it has taken already is to develop a centralized method for obtaining sales and use, alcohol, and tobacco tax licenses; opening income tax withholding and unemployment insurance accounts; and establishing admissions, amusement, and motor fuel tax accounts. To accomplish this, business owners simply complete a *Combined Business Registration Application*, which is available from the state comptroller's office or any office of the circuit court. See Chapter 3 for details on registering to pay taxes and Appendix C for the Maryland Comptroller of the Treasury.

To support the second objective, Maryland is actively marketing itself to larger industries in the hopes of attracting both more business and more attention as a growing business center. The state is also providing more financing for smaller businesses, particularly in growth industry sectors, and improving the state's technology, communication, and transportation systems for all businesses. Maryland is also working to improve workforce training to ensure its existing and up-and-coming labor force is equal to the tasks of the new technology-based industries that are capturing the world markets.

With all this interest and activity aimed at launching and protecting new businesses, there couldn't be a better time to smartstart your business here.

ACCESS TO MARKETS

The Baltimore-Washington corridor is a sprawling, urbanized area that actually stretches as far north as Boston, Massachusetts. Baltimore is a principal industrial center, and its harbor is the 2nd largest East Coast seaport. This large city is a renowned national and international trade center, increasing the state's reputation as a focal point for trade and export. From Baltimore, your business can quickly reach any East Coast market and easily access the world market as well.

From the beginning, trade has been important to Maryland. The Baltimore and Ohio (B&O) Railroad was the first railway system in the nation — largely funded by businessmen who wanted to profit from trade with the vast western territories. A few years later, the B&O was the first railroad to offer passenger service, thereby helping to populate the very country it wanted to serve by freight. Today, passenger travel is covered by AMTRAK (cross country), local commuter trains (along the Baltimore-Washington corridor), light rail, and subways.

Today, most passengers and all world courier services travel by air. The Baltimore-Washington International Airport is convenient to most of the state and assures your business timely travel options to any corner of the globe. Most Maryland residents and businesses are also within easy travel distance of Washington National Airport in Washington, D.C. (about 35 miles south of Baltimore) or Dulles International Airport, located west of the District of Columbia.

LABOR FORCE OUTLOOK

The workforce in this state is well educated (the state ranks among the top five in the nation for percentage of college-educated residents), highly skilled, and known for its strong work ethic. As part of its commitment to labor, Maryland was the first state (in 1902) to pass a workers' compensation law, and the state currently offers innovative training and support programs (described in the last section of this chapter) to ensure that its workforce is among the best prepared in the nation.

Unfortunately, the percentage of residents participating in the labor force has shown a slight downward trend since 1990, particularly among male workers. Female workers are projected to increase as a percentage of the workforce until about 2010 as the male percentage continues to decrease, causing a leveling-off effect for the workforce in general. However, unless the economy changes dramatically, Maryland predicts that the entire workforce participation rate will begin to steadily decline after 2010, as population exceeds job availability. To encourage job creation so this does not happen, Maryland offers new and expanding businesses a number of workforce support and incentive programs, such as low-cost, customized training, free employment screening, and job creation tax incentives such as those described in the following section.

TAX INCENTIVES

According to a recent study, the business tax burden accounts for a lower percentage of total tax revenue in Maryland than in any other state. The corporate income tax in this state has held steady at 7% for a number of years now, and there are no taxes at all on gross receipts or corporate franchises. In addition, numerous specific state and county corporate income tax credits and county and enterprise zone property tax credits are available. Some of these are discussed briefly in this section. Contact the Maryland Comptroller of the Treasury (see Appendix C) for more information on state business tax incentive programs and for free publications that will answer your questions about when and how you can take advantage of the tax exemptions and credits described below.

Production Activity Exemptions

Machinery and equipment used in production activities and property sold for consumption in production activities (or for resale or incorporation as a material or part of other tangible personal property produced for sale) are exempt from state sales and use tax. For the purposes of this exemption, "production activities" are defined as those that involve:

- Assembling, manufacturing, processing, or refining tangible personal property for resale;
- Generating electricity;
- Preparing textiles, such as uniforms and linens for rental;
- Establishing or maintaining clean rooms or zones, as required for the manufacture of drugs; or
- Producing or repairing machinery or equipment used in a production activity.

Equipment purchases and lease payments also qualify for the exemption, subject to some restrictions. Generally, if machinery or equipment is used both in a production activity and for other operations, the exemption applies if it is used at least 50% of the time in a production activity.

For the exemption to apply to a sale of consumable property, the consumption must occur within one year after the property is first used in a production activity. The comptroller warns that obsolescence is not consumption, and offers the following example: "A mold that wears out before finishing an order of 10,000 widgets qualifies for exemption, but a mold that is not worn out and finishes the same order is taxable, assuming the buyer does not have further need for it within a year. If the mold wears out while completing a subsequent order within a year, it then qualifies for exemption."

Utilities and Fuel Exemptions

Utilities and fuel purchased for production activities qualify for exemption from sales tax under the same terms as other production consumables. Utilities sold through a single meter for both taxable and exempt uses are taxed or exempt depending upon majority usage. To claim the exemption for utilities and fuel, you must obtain *Form ST206* and forward it directly to the vendor. Contact the Maryland Taxpayer Registration Assistance Center (TRAC) as listed in Appendix C.

Research and Development Exemptions

Purchases of tangible personal property for use in basic and applied research in science or engineering or in the design, development, and mandated premarket testing of prototypes and processes are also exempt from sales and use taxes. No special forms are required to claim the research and development exemption, although your vendors may request written certification from your business that proves the property will qualify under this exemption.

Agricultural Equipment and Supply Exemptions

When sold or rented to a farmer, farm equipment (including vehicles used only in the farming business and about the farmer's home) and replacement parts and components, including hydraulic oil, are also exempt from sales and use taxes. A farm vehicle is one that qualifies for a registration plate containing the word "farm," if titled and registered in Maryland. Farmers engaged in processing food for sale can claim the exemptions available for production activities (see above). Agricultural supplies, such as seeds (including plants and seedlings), fertilizer, lime, fungicide, herbicide, and insecticide are also exempt when sold for agricultural purposes. Neither does the tax apply to sales of: containers used by a farmer to transport farm products to market; baler twine or wire; or fuel for use in farm equipment such as a farm tractor.

LIFESTYLE

By now you are probably convinced that Maryland wants your business and will take whatever steps are necessary to make certain your company and others like it thrive in this state. But your life is not entirely consumed by business, although it may seem to be in the first few years. What does Maryland offer you and your family in the way of quality of life? The answer: Everything! Maryland boasts great schools, varied cultural experiences, and outstanding recreational opportunities. And don't forget that the national treasures of Washington, D.C. — the U.S. Capitol Building, the Smithsonian Institution, the National Archives, the National Gallery of Art, and the U.S. Supreme Court — are not much more than an hour's travel from most of the population.

Education

Maryland's approach to student assessment and accountability in the public grade schools is already a national model. The governor has stressed that all public schools be encouraged to better themselves year after year, to show relative improvement against the prior year's benchmark until all the state's schools are the best they can possibly be. Maryland's school systems are currently undergoing a tremendous growth in their access to and use of technology in the classroom. State-funded research indicates that this feature should significantly raise student achievement rates, especially for lower ability and at-risk students. Not only does technology in education help prepare students for the challenges of the workplace, but the Maryland Blue Ribbon Committee on Technology in Education reports that technology helps increase self-esteem and self-confidence and is expected to help raise enrollment and attendance and lower the overall dropout rate.

The governor's 1995 Educational Policy Transition Committee, which prioritized the state's educational goals, reports that school construction priorities will focus on adding or updating science wings and providing advanced information technology and computers. The 1996 construction budget was the highest in 20 years, and similar funding levels have been promised for the near future to ensure all schools are outfitted for the technology needs of the information age. Programs are also being developed to strengthen reading, writing, and math skills from kindergarten through the 12th grade so that graduates in the twenty-first century will be able to compete in the highly language-literate and mathematically-literate global workforce.

A wide variety of higher and continuing education options are also available to Maryland residents. According to the governor's office, the state's secondary education system ranks among the best in the nation. In addition to the much praised University of Maryland system, major universities and other specialized institutions of higher learning include Johns Hopkins University, Loyola College, and the United States Naval Academy at Annapolis. The state supports funding of public and private colleges and universities to ensure that the door of opportunity is not closed on students simply because of financial restrictions such as rising tuition.

Maryland also offers its own fine, although historically underfunded, state college (four-year) and community college (certificate and two-year program) system — a system that is getting a facelift under recent educational priority programs. For example, in 1995 the state began development of regional career technology centers in community colleges throughout the state. These centers feature distance learning and offer training in high-tech process, and provide space for industry incubators, thus strengthening ties between industry and education. Also in 1995, funding was increased for Maryland's four historically black institutions: Bowie

State University, Coppin State College, Morgan State University, and the University of Maryland, Eastern Shore.

History and Culture

Maryland is one of the original 13 states (7th to ratify the U.S. Constitution), but its rich history dates back long before the American Revolution. Originally (before the 1600s) the region that became Maryland was home to native people of the Algonquian language group, who lived in peace with early trappers and settlers. By 1635, Maryland colonists were farming tobacco for trade with the old world. The colony's boundaries and governing religious and political philosophies shifted numerous times, both pre- and post-statehood — all of which make for fascinating weekend research and museum-hopping today. A wonderful place to start, of course, is the Museum of Maryland History, which is located in Baltimore.

Numerous historic battlefields honor America's major conflicts on native soil: the American Revolutionary War, the War of 1812, and the Civil War. You can visit Fort McHenry, where "o'er the ramparts" Frances Scott Key kept watch on "The Star-Spangled Banner" in 1814. While in the Baltimore area, you will also want to catch the Baltimore Maritime Museum, the *U.S. Frigate Constellation*, and the United States Naval Academy at Annapolis. If you would prefer to commemorate something that wasn't the cause or result of bloodshed, how about the fact that Baltimore has had public schools since 1826 and a public circulating library since 1882? Or that the first American-built locomotive, named Tom Thumb, began its first trip from the grand old city of Baltimore? If the age of transportation and industry interests you, be sure to visit the B&O Railroad Museum, the Baltimore Streetcar Museum, and the Baltimore Museum of Industry.

If science and other highly intellectual pursuits are more your style, check out the Maryland Science Center, visit the National Aquarium or arrange to attend one of the monthly lectures at the Space Telescope Science Institute, which operates the fascinating Hubble Space Telescope Web site at *oposite.stsci.edu/pubinfo/edugrioup/educational-activities.html*.

The classic cultural pursuits of art, symphony, opera, and theater are also available in fine form in Maryland. Contact the Baltimore Area Visitors Center (address and phone information is presented Appendix C) for more information on area attractions.

Sports and Recreation

Maryland has few lakes, but rivers abound everywhere. Fishing, boating, and bird watching are popular sports across the state. And beaches abound, although most are along the bay rather than the ocean. In fact, Maryland can boast more than 100 times the coastline along its section of Chesapeake Bay — 3,190 miles in all — than it has along the Atlantic coast (a mere 31 miles). Still, Ocean City is a big tourist draw, and Assateague Island (State Park and National Seashore) is a mecca for swimmers and sunbathers alike. Herons and egrets are plentiful in the Deal Island Wildlife Management Area in eastern Maryland, or you can hunt for fossils at Calvert Cliffs State Park in the southern part of the state.

Spring is the season for thoroughbred horse racing, notably the Preakness Stakes at Pimilico; hot air balloon races; or a visit to the Kennedy Center for the Performing Arts in Baltimore. While on the waterfront, have some of the oysters the Chesapeake Bay area is so well known for. Rolling into summer, catch a ball game at the new Oriole Park at Camden Yards, or hike the 120,000 acres of parks and forest of the Blue Ridge and Allegheny Mountains in western Maryland. Fall is for hunting, canoeing, and visiting harvest fairs before the year winds down with a little downhill and cross country skiing, sumptuous theater, and Christmas shopping from among the nation's finest art and retail collections. Whatever you are looking for in your physical and social environment, you will find it in Maryland.

RESEARCH AND DEVELOPMENT, FINANCING, AND SUPPORT SERVICES

Maryland's Baltimore-Washington corridor is home to one of the highest concentrations of engineers and research scientists in the world, and many of the state's well-known research institutions have created strong links to industry. Space and aeronautics companies, for example, are clustered around two world-class research and development centers: the Goddard Space Flight Center and the Patuxent Naval Air Warfare Center. These centers, and other federal agencies — from the military to the National Science Foundation — involved in related work, feed Maryland's commercial aviation, satellite communications, and information technology sectors.

Cooperative Research Programs

The Division of Regional Development's Office of Federal Response and Technology Commercialization (OFRTC) offers two programs designed to help your company develop and market new products or processes. The OFRTC's Strategic Assistance Fund can help you gain market analysis and information to help your company assess its potential commercial markets and develop and implement strategies for successfully reaching them. The fund provides matching grant investments to help you engage the appropriate consultants for these efforts. While designed for defense contractors evaluating diversification opportunities, the fund is also available to other enterprises, primarily those formed by former defense workers or technology-based companies interested in moving into new markets. The second OFRTC program is the Maryland Health Care Product Alliance (MHCPA), which provides equity funding for companies involved in adapting defense technologies for medical uses. MHCPA funds must be matched equally by private investment.

The University of Maryland also operates several industry research and support programs through its Engineering Research Center. The first of these is the Maryland Industrial Partnerships Program (MIPS), which will share (with your company) the cost of collaborative research on new products or processes or improvements to products or processes. When a project's resultant intellectual property is attributable to one of its faculty members, MIPS receives about 15% of all royalties (at 2% rate) paid to the university. Two rounds of competition are held each year. Large, small, and start-up companies statewide are eligible.

Other Engineering Research Center programs include the Technology Extension Service, which offers on-site technical assistance to Maryland companies; the Technology Advancement Program, which provides business and technical support for start-up technology firms; and the Technology Initiatives Program (TIP), which helps businesses develop research capabilities within the university in important technical growth areas. One of the major TIP programs is the Bioprocess Scale-up Facility. This facility can be used to conduct scale-up biotechnology projects.

Job Training Programs

Maryland's Advanced Technology Centers provide high-tech workforce training focused on the growth sectors of aerospace, agriculture and aquaculture, biotechnology, distribution and warehousing, health care, information technology, manufacturing, minority business, telecommunications, and tourism. The Advanced Technology Center network is a partnership between the Maryland Higher Education Commission and the Maryland Department of Business and Economic Development, in cooperation with the Maryland Association of Community Colleges. Contact any of these agencies for more information.

The state's Partnership for Workforce Quality (PWQ) program largely consists of grants to businesses like yours. These grants are designed to help your business upgrade the skills of your existing workforce for new technology or to increase worker productivity. A PWQ grant will provide 50% reimbursement to your business for selected program training expenses. PWQ grants are administered through the Office of Regional Response (ORR), so check with your local regional development office about this program.

Another ORR program is the Maryland Industrial Training Program, which addresses the need for industrial assistance programs to attract new industries to the state and to retain or assist in the expansion of existing industries in Maryland. The program can provide your business with grant assistance to reimburse you for costs associated with new workforce development and training activities in your start-up or expanding operation. For more on grants and loans available to businesses in this state, see Appendix D.

Maryland also offers training through federally-funded, state- and regionally-administered programs under the federal Job Training Partnership Act (JTPA). JTPA is designed to develop employment and training programs to help low-income residents who face serious employment barriers. It also provides retraining and re-employment assistance to eligible dislocated workers. JTPA services include providing assessments of skills and needs, counseling, job search skills training, and occupational skills and on-the-job training to prospective workers.

Federal funds for JTPA programs flow through the Office of Employment Training (OET) of the Maryland Department of Labor, Licensing, and Regulation. The OET then allocates the JTPA funds to Service Delivery Areas (SDAs) — or regions with 200,000 or more residents and a common labor pool — throughout the state. For each SDA there is a Private Industry Council (PIC) charged with developing and overseeing its job training programs. The PIC also determines which companies, educational institutions, and community organizations will receive funding. Your local PIC will be listed in the government pages of the phone directory.

Other Support Services

The Maryland Business School at the University of Maryland at College Park operates the Dingman Center for Entrepreneurship, dedicated to facilitating, supporting, and encouraging entrepreneurship and new enterprise growth. The center offers a variety of services, including a mentor program for new and mature emerging growth companies at a reasonable cost. The center also manages the operation of the Baltimore-Washington Venture Group, which provides a forum for entrepreneurs to meet with groups that can supply capital and management. The Venture Group has formed a partnership with the Private Investors Network (PIN) to provide young companies the maximum opportunity to gain financing. Only Venture Group members are eligible to present business plans to PIN investors.

The Office of Regional Response also operates two general assistance programs, one aimed at failing businesses, the other at building market recognition. The At-Risk Business Assistance Program can offer early intervention and rapid response services if your business begins to flounder. The service principally coordinates turnaround assistance. The Maryland With Pride Program, on the other hand, will help to promote your Maryland business and products in both domestic and international markets. The program works to increase customer awareness of Maryland products and services at each level of the marketing chain from distributors to customers.

CHAPTER WRAP-UP

Clearly, the small state of Maryland has some big plans for the future of business within the state, with a renewed commitment to both education for the future (particularly in the use of technology) and business development and growth. Friendlier regulatory policies, increased financial assistance, greater tax incentives, numerous avenues for assistance and support, workplace training, and cooperative research and development programs all make Maryland a truly smart place to start your new business.

MAP OF MARYLAND

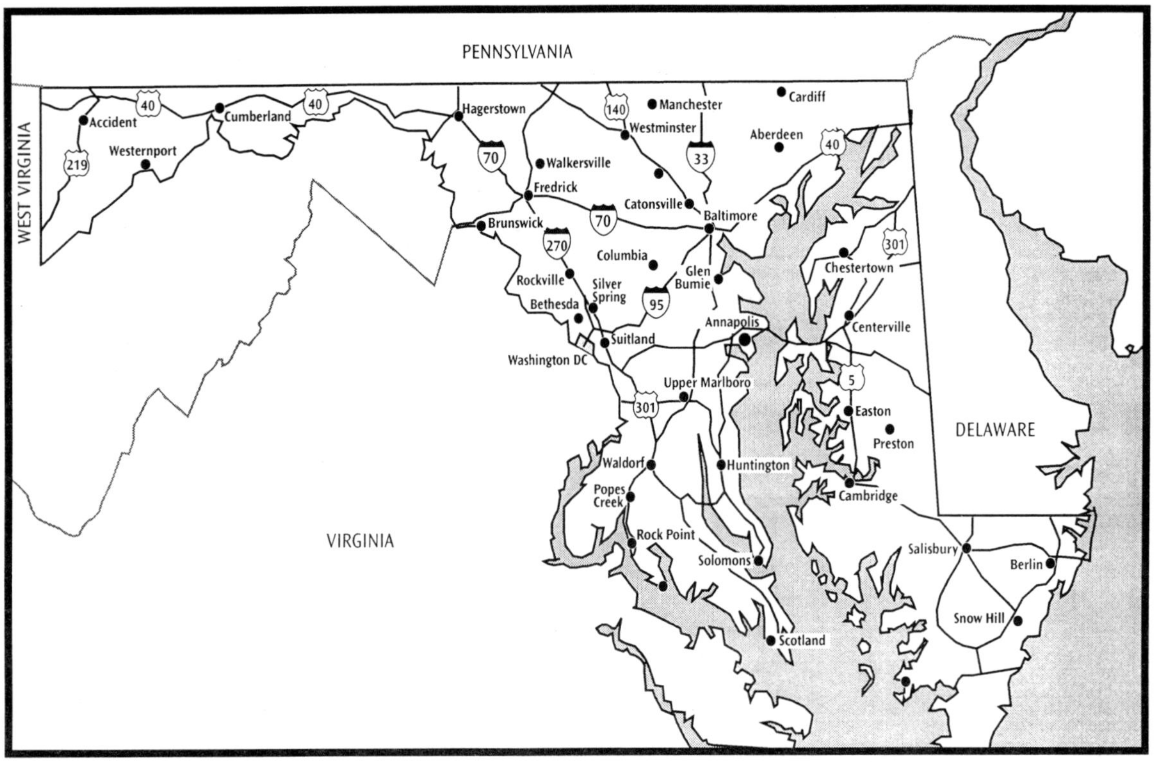

APPENDIX A

Forms You'll Need to Get Started

This appendix contains the many forms referenced throughout each chapter of this book. The following table tells you where each form is mentioned in the book and on which page the form is located in this appendix.

What forms are included?	Mentioned in Chapter	Located on Page
Form 2553 – Election by a Small Business Corporation	2	A.2
Form SS-4 – Application for Employer Identification Number	3	A.4
Form COT/ST 75 – Maryland Combined Registration Application	3	A.8
Form I-9 – Employment Eligibility Verification	4	A.14
Sample Income Statement (Profit & Loss Statement)	9	A.16
Sample Balance Sheet	9	A.18
Sample Cash Flow Statement	9	A.19
Sample Purchase Order	9	A.21
Sample Invoice	9	A.22
Sample Job Description	10	A.23
Sample Job Application	10	A.24
Form W-4 – Employee's Withholding Allowance Certificate	10	A.28
Sample Performance Review	10	A.30

Form 2553 – Election by a Small Business Corporation

Form **2553** (Rev. September 1997) Department of the Treasury Internal Revenue Service

Election by a Small Business Corporation
(Under section 1362 of the Internal Revenue Code)
▶ **For Paperwork Reduction Act Notice, see page 2 of instructions.**
▶ **See separate instructions.**

OMB No. 1545-0146

Notes: 1. *This election to be an S corporation can be accepted only if all the tests are met under* ***Who May Elect*** *on page 1 of the instructions; all signatures in Parts I and III are originals (no photocopies); and the exact name and address of the corporation and other required form information are provided.*

2. *Do not file* ***Form 1120S,*** *U.S. Income Tax Return for an S Corporation, for any tax year before the year the election takes effect.*

3. *If the corporation was in existence before the effective date of this election, see* ***Taxes an S Corporation May Owe*** *on page 1 of the instructions.*

Part I Election Information

Please Type or Print	Name of corporation (see instructions)	**A** Employer identification number
	Number, street, and room or suite no. (If a P.O. box, see instructions.)	**B** Date incorporated
	City or town, state, and ZIP code	**C** State of incorporation

D Election is to be effective for tax year beginning (month, day, year) . . . . ▶ / /

E Name and title of officer or legal representative who the IRS may call for more information

F Telephone number of officer or legal representative ( )

G If the corporation changed its name or address after applying for the EIN shown in **A** above, check this box . . . . ▶ ☐

H If this election takes effect for the first tax year the corporation exists, enter month, day, and year of the **earliest** of the following: (1) date the corporation first had shareholders, (2) date the corporation first had assets, or (3) date the corporation began doing business . . . . ▶ / /

I Selected tax year: Annual return will be filed for tax year ending (month and day) ▶ ....

If the tax year ends on any date other than December 31, except for an automatic 52-53-week tax year ending with reference to the month of December, you **must** complete Part II on the back. If the date you enter is the ending date of an automatic 52-53-week tax year, write "52-53-week year" to the right of the date. See Temporary Regulations section 1.441-2T(e)(3).

J Name and address of each shareholder; shareholder's spouse having a community property interest in the corporation's stock; and each tenant in common, joint tenant, and tenant by the entirety. (A husband and wife (and their estates) are counted as one shareholder in determining the number of shareholders without regard to the manner in which the stock is owned.)	**K** Shareholders' Consent Statement. Under penalties of perjury, we declare that we consent to the election of the above-named corporation to be an S corporation under section 1362(a) and that we have examined this consent statement, including accompanying schedules and statements, and to the best of our knowledge and belief, it is true, correct, and complete. We understand our consent is binding and may not be withdrawn after the corporation has made a valid election. (Shareholders sign and date below.)		**L** Stock owned		**M** Social security number or employer identification number (see instructions)	**N** Share-holder's tax year ends (month and day)
	Signature	Date	Number of shares	Dates acquired		

Under penalties of perjury, I declare that I have examined this election, including accompanying schedules and statements, and to the best of my knowledge and belief, it is true, correct, and complete.

Signature of officer ▶ **Title** ▶ **Date** ▶

See Parts II and III on back. Cat. No. 18629R Form **2553** (Rev. 9-97)

Form 2553 – Election by a Small Business Corporation (continued)

Form 2553 (Rev. 9-97) Page 2

Part II **Selection of Fiscal Tax Year** (All corporations using this part must complete item O and item P, Q, or R.)

O Check the applicable box to indicate whether the corporation is:

1. ☐ A new corporation adopting the tax year entered in item I, Part I.
2. ☐ An existing corporation retaining the tax year entered in item I, Part I.
3. ☐ An existing corporation changing to the tax year entered in item I, Part I.

P Complete item P if the corporation is using the expeditious approval provisions of Rev. Proc. 87-32, 1987-2 C.B. 396, to request (1) a natural business year (as defined in section 4.01(1) of Rev. Proc. 87-32) or (2) a year that satisfies the ownership tax year test in section 4.01(2) of Rev. Proc. 87-32. Check the applicable box below to indicate the representation statement the corporation is making as required under section 4 of Rev. Proc. 87-32.

1. Natural Business Year ▶ ☐ I represent that the corporation is retaining or changing to a tax year that coincides with its natural business year as defined in section 4.01(1) of Rev. Proc. 87-32 and as verified by its satisfaction of the requirements of section 4.02(1) of Rev. Proc. 87-32. In addition, if the corporation is changing to a natural business year as defined in section 4.01(1), I further represent that such tax year results in less deferral of income to the owners than the corporation's present tax year. I also represent that the corporation is not described in section 3.01(2) of Rev. Proc. 87-32. (See instructions for additional information that must be attached.)

2. Ownership Tax Year ▶ ☐ I represent that shareholders holding more than half of the shares of the stock (as of the first day of the tax year to which the request relates) of the corporation have the same tax year or are concurrently changing to the tax year that the corporation adopts, retains, or changes to per item I, Part I. I also represent that the corporation is not described in section 3.01(2) of Rev. Proc. 87-32.

Note: *If you do not use item P and the corporation wants a fiscal tax year, complete either item Q or R below. Item Q is used to request a fiscal tax year based on a business purpose and to make a back-up section 444 election. Item R is used to make a regular section 444 election.*

Q Business Purpose—To request a fiscal tax year based on a business purpose, you must check box Q1 and pay a user fee. See instructions for details. You may also check box Q2 and/or box Q3.

1. Check here ▶ ☐ if the fiscal year entered in item I, Part I, is requested under the provisions of section 6.03 of Rev. Proc. 87-32. Attach to Form 2553 a statement showing the business purpose for the requested fiscal year. See instructions for additional information that must be attached.

2. Check here ▶ ☐ to show that the corporation intends to make a back-up section 444 election in the event the corporation's business purpose request is not approved by the IRS. (See instructions for more information.)

3. Check here ▶ ☐ to show that the corporation agrees to adopt or change to a tax year ending December 31 if necessary for the IRS to accept this election for S corporation status in the event (1) the corporation's business purpose request is not approved and the corporation makes a back-up section 444 election, but is ultimately not qualified to make a section 444 election, or (2) the corporation's business purpose request is not approved and the corporation did not make a back-up section 444 election.

R Section 444 Election—To make a section 444 election, you must check box R1 and you may also check box R2.

1. Check here ▶ ☐ to show the corporation will make, if qualified, a section 444 election to have the fiscal tax year shown in item I, Part I. To make the election, you must complete **Form 8716**, Election To Have a Tax Year Other Than a Required Tax Year, and either attach it to Form 2553 or file it separately.

2. Check here ▶ ☐ to show that the corporation agrees to adopt or change to a tax year ending December 31 if necessary for the IRS to accept this election for S corporation status in the event the corporation is ultimately not qualified to make a section 444 election.

Part III **Qualified Subchapter S Trust (QSST) Election Under Section 1361(d)(2)***

Income beneficiary's name and address	Social security number
	: – :
Trust's name and address	Employer identification number

Date on which stock of the corporation was transferred to the trust (month, day, year) . . . . ▶ / /

In order for the trust named above to be a QSST and thus a qualifying shareholder of the S corporation for which this Form 2553 is filed, I hereby make the election under section 1361(d)(2). Under penalties of perjury, I certify that the trust meets the definitional requirements of section 1361(d)(3) and that all other information provided in Part III is true, correct, and complete.

Signature of income beneficiary or signature and title of legal representative or other qualified person making the election | Date

*Use Part III to make the QSST election only if stock of the corporation has been transferred to the trust on or before the date on which the corporation makes its election to be an S corporation. The QSST election must be made and filed separately if stock of the corporation is transferred to the trust after the date on which the corporation makes the S election.

Form SS-4 – Application for Employer Identification Number

Form **SS-4**
(Rev. December 1995)
Department of the Treasury
Internal Revenue Service

Application for Employer Identification Number

(For use by employers, corporations, partnerships, trusts, estates, churches, government agencies, certain individuals, and others. See instructions.)

▶ Keep a copy for your records.

EIN

OMB No. 1545-0003

Please type or print clearly.

1 Name of applicant (Legal name) (See instructions.)

2 Trade name of business (if different from name on line 1)

3 Executor, trustee, "care of" name

4a Mailing address (street address) (room, apt., or suite no.)

5a Business address (if different from address on lines 4a and 4b)

4b City, state, and ZIP code

5b City, state, and ZIP code

6 County and state where principal business is located

7 Name of principal officer, general partner, grantor, owner, or trustor—SSN required (See instructions.) ▶

8a Type of entity (Check only one box.) (See instructions.)
☐ Sole proprietor (SSN)
☐ Partnership
☐ REMIC
☐ State/local government
☐ Other nonprofit organization (specify) ▶ (enter GEN if applicable)
☐ Other (specify) ▶
☐ Personal service corp.
☐ Limited liability co.
☐ National Guard
☐ Estate (SSN of decedent)
☐ Plan administrator-SSN
☐ Other corporation (specify) ▶
☐ Trust
☐ Federal Government/military
☐ Farmers' cooperative
☐ Church or church-controlled organization

8b If a corporation, name the state or foreign country (if applicable) where incorporated | State | Foreign country

9 Reason for applying (Check only one box.)
☐ Started new business (specify) ▶
☐ Hired employees
☐ Created a pension plan (specify type) ▶
☐ Banking purpose (specify) ▶
☐ Changed type of organization (specify) ▶
☐ Purchased going business
☐ Created a trust (specify) ▶
☐ Other (specify) ▶

10 Date business started or acquired (Mo., day, year) (See instructions.)

11 Closing month of accounting year (See instructions.)

12 First date wages or annuities were paid or will be paid (Mo., day, year). **Note:** *If applicant is a withholding agent, enter date income will first be paid to nonresident alien. (Mo., day, year)* ▶

13 Highest number of employees expected in the next 12 months. **Note:** *If the applicant does not expect to have any employees during the period, enter -0-. (See instructions.)* ▶ | Nonagricultural | Agricultural | Household

14 Principal activity (See instructions.) ▶

15 Is the principal business activity manufacturing? ☐ **Yes** ☐ **No**
If "Yes," principal product and raw material used ▶

16 To whom are most of the products or services sold? Please check the appropriate box. ☐ Business (wholesale)
☐ Public (retail) ☐ Other (specify) ▶ ☐ N/A

17a Has the applicant ever applied for an identification number for this or any other business? ☐ **Yes** ☐ **No**
Note: *If "Yes," please complete lines 17b and 17c.*

17b If you checked "Yes" on line 17a, give applicant's legal name and trade name shown on prior application, if different from line 1 or 2 above.
Legal name ▶ Trade name ▶

17c Approximate date when and city and state where the application was filed. Enter previous employer identification number if known.
Approximate date when filed (Mo., day, year) | City and state where filed | Previous EIN

Under penalties of perjury, I declare that I have examined this application, and to the best of my knowledge and belief, it is true, correct, and complete.

Business telephone number (include area code)

Fax telephone number (include area code)

Name and title (Please type or print clearly.) ▶

Signature ▶ Date ▶

Note: *Do not write below this line. For official use only.*

Please leave blank ▶	Geo.	Ind.	Class	Size	Reason for applying

For Paperwork Reduction Act Notice, see page 4. Cat. No. 16055N Form **SS-4** (Rev. 12-95)

Form SS-4 – Application for Employer Identification Number (continued)

General Instructions

Section references are to the Internal Revenue Code unless otherwise noted.

Purpose of Form

Use Form SS-4 to apply for an employer identification number (EIN). An EIN is a nine-digit number (for example, 12-3456789) assigned to sole proprietors, corporations, partnerships, estates, trusts, and other entities for filing and reporting purposes. The information you provide on this form will establish your filing and reporting requirements.

Who Must File

You must file this form if you have not obtained an EIN before and:

- You pay wages to one or more employees including household employees.
- You are required to have an EIN to use on any return, statement, or other document, even if you are not an employer.
- You are a withholding agent required to withhold taxes on income, other than wages, paid to a nonresident alien (individual, corporation, partnership, etc.). A withholding agent may be an agent, broker, fiduciary, manager, tenant, or spouse, and is required to file **Form 1042,** Annual Withholding Tax Return for U.S. Source Income of Foreign Persons.
- You file **Schedule C,** Profit or Loss From Business, or **Schedule F,** Profit or Loss From Farming, of **Form 1040,** U.S. Individual Income Tax Return, **and** have a Keogh plan or are required to file excise, employment, information, or alcohol, tobacco, or firearms returns.

The following must use EINs even if they do not have any employees:

- State and local agencies who serve as tax reporting agents for public assistance recipients, under Rev. Proc. 80-4, 1980-1 C.B. 581, should obtain a separate EIN for this reporting. See **Household employer** on page 3.
- Trusts, except the following:

1. Certain grantor-owned revocable trusts. (See the **Instructions for Form 1041.**)

2. Individual Retirement Arrangement (IRA) trusts, unless the trust has to file **Form 990-T,** Exempt Organization Business Income Tax Return. (See the **Instructions for Form 990-T.**)

3. Certain trusts that are considered household employers can use the trust EIN to report and pay the social security and Medicare taxes, Federal unemployment tax (FUTA) and withheld Federal income tax. A separate EIN is not necessary.

- Estates
- Partnerships
- REMICs (real estate mortgage investment conduits) (See the **Instructions for Form 1066,** U.S. Real Estate Mortgage Investment Conduit Income Tax Return.)
- Corporations
- Nonprofit organizations (churches, clubs, etc.)
- Farmers' cooperatives
- Plan administrators (A plan administrator is the person or group of persons specified as the administrator by the instrument under which the plan is operated.)

When To Apply for a New EIN

New Business.—If you become the new owner of an existing business, **do not** use the EIN of the former owner. IF YOU ALREADY HAVE AN EIN, USE THAT NUMBER. If you do not have an EIN, apply for one on this form. If you become the "owner" of a corporation by acquiring its stock, use the corporation's EIN.

Changes in Organization or Ownership.—If you already have an EIN, you may need to get a new one if either the organization or ownership of your business changes. If you incorporate a sole proprietorship or form a partnership, you must get a new EIN. However, **do not** apply for a new EIN if you change only the name of your business.

Note: *If you are electing to be an "S corporation," be sure you file* ***Form 2553,*** *Election by a Small Business Corporation.*

File Only One Form SS-4.—File only one Form SS-4, regardless of the number of businesses operated or trade names under which a business operates. However, each corporation in an affiliated group must file a separate application.

EIN Applied For, But Not Received.—If you do not have an EIN by the time a return is due, write "Applied for" and the date you applied in the space shown for the number. **Do not** show your social security number as an EIN on returns.

If you do not have an EIN by the time a tax deposit is due, send your payment to the Internal Revenue Service Center for your filing area. (See **Where To Apply** below.) Make your check or money order payable to Internal Revenue Service and show your name (as shown on Form SS-4), address, type of tax, period covered, and date you applied for an EIN. Send an explanation with the deposit.

For more information about EINs, see **Pub. 583,** Starting a Business and Keeping Records, and **Pub. 1635,** Understanding Your EIN.

How To Apply

You can apply for an EIN either by mail or by telephone. You can get an EIN immediately by calling the Tele-TIN phone number for the service center for your state, or you can send the completed Form SS-4 directly to the service center to receive your EIN in the mail.

Application by Tele-TIN.—Under the Tele-TIN program, you can receive your EIN over the telephone and use it immediately to file a return or make a payment. To receive an EIN by phone, complete Form SS-4, then call the Tele-TIN phone number listed for your state under **Where To Apply.** The person making the call must be authorized to sign the form. (See **Signature block** on page 4.)

An IRS representative will use the information from the Form SS-4 to establish your account and assign you an EIN. Write the number you are given on the upper right-hand corner of the form, sign and date it.

Mail or FAX the signed SS-4 ***within 24 hours*** *to the Tele-TIN Unit at the service center address for your state.* The IRS representative will give you the FAX number. The FAX numbers are also listed in Pub. 1635.

Taxpayer representatives can receive their client's EIN by phone if they first send a facsimile (FAX) of a completed **Form 2848,** Power of Attorney and Declaration of Representative, or **Form 8821,** Tax Information Authorization, to the Tele-TIN unit. The Form 2848 or Form 8821 will be used solely to release the EIN to the representative authorized on the form.

Application by Mail.—Complete Form SS-4 at least 4 to 5 weeks before you will need an EIN. Sign and date the application and mail it to the service center address for your state. You will receive your EIN in the mail in approximately 4 weeks.

Where To Apply

The Tele-TIN phone numbers listed below will involve a long-distance charge to callers outside of the local calling area and can be used only to apply for an EIN. THE NUMBERS MAY CHANGE WITHOUT NOTICE. Use 1-800-829-1040 to verify a number or to ask about an application by mail or other Federal tax matters.

If your principal business, office or agency, or legal residence in the case of an individual, is located in:	**Call the Tele-TIN phone number shown or file with the Internal Revenue Service Center at:**
Florida, Georgia, South Carolina	Attn: Entity Control Atlanta, GA 39901 (404) 455-2360
New Jersey, New York City and counties of Nassau, Rockland, Suffolk, and Westchester	Attn: Entity Control Holtsville, NY 00501 (516) 447-4955
New York (all other counties), Connecticut, Maine, Massachusetts, New Hampshire, Rhode Island, Vermont	Attn: Entity Control Andover, MA 05501 (508) 474-9717
Illinois, Iowa, Minnesota, Missouri, Wisconsin	Attn: Entity Control Stop 57A 2306 E. Bannister Rd. Kansas City, MO 64131 (816) 926-5999
Delaware, District of Columbia, Maryland, Pennsylvania, Virginia	Attn: Entity Control Philadelphia, PA 19255 (215) 574-2400
Indiana, Kentucky, Michigan, Ohio, West Virginia	Attn: Entity Control Cincinnati, OH 45999 (606) 292-5467
Kansas, New Mexico, Oklahoma, Texas	Attn: Entity Control Austin, TX 73301 (512) 460-7843

Form SS-4 – Application for Employer Identification Number (continued)

Alaska, Arizona, California (counties of Alpine, Amador, Butte, Calaveras, Colusa, Contra Costa, Del Norte, El Dorado, Glenn, Humboldt, Lake, Lassen, Marin, Mendocino, Modoc, Napa, Nevada, Placer, Plumas, Sacramento, San Joaquin, Shasta, Sierra, Siskiyou, Solano, Sonoma, Sutter, Tehama, Trinity, Yolo, and Yuba), Colorado, Idaho, Montana, Nebraska, Nevada, North Dakota, Oregon, South Dakota, Utah, Washington, Wyoming	Attn: Entity Control Mail Stop 6271-T P.O. Box 9950 Ogden, UT 84409 (801) 620-7645
California (all other counties), Hawaii	Attn: Entity Control Fresno, CA 93888 (209) 452-4010
Alabama, Arkansas, Louisiana, Mississippi, North Carolina, Tennessee	Attn: Entity Control Memphis, TN 37501 (901) 365-5970

If you have no legal residence, principal place of business, or principal office or agency in any state, file your form with the Internal Revenue Service Center, Philadelphia, PA 19255 or call 215-574-2400.

Specific Instructions

The instructions that follow are for those items that are not self-explanatory. Enter N/A (nonapplicable) on the lines that do not apply.

Line 1.—Enter the legal name of the entity applying for the EIN exactly as it appears on the social security card, charter, or other applicable legal document.

Individuals.—Enter the first name, middle initial, and last name. If you are a sole proprietor, enter your individual name, not your business name. Do not use abbreviations or nicknames.

Trusts.—Enter the name of the trust.

Estate of a decedent.—Enter the name of the estate.

Partnerships.—Enter the legal name of the partnership as it appears in the partnership agreement. **Do not** list the names of the partners on line 1. See the specific instructions for line 7.

Corporations.—Enter the corporate name as it appears in the corporation charter or other legal document creating it.

Plan administrators.—Enter the name of the plan administrator. A plan administrator who already has an EIN should use that number.

Line 2.—Enter the trade name of the business if different from the legal name. The trade name is the "doing business as" name.

Note: *Use the full legal name on line 1 on all tax returns filed for the entity. However, if you enter a trade name on line 2 and choose to use the trade name instead of the legal name, enter the trade name on all returns you file. To prevent processing delays and errors,* ***always*** *use either the legal name only or the trade name only on all tax returns.*

Line 3.—Trusts enter the name of the trustee. Estates enter the name of the executor, administrator, or other fiduciary. If the entity applying has a designated person to receive tax information, enter that person's name as the "care of" person. Print or type the first name, middle initial, and last name.

Line 7.—Enter the first name, middle initial, last name, and social security number (SSN) of a principal officer if the business is a corporation; of a general partner if a partnership; or of a grantor, owner, or trustor if a trust.

Line 8a.—Check the box that best describes the type of entity applying for the EIN. If not specifically mentioned, check the "Other" box and enter the type of entity. Do not enter N/A.

Sole proprietor.—Check this box if you file Schedule C or F (Form 1040) and have a Keogh plan, or are required to file excise, employment, information, or alcohol, tobacco, or firearms returns. Enter your SSN in the space provided.

REMIC.—Check this box if the entity has elected to be treated as a real estate mortgage investment conduit (REMIC). See the **Instructions for Form 1066** for more information.

Other nonprofit organization.—Check this box if the nonprofit organization is other than a church or church-controlled organization and specify the type of nonprofit organization (for example, an educational organization).

If the organization also seeks tax-exempt status, you must file either **Package 1023** or **Package 1024,** Application for Recognition of Exemption. Get **Pub. 557,** Tax-Exempt Status for Your Organization, for more information.

Group exemption number (GEN).—If the organization is covered by a group exemption letter, enter the four-digit GEN. (Do not confuse the GEN with the nine-digit EIN.) If you do not know the GEN, contact the parent organization. Get Pub. 557 for more information about group exemption numbers.

Withholding agent.—If you are a withholding agent required to file Form 1042, check the "Other" box and enter "Withholding agent."

Personal service corporation.—Check this box if the entity is a personal service corporation. An entity is a personal service corporation for a tax year only if:

- The principal activity of the entity during the testing period (prior tax year) for the tax year is the performance of personal services substantially by employee-owners, and
- The employee-owners own 10% of the fair market value of the outstanding stock in the entity on the last day of the testing period.

Personal services include performance of services in such fields as health, law, accounting, or consulting. For more information about personal service corporations, see the **Instructions for Form 1120,** U.S. Corporation Income Tax Return, and **Pub. 542,** Tax Information on Corporations.

Limited liability co.—See the definition of limited liability company in the **Instructions for Form 1065.** If you are classified as a partnership for Federal income tax purposes, mark the "Limited liability co." checkbox. If you are classified as a corporation for Federal income tax purposes, mark the "Other corporation" checkbox and write "Limited liability co." in the space provided.

Plan administrator.—If the plan administrator is an individual, enter the plan administrator's SSN in the space provided.

Other corporation.—This box is for any corporation other than a personal service corporation. If you check this box, enter the type of corporation (such as insurance company) in the space provided.

Household employer.—If you are an individual, check the "Other" box and enter "Household employer" and your SSN. If you are a state or local agency serving as a tax reporting agent for public assistance recipients who become household employers, check the "Other" box and enter "Household employer agent." If you are a trust that qualifies as a household employer, you do not need a separate EIN for reporting tax information relating to household employees; use the EIN of the trust.

Line 9.—Check only **one** box. Do not enter N/A.

Started new business.—Check this box if you are starting a new business that requires an EIN. If you check this box, enter the type of business being started. **Do not** apply if you already have an EIN and are only adding another place of business.

Hired employees.—Check this box if the existing business is requesting an EIN because it has hired or is hiring employees and is therefore required to file employment tax returns. **Do not** apply if you already have an EIN and are only hiring employees. For information on the applicable employment taxes for family members, see **Circular E,** Employer's Tax Guide (Publication 15).

Created a pension plan.—Check this box if you have created a pension plan and need this number for reporting purposes. Also, enter the type of plan created.

Banking purpose.—Check this box if you are requesting an EIN for banking purposes only, and enter the banking purpose (for example, a bowling league for depositing dues or an investment club for dividend and interest reporting).

Changed type of organization.—Check this box if the business is changing its type of organization, for example, if the business was a sole proprietorship and has been incorporated or has become a partnership. If you check this box, specify in the space provided the type of change made, for example, "from sole proprietorship to partnership."

Purchased going business.—Check this box if you purchased an existing business. **Do not** use the former owner's EIN. **Do not** apply for a new EIN if you already have one. Use your own EIN.

Created a trust.—Check this box if you created a trust, and enter the type of trust created.

Form SS-4 – Application for Employer Identification Number (continued)

Note: *Do not file this form if you are the grantor/owner of certain revocable trusts. You must use your SSN for the trust. See the Instructions for Form 1041.*

Other (specify).—Check this box if you are requesting an EIN for any reason other than those for which there are checkboxes, and enter the reason.

Line 10.—If you are starting a new business, enter the starting date of the business. If the business you acquired is already operating, enter the date you acquired the business. Trusts should enter the date the trust was legally created. Estates should enter the date of death of the decedent whose name appears on line 1 or the date when the estate was legally funded.

Line 11.—Enter the last month of your accounting year or tax year. An accounting or tax year is usually 12 consecutive months, either a calendar year or a fiscal year (including a period of 52 or 53 weeks). A calendar year is 12 consecutive months ending on December 31. A fiscal year is either 12 consecutive months ending on the last day of any month other than December or a 52-53 week year. For more information on accounting periods, see **Pub. 538,** Accounting Periods and Methods.

Individuals.—Your tax year generally will be a calendar year.

Partnerships.—Partnerships generally must adopt the tax year of either (a) the majority partners; (b) the principal partners; (c) the tax year that results in the least aggregate (total) deferral of income; or (d) some other tax year. (See the **Instructions for Form 1065,** U.S. Partnership Return of Income, for more information.)

REMIC.—REMICs must have a calendar year as their tax year.

Personal service corporations.—A personal service corporation generally must adopt a calendar year unless:

- It can establish a business purpose for having a different tax year, or
- It elects under section 444 to have a tax year other than a calendar year.

Trusts.—Generally, a trust must adopt a calendar year except for the following:

- Tax-exempt trusts,
- Charitable trusts, and
- Grantor-owned trusts.

Line 12.—If the business has or will have employees, enter the date on which the business began or will begin to pay wages. If the business does not plan to have employees, enter N/A.

Withholding agent.—Enter the date you began or will begin to pay income to a nonresident alien. This also applies to individuals who are required to file Form 1042 to report alimony paid to a nonresident alien.

Line 13.—For a definition of agricultural labor (farmworker), see **Circular A,** Agricultural Employer's Tax Guide (Publication 51).

Line 14.—Generally, enter the exact type of business being operated (for example, advertising agency, farm, food or beverage establishment, labor union, real estate agency, steam laundry, rental of coin-operated vending machine, or investment club). Also state if the business will involve the sale or distribution of alcoholic beverages.

Governmental.—Enter the type of organization (state, county, school district, municipality, etc.).

Nonprofit organization (other than governmental).—Enter whether organized for religious, educational, or humane purposes, and the principal activity (for example, religious organization—hospital, charitable).

Mining and quarrying.—Specify the process and the principal product (for example, mining bituminous coal, contract drilling for oil, or quarrying dimension stone).

Contract construction.—Specify whether general contracting or special trade contracting. Also, show the type of work normally performed (for example, general contractor for residential buildings or electrical subcontractor).

Food or beverage establishments.—Specify the type of establishment and state whether you employ workers who receive tips (for example, lounge—yes).

Trade.—Specify the type of sales and the principal line of goods sold (for example, wholesale dairy products, manufacturer's representative for mining machinery, or retail hardware).

Manufacturing.—Specify the type of establishment operated (for example, sawmill or vegetable cannery).

Signature block.—The application must be signed by (a) the individual, if the applicant is an individual, (b) the president, vice president, or other principal officer, if the applicant is a corporation, (c) a responsible and duly authorized member or officer having knowledge of its affairs, if the applicant is a partnership or other unincorporated organization, or (d) the fiduciary, if the applicant is a trust or estate.

Some Useful Publications

You may get the following publications for additional information on the subjects covered on this form. To get these and other free forms and publications, call 1-800-TAX-FORM (1-800-829-3676). You should receive your order or notification of its status within 7 to 15 workdays of your call.

Use your computer.—If you subscribe to an on-line service, ask if IRS information is available and, if so, how to access it. You can also get information through IRIS, the Internal Revenue Information Services, on FedWorld, a government bulletin board. Tax forms, instructions, publications, and other IRS information, are available through IRIS.

IRIS is accessible directly by calling 703-321-8020. On the Internet, you can telnet to fedworld.gov. or, for file transfer protocol services, connect to ftp.fedworld.gov. If you are using the WorldWide Web, connect to http://www.ustreas.gov

FedWorld's help desk offers technical assistance on accessing IRIS (not tax help) during regular business hours at 703-487-4608. The IRIS menus offer information on available file formats and software needed to read and print files. You must print the forms to use them; the forms are not designed to be filled out on-screen.

Tax forms, instructions, and publications are also available on CD-ROM, including prior-year forms starting with the 1991 tax year. For ordering information and software requirements, contact the Government Printing Office's Superintendent of Documents (202-512-1800) or Federal Bulletin Board (202-512-1387).

Pub. 1635, Understanding Your EIN

Pub. 15, Employer's Tax Guide

Pub. 15-A, Employer's Supplemental Tax Guide

Pub. 538, Accounting Periods and Methods

Pub. 541, Tax Information on Partnerships

Pub. 542, Tax Information on Corporations

Pub. 557, Tax-Exempt Status for Your Organization

Pub. 583, Starting a Business and Keeping Records

Package 1023, Application for Recognition of Exemption

Package 1024, Application for Recognition of Exemption Under Section 501(a) or for Determination Under Section 120

Paperwork Reduction Act Notice

We ask for the information on this form to carry out the Internal Revenue laws of the United States. You are required to give us the information. We need it to ensure that you are complying with these laws and to allow us to figure and collect the right amount of tax.

The time needed to complete and file this form will vary depending on individual circumstances. The estimated average time is:

Recordkeeping	7 min.
Learning about the law or the form	18 min.
Preparing the form	45 min.
Copying, assembling, and sending the form to the IRS	20 min.

If you have comments concerning the accuracy of these time estimates or suggestions for making this form simpler, we would be happy to hear from you. You can write to the Tax Forms Committee, Western Area Distribution Center, Rancho Cordova, CA 95743-0001. **Do not** send this form to this address. Instead, see **Where To Apply** on page 2.

Form COT/ST 75 – Combined Registration Application

State of Maryland Comptroller of the Treasury

Combined Registration Application

This application may be used for:

- **Admissions and amusement tax account**
- **Alcohol tax license**
- **Income tax withholding account**
- **Motor fuel tax account**
- **Sales and use tax license**
- **Use tax account**
- **Sales and use tax exemption certificate (for non-profit organizations)**
- **Tire recycling fee account**
- **Tobacco tax license**
- **Transient vendor license**
- **Unemployment insurance account**

Further registration is required for motor fuel, alcohol or tobacco taxes before engaging in business. The appropriate division of the Comptroller's Office will contact you and provide the necessary forms.

Other requirements

Depending on the nature of your business, you may be required to contact or register with some of the following agencies.

- **Local Licenses** may be required for corporations or individuals doing business in Maryland. Local licenses may be obtained from the Clerk of the Circuit Court for the jurisdiction in which the business is to be located.
- **Domestic and foreign corporations and limited liability companies** must register with the Department of Assessments and Taxation, Charter Division, at 301 West Preston Street, Baltimore, Maryland 21201-2395, (410) 767-1340. Each entity must file an annual personal property return.
- **Individuals, sole proprietorships and partnerships** which possess personal property (furniture, fixtures, tools, machinery, equipment, etc.) or need a business license must register and file an annual personal property return with the Department of Assessments and Taxation, Unincorporated Personal Property Unit, 301 West Preston Street, Room 806, Baltimore, Maryland 21201-2395, (410) 767-4991.
- **Every corporation and association** (domestic or foreign) having income allocable to Maryland must file a state income tax return.
- **All corporations** whose total Maryland income tax for the current taxable year can reasonably be expected to exceed $1,000 must file a declaration of estimated tax. (410) 974-3981 or 1-800-MD TAXES.
- **To form a corporation,** contact the State Department of Assessments & Taxation, 301 West Preston Street, Baltimore, Maryland 21201-2315. (410) 767-1340.
- **Worker's compensation insurance** coverage for employees is required of every employer in Maryland. This coverage may be obtained from a private carrier, the Injured Worker's Insurance Fund or by becoming self-insured. Contact the IWIF, 8722 Loch Raven Boulevard, Towson, Maryland 21204-6285. (410) 494-2000 or 1-800-492-0197.
- **Unclaimed property.** The Maryland abandoned property law requires businesses to review their records each year to determine whether they are in possession of any unclaimed funds and securities due and owing Maryland residents that have remained unclaimed for more than five years, and to file an annual report. Contact the Comptroller of the Treasury, Unclaimed Property Section, 301 W. Preston Street, Baltimore, Maryland 21201-2385. (410) 767-1700 or 1-800-782-7383.
- **Charitable organizations** may be required to register with the secretary of state if they solicit the public for contributions. Contact the Secretary of State's Office, Annapolis, Maryland 21401. (410) 974-5534.
- **Weights and measures.** If you buy or sell commodities on the basis of weight or measure, or use a weighing or measuring device commercially, your firm is subject to the Maryland Weights and Measures Law. To obtain information, call the Department of Agriculture, Weights and Measures Section at (410) 841-5790.
- **Food businesses** are required to be licensed with the Department of Health and Mental Hygiene. Contact your local county health department or call DHMH at (410) 767-8400.

Form COT/ST 75 – Combined Registration Application (continued)

Page I

State of Maryland - Comptroller of the Treasury

Combined Registration Application

See instructions on page IV

Office use only

SECTION A: All applicants must complete this section.

1 a) Federal Employer Identification Number (See instructions)

☐☐-☐☐☐☐☐☐☐ AND

b) Social security number of owner, officer or agent responsible for taxes (must be supplied)

☐☐☐-☐☐-☐☐☐☐

2. Legal name of dealer, employer, corporation, or owner

3. Trade name (if different from above)

4. Street address of business location (Post office box not acceptable)

City, County and State Zip code (nine digits if known)

Telephone number (___) ___-____

Fax number (___) ___-____

5. Mailing address (post office box acceptable)

City, State Zip code (nine digits if known)

6. Reason for applying:

- ☐ New business
- ☐ Merger
- ☐ Change of entity
- ☐ Reorganization
- ☐ Additional location(s)
- ☐ Purchased going business
- ☐ Remit use tax on purchases
- ☐ Other (describe)

7. List previous owner's name and address:

8. Indicate registration sought: Number if registered:

- a ☐ Sales and use tax ______
- b ☐ Sales and use tax exemption for non-profit organizations ______
- c ☐ Tire recycling fee ______
- d ☐ Admissions & amusement tax ______
- e ☐ Employer withholding tax ______
- f ☐ Unemployment insurance ______
- g ☐ Alcohol tax ______
- h ☐ Tobacco tax ______
- i ☐ Motor fuel tax ______
- j ☐ Transient vendor license ______

9. Type of ownership: (Check appropriate box)

- a ☐ Sole proprietorship
- b ☐ Partnership
- c ☐ Non-profit corporation
- d ☐ Maryland corporation
- e ☐ Limited liability company
- f ☐ Non-Maryland corporation
- j ☐ Governmental
- k ☐ Fiduciary

10. Date first sales made in Maryland:

11. Date first wages paid in Maryland subject to withholding:

12. If you currently file a consolidated sales and use tax return, enter the number of your consolidated account:

13. If you have employees enter the number of your workers' compensation insurance policy or binder:

14. Date first wages paid to employees performing services in Maryland (Write N/A if no services performed in Maryland):

15. Number of employees:

16. Estimated gross wages paid in first quarter of operations:

17. Do you need a sales and use tax account only to remit taxes on untaxed purchases? ☐ Yes ☐ No

18. Describe business activity which generates revenue. Specify the product manufactured and/or sold, or the type of service performed.

19. Are you a non-profit organization applying for an exemption certificate? ☐ Yes ☐ No
If yes, enclose a non-returnable copy of IRS determination letter, articles of incorporation, by-laws, and other organization documents.

20. If the location described above is primarily engaged in providing support services to other units of the company, please indicate the nature of these activities. ☐ Administrative ☐ R&D ☐ Storage ☐ Other (specify) ______

21. Identify owners, partners, corporate officers, trustees, or members: (Please list person whose social security number is listed in Section A.1b first.)

Name and social security number	Title	Home address, city, state, zip code	Telephone number

Form COT/ST 75 – Combined Registration Application (continued)

Page IV

Instructions for completing the Maryland Combined Registration Application

General instructions

NOTE: Incomplete applications cannot be processed and will be returned. To ensure that your application is processed without delay, be sure to provide all requested information. Please type or print clearly using a dark ink pen. Before mailing this application, be sure to:

1. Complete all of Section A.
2. Answer all questions in all the other sections that pertain to your business.
3. Sign the application in Section E.
4. Detach this instruction sheet from the application.
5. Mail the application to:
   Comptroller of the Treasury
   Central Registration
   Revenue Administration Center
   Annapolis, MD 21411-0001

Instructions for page 1

Item 1 (a) A Federal Employer Identification Number (FEIN) is required by: all Corporations (Regular, Closed, or S), all Partnerships, all Non-Profit Organizations, and Sole Proprietorships who pay wages to one or more employees (a Sole Proprietorship with no employees, other than self, is not required to have a FEIN). If you don't have a FEIN at the time you submit this application, and one is required, leave this space blank and submit the number to Central Registration when you receive it from the Internal Revenue Service.

Item 1 (b) The social security number of the individual owner of the company or officer or agent of a corporation responsible for remitting the taxes is required. Also enter the name of the individual owner, officer or agent responsible for the taxes on the first line of Item 21.

Item 2. Enter the true name of the business, organization, corporation (John Smith, Inc.), partnership (Smith & Jones), individual proprietor or professional (Smith, John T.), or governmental agency.

Item 3. Enter the name by which your business is known to the public (Example: Smith's Ceramics).

Item 8 If you are already registered for any of the taxes listed, enter your registration number.

Item 8 (b) Sales and use tax exemption: Exemption certificates are issued to non-profit charitable, educational or religious organizations, volunteer fire or ambulance companies or volunteer rescue squads located in this state. Possession of an effective determination letter from the Internal Revenue Service stating that the organization qualifies under 501(c)(3) of the Internal Revenue Code may be treated as evidence that an organization qualifies for this exemption. You must enclose a non-returnable copy of the IRS determination letter, articles of incorporation, by-laws, and other organizational documents.

Item 8 (c) Tire recycling fee: You must register for a tire fee account if you will make any sales of tires to a retailer or you are a retailer who purchases tires from an out-of-state tire wholesaler or other person who does not show payment of Maryland's used tire recycling fees on invoices to you.

Item 8 (d) Admissions and amusement tax: Typical activities subject to the admissions and amusement tax include admissions to any place, including motion pictures, athletic events, races, shows and exhibits. Also subject to tax are receipts from athletic equipment rentals, bingo, coin-operated amusement devices, boat rides and excursions, amusement rides, golf greens fees, golf cart rentals, skating, bowling shoe rentals, lift tickets, riding academies, horse rentals, and merchandise, refreshments, or a service sold or served in connection with entertainment at a night club or room in a hotel, restaurant, hall, or other place where dancing privileges, music or other entertainment is provided.

Item 8 (j) Transient vendor license. If you make sales of property subject to the sales and use tax from either motor vehicles or from roadside or temporary locations, you must, in addition to any other license required by law, obtain and display a transient vendor license. Transient vendor licenses will be issued and reissued only to persons who have sales and use tax and trader's licenses and who are not delinquent in the payment of any state taxes.

Exhibitors at fairs, trade shows, flea markets and individuals who sell by catalogues, samples or brochures for future delivery do not need transient vendor licenses.

Form COT/ST 75 – Combined Registration Application (continued)

Page II - See instructions on page III FEIN or SSN

SECTION B: Complete this section to register for an unemployment insurance account.

PART 1.

1. Will corporate officers receive compensation, salary or distribution of profits? ❑ Yes ❑ No

2. Do you operate more than one location in Maryland? ❑ Yes ❑ No

3. Did you acquire by sale or otherwise all or part of the assets, business, organization or trade of another employer? ❑ Yes ❑ No

4. If your answer to question 3 is "No", proceed to item 6 of this section. If your answer to question 3 is "Yes", provide the information below and answer question 5, if applicable:
   a. Percentage of common ownership between current business and former business: ________
   b. Percentage of assets acquired from former business: ________
   c. Date former business was acquired by current business: ________
   d. Unemployment insurance number of former business, if known: ________

5. If the percentage of common ownership, as shown in item 4(a), is 50% or less, choose the type of tax rate you desire from the following:
   ❑ rate based on former employer's experience with unemployment insurance claims and taxable payrolls.
   ❑ new employer rate (approximately 2.3%)

6. **For employers of domestic help only:**
   a) Have you or will you have as an individual or local college club, college fraternity or sorority a total payroll of $1,000 or more in the state of Maryland during any calendar quarter?
   ❑ Yes ❑ No
   b) If yes, indicate the earliest quarter and calendar year.

7. **For agricultural operations only:**
   a) Have you had or will you have 10 or more workers for 20 weeks or more in any calendar year or have you paid or will you pay $20,000 or more in wages during any calendar quarter?
   ❑ Yes ❑ No
   b) If yes, indicate the earliest quarter and calendar year.

PART 2. COMPLETE THIS PART IF YOU ARE A NON-PROFIT ORGANIZATION.

1. Are you covered by the Federal Unemployment Tax Act? ❑ Yes ❑ No

2. If not, are you exempt under Section 3306(c)(8) of the Federal Unemployment Tax Act? ❑ Yes ❑ No

3. Are you a non-profit organization as described in Section 501(c)(3) of the United States Internal Revenue Code which is exempt from Income Tax under Section 501(a) of such code? If YES, attach a copy of your exemption from Internal Revenue Service. ❑ Yes ❑ No

4. Elect option to finance unemployment insurance coverage. See instructions.
   a ❑ Contributions
   b ❑ Reimbursement of trust fund If b) is checked, indicate the total taxable payroll ($8,500 maximum per individual per calendar year)
   $________ for 19________ ❑ Letter of credit ❑ Surety bond ❑ Security deposit ❑ Cash in escrow

SECTION C: Complete this section if you are applying for an alcohol or tobacco tax license.

1. Will you engage in any business activity pertaining to the manufacture, sale, distribution, or storage of alcoholic beverages?
   ❑ Yes ❑ No

2. Will you engage in any wholesale activity regarding the sale and/or distribution of cigarettes in Maryland?
   ❑ Yes ❑ No

SECTION D: Complete this section if you plan to sell, use or transport any fuels in Maryland.

1. Do you import any of the following fuels into Maryland?
   ❑ Gasoline (including av/gas)
   ❑ Special fuel (any fuel other than gasoline)
   ❑ Turbine fuel (jet fuel)

2. Do you buy or manufacture any of the following fuels for resale or distribution?
   ❑ Gasoline (including av/gas)
   ❑ Special fuel (any fuel other than gasoline)
   ❑ Turbine fuel (jet fuel)

3. Do you operate any motor vehicle which exceeds 26,000 lbs. (registered, operating, or in combination with another vehicle on a Maryland highway)?
   ❑ Yes ❑ No

4. Do you operate a retail service station?
   ❑ Yes ❑ No

5. Do you transport petroleum in any transporting device exceeding 50 gallons? ❑ Yes ❑ No

SECTION E: All applicants must complete this section.

I DECLARE UNDER THE PENALTY OF PERJURY THAT THIS APPLICATION HAS BEEN EXAMINED BY ME AND TO THE BEST OF MY KNOWLEDGE AND BELIEF IS TRUE, CORRECT, AND COMPLETE.

SIGN HERE ➤ ________________ Title ________________ Date ________________

If the business is a corporation, an officer of the corporation authorized to sign on behalf of the corporation must sign; if a partnership, one partner must sign; if an unincorporated association, one member must sign; if a sole proprietorship, the proprietor must sign. (The signature of any other person will not be accepted.)

Form COT/ST 75 – Combined Registration Application (continued)

Page III

Instructions for page II

SECTION B. Complete this section if you are an employer registering for unemployment insurance.

PART 1. All industrial and commercial employers and many nonprofit charitable, educational and religious institutions in Maryland are covered by the state unemployment insurance law. There is no employee contribution. An employer must register upon establishing a new business in the state. If an employer is found liable to provide unemployment coverage, an account number and tax rate will be assigned. The employer must report and pay contributions on a report mailed to the employer each quarter by the Office of Unemployment Insurance.

PART 2. Complete this part if you are a non-profit organization.

Item 1. Your exemption from the Internal Revenue Service should state if you are exempt from Federal Unemployment Taxes.

Item 2. Check the appropriate box and include a copy of the Internal Revenue Service exemption, if applicable.

Item 4. Indicate your option to finance unemployment insurance coverage:

Option (a) - Contributions.

The employer has the option to pay contributions. A rate assigned by the administration is applied to the first $8,500.00 of wages paid to each employee during a calendar year. Contributions are paid on a calendar quarter basis.

An employer who has not been subject to the Maryland Unemployment Insurance Law for a sufficient period of time to have its rates computed is required to pay at the new account rate, which is approximately 2.3%. Thereafter, the employer will be assigned a rate reflecting its own experience with layoffs. If the employer's former employees receive benefits regularly which result in benefit charges, the employer will have a higher tax rate. Employers which incur little or no benefit charges will have a lower tax rate.

Option (b) - Reimbursement Of Trust Fund.

The employer may elect to reimburse the Trust Fund. At the end of each calendar quarter, the employer is billed for unemployment benefits paid to its former employees during the quarter. A nonprofit organization that elects to reimburse must also provide collateral to protect the administration from default in reimbursement.

If (b) is checked, indicate which method of providing collateral you will use.

For more information on the financing options, call (410) 767-2691. Toll Free 1-800-492-5524.

Executive order on privacy and state data system security notice

The information on this application will be used to determine if you are liable for certain taxes, to register you and, where appropriate, to issue a required license.

If you fail to provide required information, you will not be properly registered with state tax authorities, and necessary licenses may not be issued. If you operate a business without the appropriate registration and licenses, you may be subject to civil and criminal penalties, including confiscation in some instances.

If you are a sole proprietor, partner or officer in a corporation, you have the right to inspect any tax records for which you are responsible, and you may ask the tax authorities to correct any inaccurate or incomplete information on those records.

This application and the information you provide on it are generally not available for public inspection. This information will be shared with the state tax authorities with whom you should be registered.

Form COT/ST 75 – Combined Registration Application (continued)

Other licenses you may need

In addition to a sales and use tax license, you may also need to obtain one or more of the licenses listed below from your local Clerk of the Court to operate your business in the state of Maryland:

Traders	Plumber & gas fitter	Junk dealer	Music box
Restaurant	Laundry	Auctioneer	Vending machine
Cigarette	Chain store	Hawkers & peddlers	Console machine
Special cigarette	Commercial garage	Billiard table	Wholesale dealer - farm machinery
Construction firm	Storage warehouse	Pinball	

These licenses are issued by the Clerk of the Circuit Court in the County (or Baltimore City) where the business is located. If your business falls into one or more of the above categories, please contact the Clerk of the Court in your county courthouse. Check the blue government pages of your local telephone directory for the street address and phone number. The clerk can also advise you on any local licensing requirements.

Get on the right 'TRAC'

The Taxpayer Registration Assistance Center (TRAC), located in Room 206, 301 West Preston Street, Baltimore, Maryland, offers you on-the-spot help in determining the tax registrations you need, in completing this application and in understanding basic Maryland business tax requirements.

Personnel at the center can see that you talk to the right people and get the correct information to get your new business off to the right start. No appointment is necessary. If you wish to register for a sales and use tax license in person, you may apply in Room 206, State Office Building, 301 West Preston Street, Baltimore, Maryland. Anyone needing a reasonable accommodation due to a disability should contact us in advance of a visit.

Register by fax

You can now file your Maryland Combined Registration Application by fax 24 hours a day. When applying by fax, be sure to complete Sections A and E of the application and any other sections that apply to your business. You *must* provide your federal employer ID number, if available, and social security number requested in Section A-1 and describe your business in Section A-18. Fax pages I and II of the application separately. Please *do not* fax a cover sheet or our instructions. The Central Registration fax number is (410) 767-1571.

Add registrations by telephone

If you have (or recently had) a business tax registration with the Comptroller's Office, an account with the Unemployment Insurance Division or a business license issued by a clerk of the circuit court, we can open a sales and use tax, admissions and amusement tax or tire recycling fee account for you in just minutes by telephone. Telephone registration eliminates the need for you to fill out a Combined Registration Application. Just give us a call at: (410) 767-1300 or 1-800-492-1751.

Questions?

☎ Call Central Registration at (410) 767-1313 in Baltimore

☎ Toll free from elsewhere in Maryland 1-800-492-1751

For the hearing impaired: Maryland Relay Service 1-800-735-2258

Maryland tax forms and publications are available on our Forms-by-Fax System 410-974-FAXX (974-3299) and on the world wide web www.comp.state.us

State of Maryland
Comptroller of the Treasury
Central Registration
Revenue Administration Center
Annapolis, MD 21411-0001

Form I-9 – Employment Eligibility Verification

U.S. Department of Justice
Immigration and Naturalization Service

OMB No. 1115-0136
Employment Eligibility Verification

Please read instructions carefully before completing this form. The instructions must be available during completion of this form. ANTI-DISCRIMINATION NOTICE. It is illegal to discriminate against work eligible individuals. Employers CANNOT specify which document(s) they will accept from an employee. The refusal to hire an individual because of a future expiration date may also constitute illegal discrimination.

Section 1. Employee Information and Verification. To be completed and signed by employee at the time employment begins

Print Name: Last | First | Middle Initial | Maiden Name

Address *(Street Name and Number)* | Apt. # | Date of Birth *(month/day/year)*

City | State | Zip Code | Social Security #

I am aware that federal law provides for imprisonment and/or fines for false statements or use of false documents in connection with the completion of this form.

I attest, under penalty of perjury, that I am (check one of the following):
A citizen or national of the United States
A Lawful Permanent Resident (Alien # A__________
An alien authorized to work until___/___/___
(Alien # or Admission #__________________

Employee's Signature | Date *(month/day/year)*

Preparer and/or Translator Certification. *(To be completed and signed if Section 1 is prepared by a person other than the employee.) I attest, under penalty of perjury, that I have assisted in the completion of this form and that to the best of my knowledge the information is true and correct.*

Preparer's/Translator's Signature | Print Name

Address *(Street Name and Number, City, State, Zip Code)* | Date *(month/day/year)*

Section 2. Employer Review and Verification. To be completed and signed by employer. **Examine one document from List A OR examine one document from List B and one from List C** as listed on the reverse of this form and record the title, number and expiration date, if any, of the document(s)

	List A	OR	List B	AND	List C
Document title:	__________		__________		__________
Issuing authority:	__________		__________		__________
Document #:	__________		__________		__________
Expiration Date *(if any)*:	__/__/__		__/__/__		__/__/__
Document #:	__________				
Expiration Date *(if any)*:	__/__/__				

CERTIFICATION - I attest, under penalty of perjury, that I have examined the document(s) presented by the above-named employee, that the above-listed document(s) appear to be genuine and to relate to the employee named, that the employee began employment on *(month/day/year)* **___/___/___and that to the best of my knowledge the employee is eligible to work in the United States. (State employment agencies may omit the date the employee began employment).**

Signature of Employer or Authorized Representative | Print Name | Title

Business or Organization Name | Address *(Street Name and Number, City, State, Zip Code)* | Date *(month/day/year)*

Section 3. Updating and Reverification. To be completed and signed by employer

A. New Name *(if applicable)* | B. Date of rehire *(month/day/year) (if applicable)*

C. If employee's previous grant of work authorization has expired, provide the information below for the document that establishes current employment eligibility.

Document Title:__________Document #:__________Expiration Date (if any):__/__/__

I attest, under penalty of perjury, that to the best of my knowledge, this employee is eligible to work in the United States, and if the employee presented document(s), the document(s) I have examined appear to be genuine and to relate to the individual.

Signature of Employer or Authorized Representative | Date *(month/day/year)*

Form I-9 (Rev. 11-21-91) N

Form I-9 – Employment Eligibility Verification (continued)

LISTS OF ACCEPTABLE DOCUMENTS

LIST A		LIST B		LIST C
Documents that Establish Both Identity and Employment Eligibility	**OR**	**Documents that Establish Identity**	**AND**	**Documents that Establish Employment Eligibility**
1. U.S. Passport (unexpired or expired)		1. Driver's license or ID card issued by a state or outlying possession of the United States provided it contains a photograph or information such as name, date of birth, sex, height, eye color, and address		1. U.S. social security card issued by the Social Security Administration *(other than a card stating it is not valid for employment)*
2. Certificate of U.S. Citizenship *(INS Form N-560 or N-561)*		2. ID card issued by federal, state, or local government agencies or entities provided it contains a photograph or information such as name, date of birth, sex, height, eye color, and address		2. Certification of Birth Abroad issued by the Department of State *(Form FS-545 or Form DS-1350)*
3. Certificate of Naturalization *(INS Form N-550 or N-570)*		3. School ID card with a photograph		3. Original or certified copy of a birth certificate issued by a state, county, municipal authority or outlying possession of the United States bearing an official seal
4. Unexpired foreign passport, with *I-551 stamp or* attached *INS Form I-94* indicating unexpired employment authorization		4. Voter's registration card		4. Native American tribal document
5. Alien Registration Receipt Card with photograph *(INS Form I-151 or I-551)*		5. U.S. Military card or draft record		5. U.S. Citizen ID Card *(INS Form I-197)*
6. Unexpired Temporary Resident Card *(INS Form I-688)*		6. Military dependent's ID card		6. ID Card for use of Resident Citizen in the United States *(INS Form I-179)*
7. Unexpired Employment Authorization Card *(INS Form I-688A)*		7. U.S. Coast Guard Merchant Mariner Card		7. Unexpired employment authorization document issued by the INS *(other than those listed under List A)*
8. Unexpired Reentry Permit *(INS Form I-327)*		8. Native American tribal document		
9. Unexpired Refugee Travel Document *(INS Form I-571)*		9. Driver's license issued by a Canadian government authority		
10. Unexpired Employment Authorization Document issued by the INS which contains a photograph *(INS Form I-688B)*		**For persons under age 18 who are unable to present a document listed above:**		
		10. School record or report card		
		11. Clinic, doctor, or hospital record		
		12. Day-care or nursery school record		

Illustrations of many of these documents appear in Part 8 of the Handbook for Employers (M-274)

Form I-9 (Rev. 11-21-91) N

Sample Income Statement (Profit & Loss Statement)

For Year: __________	January	February	March	April	May
INCOME					
Gross Sales					
Less returns and allowances					
Net Sales					
Cost of Goods					
Gross Profit					
GENERAL & ADMINISTRATIVE (G&A) EXPENSES					
Salaries and wages					
Employee benefits					
Payroll taxes					
Sales commissions					
Professional services					
Rent					
Maintenance					
Equipment rental					
Furniture and equipment purchase					
Depreciation and amortization					
Insurance					
Interest expenses					
Utilities					
Telephone					
Office supplies					
Postage and shipping					
Marketing and advertising					
Travel					
Entertainment					
Other					
Other					
TOTAL G&A EXPENSES					
Net income before taxes					
Provision for taxes on income					
NET INCOME AFTER TAXES (Net Profit)					

Sample Income Statement (continued)

June	July	August	September	October	November	December	TOTAL

Sample Balance Sheet

Company Name: ____

Balance Sheet as of: ____

ASSETS:		LIABILITIES:		
Cash	________	Accounts payable		________
Marketable securities	________	Sales tax payable		________
Accounts receivable	________	Payroll payable		________
Inventory	________	Payroll taxes payable		________
Prepaid expenses	________	Income taxes payable		________
________	________	Accruals		________
TOTAL CURRENT ASSETS	________	TOTAL CURRENT LIABILITIES		________
Land	________	Notes Payable		
Buildings	________		________	________
Equipment	________		________	________
Accumulated depreciation	________		________	________
Leasehold improvements	________		________	________
Amortization of leasehold improvements	________		________	________
TOTAL FIXED ASSETS	________	TOTAL LONG-TERM LIABILITIES		________
Deposits	________	Draws		________
Long-term investments	________	Paid-in capital		________
Deferred Assets	________	Retained earnings prior		________
________	________	Retained earnings current		________
LONG-TERM ASSETS	________	TOTAL EQUITY		________
TOTAL ASSETS	$ ________	TOTAL EQUITY & LIABILITIES		$ ________

Note: Total Assets must equal Total Equity and Liabilities.

Sample Cash Flow Statement

For the period of: ______	**January**	**February**	**March**	**April**	**May**
SALES Cash sales					
CREDIT SALES COLLECTIBLE For this month					
From last month					
From prior months					
OTHER CASH INFLOWS Sale of equipment					
Loan proceeds					
TOTAL INFLOWS					
PURCHASES Accounts payable that will be paid this month					
Salaries, wages, and benefits					
Other operating costs					
Tax payments					
Loan fees, principal, interest					
Equipment purchases					
Dividends					
Other ______					
Total Outflows					
INFLOWS MINUS OUTFLOWS EQUALS NET CASH					
COMPANY CASH BUDGET					
Opening cash balance					
Cash inflows					
Cash available					
Cash outflows					
Net end of month cash					

Sample Cash Flow Statement (continued)

June	July	August	September	October	November	December	TOTAL

Sample Purchase Order

Purchase Order Number ______________________

From ______________________ Phone ______________________

Address ______________________

____

Vendor

____
____
____
____
____

Ship to

____
____
____
____

Job Reference # ______________________ Ship Via ______________________

Delivery Date ______________________ Terms ______________________

Quantity	Item Number	Description	Unit Cost	Extended Price

Conditions:

Our purchase order number must appear on all invoices, bills of lading, shipping memos, and packing lists. Goods are subject to our inspection and approval. If shipment will be delayed for any reason, advise us immediately and state all necessary facts. To avoid errors, note specifications carefully and let us know if unable to complete orders as written.

Subtotals $__________

Freight $__________

Tax $__________

Total $__________

Approved by ______________________ Date ______________________

Sample Invoice

Invoice Number ______________________

From ______________________ Phone ______________________

Address ______________________

______________________ Order Taken by ______________________

To ______________________ Phone ______________________

Address ______________________ Date of Order ______________________

______________________ Purchase Order # ______________________

Job Location ______________________ Ordered by

______________________ Starting Time

Quantity	Material	Price	Amount

Description of Work

____

____

____

____

____

Date	Hours	Rate	Amount

Total Labor $______

Other Charges

Recap of Job Invoice

Terms ______________________

Date Completed ______________________

I hereby acknowledge the satisfactory completion of the above work.

Authorized Signature ______________________

Total Materials $______

Total Labor $______

Total Other Charges $______

Tax $______

Total Due ______________________

Sample Job Description

POSITION MINIMUM REQUIREMENTS:

Education ______________________________
____
____

Experience ______________________________
____
____

Responsibility ______________________________
____
____

Initiative ______________________________
____
____

Skills ______________________________
____
____

Physical Requirements ______________________________
____
____

Mental Requirements ______________________________
____
____

Supervision ______________________________
____
____

Equipment Used ______________________________
____
____

Other Supervision ______________________________
____
____

Prepared by______________ Date ______________

Approved by ______________ Date ______________

Sample Job Application

Our policy is to provide equal employment opportunity to all qualified persons without regard to race, creed, color, religious belief, sex, age, national origin, physical or mental disability, or veteran status.

PERSONAL INFORMATION

Name ______________________________

Home Address ______________________________

Day Phone ______________ Evening Phone ______________

Social Security Number ______________________________

Are you a citizen or authorized by INS to work? (Documentation may be required.) ☐ Yes ☐ No

Have you ever been convicted of a felony? (This will not necessarily affect your application.) ☐ Yes ☐ No

EMPLOYMENT DESIRED

Have you ever applied for employment here? ☐ Yes ☐ No

When? ______________________________

Have you ever been employed by this company? ☐ Yes ☐ No

When? ______________ Where? ______________

Are you presently employed? ☐ Yes ☐ No

May we contact your employer? ☐ Yes ☐ No

Are you available for full-time work? ☐ Yes ☐ No

Are you available for part-time work? ☐ Yes ☐ No

Will you relocate? ☐ Yes ☐ No

Are you willing to travel? ☐ Yes ☐ No If yes, what percent? ______________

Date you can start: ______________________________

Desired position: ______________________________

Desired starting salary: ______________________________

Please list applicable skills: ______________________________

EDUCATION

School	Location	Major	Degree	Grade Average

Please list any scholastic honors received and offices held in school: ______________________________

____

Are you planning to continue your studies? ☐ Yes ☐ No

If yes, where and what courses of study? ______________________________

____

Sample Job Application (continued)

WORK EXPERIENCE

Please list employment from the last ten years, starting with the most recent employer.

Company Name ________________________________

Address ________________________________

Job Title ________________________________

Responsibilities ________________________________

____

Dates of Employment — From ______________ To ______________

Reason for Leaving ________________________________

Company Name ________________________________

Address ________________________________

Job Title ________________________________

Responsibilities ________________________________

____

Dates of Employment — From ______________ To ______________

Reason for Leaving ________________________________

Company Name ________________________________

Address ________________________________

Job Title ________________________________

Responsibilities ________________________________

____

Dates of Employment — From ______________ To ______________

Reason for Leaving ________________________________

Company Name ________________________________

Address ________________________________

Job Title ________________________________

Responsibilities ________________________________

____

Dates of Employment — From ______________ To ______________

Reason for Leaving ________________________________

Attach additional sheet if necessary.

Sample Job Application (continued)

REFERENCES

List three personal references, not related to you, whom have known you more than one year:

Name ______________________ Phone ____________________ Years Known __________

Address ____

Name ______________________ Phone ____________________ Years Known __________

Address ____

Name ______________________ Phone ____________________ Years Known __________

Address ____

EMERGENCY CONTACT

In case of emergency, please notify: ____

Name ___________________________________ Phone ____________________________

Address ____

Name ___________________________________ Phone ____________________________

Address ____

PLEASE READ BEFORE SIGNING

I certify that all information provided by me on this application is true and complete to the best of my knowledge and that I have withheld nothing which, if disclosed, would alter the integrity of this application.

I authorize my previous employers, schools or persons listed as references to give any information regarding my employment or educational record. I agree that this company and my previous employers will not be held liable in any respect if a job is not extended, or is withdrawn, or employment is terminated because of false statements, omissions or answers made by myself on this application. In the event of any employment with this company I will comply with all rules and regulations as set by the company in any communication distributed to the employees.

In compliance with the Immigration Reform and Control Act of 1986, I understand that I am required to provide approved documentation to the company, which verifies my right to work in the United States on the first day of employment. I have received from the company a list of approved documents which are required.

I understand that employment at this company is "at will" which means that either I or this company can terminate the employment relationship at any time, with or without prior notice, and for any reason not prohibited by statute. All employment is continued on that basis. I hereby acknowledge that I have read and understand the above statements.

Signature ____ Date ______________________

Sample Job Application (continued)

IMMIGRATION REFORM AND CONTROL ACT REQUIREMENT

In compliance with the Immigration Reform and Control Act of 1986, you are required to provide approved documentation that verifies your right to work in the United States prior to your employment with this company. Please be prepared to provide us with the following documentation in the event you are offered and accept employment with our company.

Any one of the following: (These establish both identity and employment authorization.)

1. United States Passport.
2. Certificate of U.S. Citizenship (issued by INS).
3. Certificate of Naturalization (issued by INS).
4. Resident alien or other alien unexpired endorsement card, with photo or other approved identifying information which evidences authorizing employment.

Or one from List A and List B.

List A (These establish employment authorization.)

1. Social Security card.
2. Birth Certificate or other documentation which establishes U.S. nationality or birth.
3. Other approved documentation.

List B

1. Driver's License or similar government identification card with photo or other approved identifying information.
2. Other approved documentation of identity for applicants under age 16 or in a state which does not issue an I.D. card (other than a driver's license).

This verification process is a requirement for all employees hired after November 6, 1986.

Form W-4 – Employee's Withholding Allowance Certificate

Form W-4 (1998)

Purpose. Complete Form W-4 so your employer can withhold the correct Federal income tax from your pay. Because your tax situation may change, you may want to refigure your withholding each year.

Exemption from withholding. *If you are exempt, complete only lines 1, 2, 3, 4, and 7, and sign the form to validate it.* Your exemption for 1998 expires February 16, 1999.

Note: *You cannot claim exemption from withholding if (1) your income exceeds $700 and includes unearned income (e.g., interest and dividends) and (2) another person can claim you as a dependent on their tax return.*

Basic instructions. If you are not exempt, complete the Personal Allowances Worksheet. The worksheets on page 2 adjust your withholding allowances based on itemized deductions, adjustments to income, or two-earner/two-job situations. Complete all worksheets that apply. They will help you figure the number of withholding allowances you are entitled to claim. However, you may claim fewer allowances.

New—Child tax and higher education credits. For details on adjusting withholding for these and other credits, see **Pub. 919,** Is My Withholding Correct for 1998?

Head of household. Generally, you may claim head of household filing status on your tax return only if you are unmarried and pay more than 50% of the costs of keeping up a home for yourself and your dependent(s) or other qualifying individuals.

Nonwage income. If you have a large amount of nonwage income, such as interest or dividends, you should consider making estimated tax payments using Form 1040-ES. Otherwise, you may owe additional tax.

Two earners/two jobs. If you have a working spouse or more than one job, figure the total number of allowances you are entitled to claim on all jobs using worksheets from only one W-4. Your withholding will usually be most accurate when all allowances are claimed on the W-4 filed for the highest paying job and zero allowances are claimed for the others.

Check your withholding. After your W-4 takes effect, use Pub. 919 to see how the dollar amount you are having withheld compares to your estimated total annual tax. Get Pub. 919 especially if you used the Two-Earner/Two-Job Worksheet and your earnings exceed $150,000 (Single) or $200,000 (Married). To order Pub. 919, call 1-800-829-3676. Check your telephone directory for the IRS assistance number for further help.

Sign this form. Form W-4 is not valid unless you sign it.

Personal Allowances Worksheet

A Enter "1" for **yourself** if no one else can claim you as a dependent . . . . . **A** ______

B Enter "1" if:
- You are single and have only one job; or
- You are married, have only one job, and your spouse does not work; or
- Your wages from a second job or your spouse's wages (or the total of both) are $1,000 or less.

. . **B** ______

C Enter "1" for your **spouse.** But, you may choose to enter -0- if you are married and have either a working spouse or more than one job. (This may help you avoid having too little tax withheld.). . . . . **C** ______

D Enter number of **dependents** (other than your spouse or yourself) you will claim on your tax return . . . . **D** ______

E Enter "1" if you will file as **head of household** on your tax return (see conditions under **Head of household** above) . **E** ______

F Enter "1" if you have at least $1,500 of **child or dependent care expenses** for which you plan to claim a credit . . **F** ______

G **New—Child Tax Credit:** • If your total income will be between $16,500 and $47,000 ($21,000 and $60,000 if married), enter "1" for each eligible child. • If your total income will be between $47,000 and $80,000 ($60,000 and $115,000 if married), enter "1" if you have two or three eligible children, or enter "2" if you have four or more . . . . **G** ______

H Add lines A through G and enter total here. **Note:** This amount may be different from the number of exemptions you claim on your return. ▶ **H** ______

For accuracy, complete all worksheets that apply.
- If you plan to **itemize or claim adjustments to income** and want to reduce your withholding, see the Deductions and Adjustments Worksheet on page 2.
- If you are **single,** have **more than one job,** and your combined earnings from all jobs exceed $32,000 OR if you are **married** and have a **working spouse or more than one job,** and the combined earnings from all jobs exceed $55,000, see the Two-Earner/Two-Job Worksheet on page 2 to avoid having too little tax withheld.
- If **neither** of the above situations applies, **stop here** and enter the number from line H on line 5 of Form W-4 below.

Cut here and give the certificate to your employer. Keep the top part for your records.

Form **W-4**
Department of the Treasury
Internal Revenue Service

Employee's Withholding Allowance Certificate

▶ **For Privacy Act and Paperwork Reduction Act Notice, see page 2.**

OMB No. 1545-0010

1998

1 Type or print your first name and middle initial	Last name	**2** Your social security number
Home address (number and street or rural route)		**3** ☐ Single ☐ Married ☐ Married, but withhold at higher Single rate. **Note:** *If married, but legally separated, or spouse is a nonresident alien, check the Single box.*
City or town, state, and ZIP code		**4** If your last name differs from that on your social security card, check here and call 1-800-772-1213 for a new card . . . . ▶ ☐

5 Total number of allowances you are claiming (from line H above or from the worksheets on page 2 if they apply) . | **5** |

6 Additional amount, if any, you want withheld from each paycheck . . . . . | **6** | $

7 I claim exemption from withholding for 1998, and I certify that I meet **BOTH** of the following conditions for exemption:
- Last year I had a right to a refund of **ALL** Federal income tax withheld because I had **NO** tax liability **AND**
- This year I expect a refund of **ALL** Federal income tax withheld because I expect to have **NO** tax liability.

If you meet both conditions, enter "EXEMPT" here . . . . . ▶ | **7** |

Under penalties of perjury, I certify that I am entitled to the number of withholding allowances claimed on this certificate or entitled to claim exempt status.

Employee's signature ▶ **Date ▶** , 19

8 Employer's name and address (Employer: Complete 8 and 10 only if sending to the IRS)	**9** Office code (optional)	**10** Employer identification number

Cat. No. 10220Q

Form W-4 – Employee's Withholding Allowance Certificate (continued)

Form W-4 (1998) Page 2

Deductions and Adjustments Worksheet

Note: *Use this worksheet only if you plan to itemize deductions or claim adjustments to income on your 1998 tax return.*

1 Enter an estimate of your 1998 itemized deductions. These include qualifying home mortgage interest, charitable contributions, state and local taxes (but not sales taxes), medical expenses in excess of 7.5% of your income, and miscellaneous deductions. (For 1998, you may have to reduce your itemized deductions if your income is over $124,500 ($62,250 if married filing separately). Get Pub. 919 for details.) . . . 1 $ ______

2 Enter: { $7,100 if married filing jointly or qualifying widow(er); $6,250 if head of household; $4,250 if single; $3,550 if married filing separately } . . . 2 $ ______

3 **Subtract** line 2 from line 1. If line 2 is greater than line 1, enter -0- . . . 3 $ ______

4 Enter an estimate of your 1998 adjustments to income, including alimony, deductible IRA contributions, and education loan interest . . . 4 $ ______

5 **Add** lines 3 and 4 and enter the total . . . 5 $ ______

6 Enter an estimate of your 1998 nonwage income (such as dividends or interest) . . . 6 $ ______

7 **Subtract** line 6 from line 5. Enter the result, but not less than -0- . . . 7 $ ______

8 **Divide** the amount on line 7 by $2,500 and enter the result here. Drop any fraction . . . 8 ______

9 Enter the number from Personal Allowances Worksheet, line H, on page 1 . . . 9 ______

10 **Add** lines 8 and 9 and enter the total here. If you plan to use the Two-Earner/Two-Job Worksheet, also enter this total on line 1 below. Otherwise, **stop here** and enter this total on Form W-4, line 5, on page 1 . . . 10 ______

Two-Earner/Two-Job Worksheet

Note: *Use this worksheet only if the instructions for line H on page 1 direct you here.*

1 Enter the number from line H on page 1 (or from line 10 above if you used the Deductions and Adjustments Worksheet) 1 ______

2 Find the number in **Table 1** below that applies to the **LOWEST** paying job and enter it here . . . 2 ______

3 If line 1 is **GREATER THAN OR EQUAL TO** line 2, subtract line 2 from line 1. Enter the result here (if zero, enter -0-) and on Form W-4, line 5, on page 1. **DO NOT** use the rest of this worksheet . . . 3 ______

Note: *If line 1 is* ***LESS THAN*** *line 2, enter -0- on Form W-4, line 5, on page 1. Complete lines 4–9 to calculate the additional withholding amount necessary to avoid a year end tax bill.*

4 Enter the number from line 2 of this worksheet . . . 4 ______

5 Enter the number from line 1 of this worksheet . . . 5 ______

6 **Subtract** line 5 from line 4 . . . 6 ______

7 Find the amount in **Table 2** below that applies to the **HIGHEST** paying job and enter it here . . . 7 $ ______

8 **Multiply** line 7 by line 6 and enter the result here. This is the additional annual withholding amount needed 8 $ ______

9 Divide line 8 by the number of pay periods remaining in 1998. (For example, divide by 26 if you are paid every other week and you complete this form in December 1997.) Enter the result here and on Form W-4, line 6, page 1. This is the additional amount to be withheld from each paycheck . . . 9 $

Table 1: Two-Earner/Two-Job Worksheet

Married Filing Jointly				All Others			
If wages from **LOWEST** paying job are—	Enter on line 2 above	If wages from **LOWEST** paying job are—	Enter on line 2 above	If wages from **LOWEST** paying job are—	Enter on line 2 above	If wages from **LOWEST** paying job are—	Enter on line 2 above
0 - $4,000	0	38,001 - 43,000	8	0 - $5,000	0	70,001 - 85,000	8
4,001 - 7,000	1	43,001 - 54,000	9	5,001 - 11,000	1	85,001 - 100,000	9
7,001 - 12,000	2	54,001 - 62,000	10	11,001 - 16,000	2	100,001 and over	10
12,001 - 18,000	3	62,001 - 70,000	11	16,001 - 21,000	3		
18,001 - 24,000	4	70,001 - 85,000	12	21,001 - 25,000	4		
24,001 - 28,000	5	85,001 - 100,000	13	25,001 - 42,000	5		
28,001 - 33,000	6	100,001 - 110,000	14	42,001 - 55,000	6		
33,001 - 38,000	7	110,001 and over	15	55,001 - 70,000	7		

Table 2: Two-Earner/Two-Job Worksheet

Married Filing Jointly		All Others	
If wages from **HIGHEST** paying job are—	Enter on line 7 above	If wages from **HIGHEST** paying job are—	Enter on line 7 above
0 - $50,000	$400	0 - $30,000	$400
50,001 - 100,000	760	30,001 - 60,000	760
100,001 - 130,000	840	60,001 - 120,000	840
130,001 - 240,000	970	120,001 - 250,000	970
240,001 and over	1,070	250,001 and over	1,070

Privacy Act and Paperwork Reduction Act Notice. We ask for the information on this form to carry out the Internal Revenue laws of the United States. The Internal Revenue Code requires this information under sections 3402(f)(2)(A) and 6109 and their regulations. Failure to provide a completed form will result in your being treated as a single person who claims no withholding allowances. Routine uses of this information include giving it to the Department of Justice for civil and criminal litigation and to cities, states, and the District of Columbia for use in administering their tax laws.

You are not required to provide the information requested on a form that is subject to the Paperwork Reduction Act unless the form displays a valid OMB control number. Books or records relating to a form or its instructions must be retained as long as their contents may become material in the administration of any Internal Revenue law. Generally, tax returns and return information are confidential, as required by Code section 6103.

The time needed to complete this form will vary depending on individual circumstances. The estimated average time is: **Recordkeeping** 46 min., **Learning about the law or the form** 10 min., **Preparing the form** 1 hr., 10 min. If you have comments concerning the accuracy of these time estimates or suggestions for making this form simpler, we would be happy to hear from you. You can write to the Tax Forms Committee, Western Area Distribution Center, Rancho Cordova, CA 95743-0001. **DO NOT** send the tax form to this address. Instead, give it to your employer.

Sample Performance Review

Name ____

Job Title ____

Department ____

Supervisor ____

Date Hired ______________ Last Review Date ____________ Today's Date ________

The following definitions apply to each factor rated below. (See page 4 for full explanation)

Level 6 — Far exceeds job requirements
Level 5 — Consistently exceeds job requirements
Level 4 — Meets and usually exceeds job requirements
Level 3 — Consistently meets job requirements
Level 2 — Inconsistent in meeting job requirements
Level 1 — Does not meet job requirements
(Circle appropriate number.)

Quantity of Work Level 1 2 3 4 5 6

Volume of work regularly produced. Speed and consistency of output .

Comments: ____

____

____

____

Quality of Work Level 1 2 3 4 5 6

Extent to which employee can be counted upon to carry out assignments to completion.

Comments: ____

____

____

____

Job Cooperation Level 1 2 3 4 5 6

Amount of interest and enthusiasm shown in work.

Comments: ____

____

____

____

Sample Performance Review (continued)

Ability to work with others Level 1 2 3 4 5 6

Extent to which employee effectively interacts with others in the performance of his/her job.

Comments: ______________________________

____

____

____

Adaptability Level 1 2 3 4 5 6

Extent to which employee is able to perform a variety of tasks within the scope of his/her job.

Comments: ______________________________

____

____

____

Job Knowledge Level 1 2 3 4 5 6

Extent of job information and understanding possessed by employee.

Comments: ______________________________

____

____

____

Initiative Level 1 2 3 4 5 6

Extent to which employee is a self starter in attaining objectives of the job.

Comments: ______________________________

____

____

____

Overall Performance Evaluation Level 1 2 3 4 5 6

Comments: ______________________________

____

____

____

____

____

____

Sample Performance Review (continued)

Attendance ☐ Problem ☐ No Problem

Volume of work regularly produced. Speed and consistency of output

Comments: ______

______

______

______

EMPLOYEE'S CAREER DEVELOPMENT

Strengths: ______

______

______

______

______

Development Needs: ______

______

______

______

______

Development Plan (Include Long Range): ______

______

______

______

EMPLOYEE'S COMMENTS (optional)

General comments about your performance: ______

______

______

______

______

Read and Acknowledged by:

Employee ______ Date ______

Approvals

Supervisor ______ Date ______

Department Manager ______ Date ______

Personnel ______ Date ______

Owner or CEO ______ Date ______

APPENDIX B

Federal Agency Contacts

FEDERAL INFORMATION CENTER (800) 688-9889	**Purpose: A one-stop phone number to help you reach other federal numbers.**
U.S. SMALL BUSINESS ADMINISTRATION (SBA) FIELD OFFICES *http://www.sba.gov* (Web site)	**Purpose: Free financial assistance and counseling on creating a marketing plan to developing a business plan.**

Maryland Regional Office
475 Allendale Road
King of Prussia, PA 19406
(610) 962-3710
(610) 962-3743 (FAX)

Maryland District Office
10 South Howard Street
Baltimore, MD 21201-2525
(410) 962-4392
(410) 962-1805 (FAX)

- ❑ **Date to contact:** ____________
- ❑ **Questions to Ask:**

____
____
____
____

- ❑ **Who you spoke with:**

____
____
____
____
____
____
____

- ❑ **Date Replied:** ____________

SBA Answer Desk
(800) UASK-SBA
(202) 205-7333 (TDD)
(202) 205-7064 (FAX)

Purpose: A 24-hour computerized phone message system for answers related to small business.

SBA OnLine
(800) 697-4636 (limited access)
(900) 463-4636 (full access)
(202) 401-9600 (D.C. metro area)

Purpose: Electronic bulletin board that gives current information on starting and running a business.

U.S. Business Advisor
Office of Technology
Mail Code 6470
409 3rd Street, SW
Washington, D.C. 20416
(202) 205-6450
(202) 205-7754
http://www.business.gov (Web site)

Purpose: Electronic one-stop center for making electronic links to all government business sites.

BUSINESS INFORMATION CENTER (BIC)

Purpose: To get counseling and training for your new or expanding business.

Business Information Center
SBA/Nations Bank/MDBA/Bell Atlantic
Small Business Resource Center
3 West Baltimore Street
Baltimore, MD 21201
(410) 605-0990
(410) 605-0995 (FAX)

- ❑ **Date to contact:** ____________
- ❑ **Questions to Ask:**

  ____
  ____
  ____
  ____
  ____
  ____
  ____
  ____

- ❑ **Who you spoke with:**

  ____
  ____
  ____

- ❑ **Date Replied:** ____________

NATIONAL BUSINESS INCUBATION ASSOCIATION (NBIA)
http://www.nbia.org (Web site)

Purpose: Will help you locate the nearest business incubator.

NBIA Headquarters
20 East Circle Drive, Suite 190
Athens, OH 45701-4331
(740) 593-4331
(740) 593-1996 (FAX)

- ❑ Date to contact: ________________
- ❑ Questions to Ask:

____
____
____
____
____

- ❑ Who you spoke with:

____
____
____
____

- ❑ Date Replied: ________________

U.S. DEPARTMENT OF COMMERCE
http://www.doc.gov (Web site)

Purpose: Serves as the umbrella agency for a variety of programs geared toward business.

Headquarters
14th and Constitution Avenue, NW
Washington, D.C. 20230
(202) 482-2000
(202) 482-5270 (FAX)

- ❑ Date to contact: ________________
- ❑ Questions to Ask:

____
____
____
____
____

- ❑ Who you spoke with:

____
____
____

- ❑ Date Replied: ________________

Bureau of Economic Analysis (BEA)
Public Information Office
Bureau of Economic Analysis
U.S. Department of Commerce, BE-53
Washington, D.C. 20230
(202) 606-9900
(202) 606-5355 (TDD)

For information on services:
STAT-USA
(202) 482-1986
http://www.stat-usa.gov (Web site)

❑ Date to contact: ________________

❑ Questions to Ask:

____

____

____

____

❑ Who you spoke with:

____

____

❑ Date Replied: ____________________

Office of Consumer Affairs
(202) 482-5001 or 8021 (Automated consumer lines)
(202) 482-6007 (FAX)
http://www.osec.doc.gov/oca (Web site)
caffairs@doc.gov (email)

❑ Date to contact: ________________

❑ Questions to Ask:

____

____

____

____

❑ Who you spoke with:

____

____

❑ Date Replied: ____________________

U.S. Census Bureau
105 South 7th Street, 1st Floor
Philadelphia, PA 19106-3395
(215) 597-4920
(215) 597-7507 (FAX)
http://www.census.gov (Web site)

❑ Date to contact: ________________

❑ Questions to Ask:

____

____

____

❑ Who you spoke with:

____

____

❑ Date Replied: ____________________

Economic Development Administration (EDA)
14th and Constitution Avenue, Room 7800B
Washington, D.C. 20230
(202) 482-5112
http://www.doc.gov/eda (Web site)

- ❑ Date to contact: ____________
- ❑ Questions to Ask:
  ____
  ____
  ____
  ____
- ❑ Who you spoke with:
  ____
  ____
- ❑ Date Replied: ____________

Philadelphia EDA Regional Office
(serving Maryland)
Curtis Center, Suite 140 South
Independence Square West
Philadelphia, PA 19106
(215) 597-4603
(215) 597-6669 (FAX)
http://www.doc.gov (Web site)

- ❑ Date to contact: ____________
- ❑ Questions to Ask:
  ____
  ____
  ____
  ____
- ❑ Who you spoke with:
  ____
  ____
- ❑ Date Replied: ____________

International Trade Administration (ITA)
Trade Information Center
(800) USA-TRADE (872-8723)
(800) TDD-TRADE (TDD, 833-8723)
(202) 482-4473 (FAX)
http://www.ita.doc.gov (Web site)

- ❑ Date to contact: ____________
- ❑ Questions to Ask:
  ____
  ____
  ____
- ❑ Who you spoke with:
  ____
  ____
- ❑ Date Replied: ____________

Minority and Business Development Agency
U.S. Department of Commerce
14th and Constitution Avenue, NW
Room 5053
Washington, D.C. 20230
(202) 482-5061
(202) 482-2678 (FAX)
http://www.mbda.gov (Web site)

Philadelphia District MBDA Office
(serving Maryland)
600 Arch Street, Room 10128
Philadelphia, PA 19106
(215) 597-9236
(215) 597-1994 (FAX)

❑ Date to contact: ______________

❑ Questions to Ask:

____
____
____
____

❑ Who you spoke with:

____
____
____
____

❑ Date Replied: ______________

U.S. CHAMBER OF COMMERCE
http://www.uschamber.org (Web site)

Purpose: Provides a link between small business and government and is the main center for a nationwide network of local chambers of commerce.

Chamber Headquarters
1615 H Street, NW
Washington, D.C. 20062-2000
(202) 659-6000
(800) 649-9719 (Nationwide)

❑ Date to contact: ______________

❑ Questions to Ask:

____
____
____
____

❑ Who you spoke with:

____
____
____
____

❑ Date Replied: ______________

INTERNAL REVENUE SERVICE (IRS)
http://www.irs.ustreas.gov (Web site)

Purpose: To register to pay withholding tax (FUTA, unemployment, SSI, FICA), income, and corporate taxes.

Taxpayer Education Coordinator
31 Hopkins Plaza, Room 1208
Baltimore, MD 21201
(410) 962-2222 (in Baltimore)
(800) 829-1040 (Nationwide)
(410) 962-0967 (FAX)

- ❑ **Date to contact:** ________________
- ❑ **Questions to Ask:**

____
____
____
____
____
____
____

- ❑ **Who you spoke with:**

____
____
____
____
____

- ❑ **Date Replied:** ________________

Tele-TIN
Entity Control
Philadelphia, PA 19255
(215) 516-6999

Purpose: To apply for an employer identification number (EIN). Note: you must complete *Form SS-4* before you call.

Tele-Tax
(410) 244-7306 (in Baltimore)
(800) 829-4477 (Nationwide)

Purpose: Recorded tax information available 24 hours a day on a wide variety of tax-related subjects.

Internal Revenue Information Services (IRIS)
(703) 321-8020
(800) TAX-FORM (For publications by mail)

Purpose: To access a government bulletin board called FedWorld for IRS publications, forms, and instructions.

EQUAL EMPLOYMENT OPPORTUNITY COMMISSION (EEOC) *http://www.eeoc.gov* (Web site)	**Purpose: To learn employer responsibilities under ADA and obtain minimum wage poster.**
EEOC Publications Information Center P.O. Box 12549 Cincinnati, OH 45212-0549 (800) 669-3362	❑ Date to contact: ____________ ❑ Questions to Ask: ____________ ____________ ____________ ____________ ❑ Who you spoke with: ____________ ____________ ____________ ____________ ❑ Date Replied: ____________
EEOC Headquarters 1801 L Street, NW Washington, D.C. 20507 (202) 663-4900 (202) 663-4494 (TDD) (800) 669-4000 (Connection to nearest EEOC field office) (800) 669-6820 (TDD for connection to nearest EEOC field office)	❑ Date to contact: ____________ ❑ Questions to Ask: ____________ ____________ ____________ ____________ ____________ ____________ ❑ Who you spoke with: ____________ ____________ ____________ ____________ ____________ ____________ ____________ ❑ Date Replied: ____________

EEOC Baltimore District Office
City Crescent Building
10 South Howard Street, 3rd Floor
Baltimore, MD 21201
(410) 962-3932
(410) 962- 6065 (TDD)
(410) 962-4270 (FAX)

❑ Date to contact: ____________

❑ Questions to Ask:

____
____
____
____
____
____

❑ Who you spoke with:

____
____
____
____

❑ Date Replied: ____________

ENVIRONMENTAL PROTECTION AGENCY
http://www.epa.gov/r3earth/ (Web site)

Purpose: For assistance in complying with federal EPA requirements.

EPA Region 3
841 Chestnut Building
Philadelphia, PA 19107
(215) 566-5000

❑ Date to contact: ____________

❑ Questions to Ask:

____
____
____
____
____
____

❑ Who you spoke with:

____
____
____
____
____

❑ Date Replied: ____________

FEDERAL TRADE COMMISSION (FTC)
http://www.ftc.gov (Web site)

Purpose: To find out federal disclosure information on franchise opportunities.

FTC Headquarters
600 Pennsylvania Avenue, NW
Washington, D.C. 20580
(202) 326-3128 or 3761 (Consumer response centers)
(202) 326-2012 (FAX)

Cleveland Regional Office (serving Maryland)
Federal Trade Commission
1111 Superior Avenue, Suite 200
Cleveland, OH 44114-2507
(216) 263-3410
(216) 263-3426 (FAX)

- ❑ **Date to contact:** ____________
- ❑ **Questions to Ask:**

____
____
____
____
____
____

- ❑ **Who you spoke with:**

____
____
____
____
____

- ❑ **Date Replied:** ____________

Bureau of Consumer Protection
Division of Service Industry Protection
601 Pennsylvania Avenue, NW
Washington, D.C. 20580
(202) 326-3220 (General questions)
http://www.ftc.gov/bcp/bcpsip.htm (Web site)

- ❑ **Date to contact:** ____________
- ❑ **Questions to Ask:**

____
____
____
____
____
____

- ❑ **Who you spoke with:**

____
____
____
____
____

- ❑ **Date Replied:** ____________

IMMIGRATION AND NATURALIZATION SERVICE (INS)
http://www.ins.usdoj.gov (Web site)

Purpose: To find the employer relations office nearest you to assist with *Form I-9*.

(800) 755-0777
(800) 870-3676 (Forms requests)

- ❑ Date to contact: ____________
- ❑ Questions to Ask:

____
____
____
____
____
____

- ❑ Who you spoke with:

____
____
____
____
____

- ❑ Date Replied: ____________

U.S. DEPARTMENT OF LABOR (DOL)
http://www.dol.gov (Web site)

Purpose: To find out about federal wage and hour and employment laws.

Wage-Hour Division
31 Hopkins Plaza
913 Federal Building
Baltimore, MD 21201
(410) 962-2265 (General information)
(410) 962-2240 (Other questions)

- ❑ Date to contact: ____________
- ❑ Questions to Ask:

____
____
____

- ❑ Who you spoke with:

____
____
____
____

- ❑ Date Replied: ____________

EMPLOYER SUPPORT OF THE GUARD AND RESERVE
http://www.ncesgr.osd.mil (Web site)

Purpose: For information and mediation on understanding and applying the law related to military leave.

National Committee
1555 Wilson Boulevard, Suite 200
Arlington, VA 22209-2405
(800) 336-4590
(703) 696-1411 (FAX)

❑ Date to contact: ____________

❑ Questions to Ask:

____
____
____
____
____
____

❑ Who you spoke with:

____
____
____

❑ Date Replied: ____________

U.S. PATENT AND TRADEMARK OFFICE
http://www.uspto.gov (Web site)

Purpose: To obtain a federal trademark, servicemark, or trade name.

For new trademark applications:
Box NEW APP FEE
Assistant Commissioner for Trademarks
2900 Crystal Drive
Arlington, VA 22202-3513
(800) 786-9199
(703) 308-HELP (Trademark assistance)
(703) 305-7785 (TDD)
(703) 305-7786 (FAX)

Trademark Assistance Center
(703) 308-9000
(703) 308-7016 (FAX)

❑ Date to contact: ____________

❑ Questions to Ask:

____
____
____
____
____
____

❑ Who you spoke with:

____
____
____

❑ Date Replied: ____________

APPENDIX C

State and Private Agency Contacts

MARYLAND SECRETARY OF STATE
http://www.sos.state.md.us (Web site)

Purpose: Registers and regulates all trademarks and servicemarks for Maryland businesses.

State House
Annapolis, MD 21401

(410) 974-5521
(888) 874-0013 (in Maryland)
(410) 974-5190 (FAX)

- ❑ **Date to contact:** ____________

- ❑ **Questions to Ask:**

____
____
____
____
____
____
____
____
____

- ❑ **Who you spoke with:**

____
____
____
____
____

- ❑ **Date Replied:** ____________

DINGMAN CENTER FOR ENTREPRENEURSHIP
http://www.mbs.umd.edu/dingman (Web site)

Purpose: Acts as the state's one-stop business assistance center.

University of Maryland
Van Munching Hall, Room 4361
College Park, MD 20742

(301) 405-2144
(301) 314-9152 (FAX)

- ❑ Date to contact: ____________
- ❑ Questions to Ask:
____
____
____
____
- ❑ Who you spoke with:
____
____
____
____
- ❑ Date Replied: ____________

MARYLAND COMPTROLLER OF THE TREASURY
http://www.comp.state.md.us (Web site)

Purpose: Collects sales, income, and unemployment taxes.

301 West Preston Street
Baltimore, MD 21201

(410) 767-1995
(410) 974-FAXX (Forms-by-FAXX)
(410) 767-1571 (FAX)

Maryland Taxpayer Registration Assistance Center (TRAC)

(410) 767-1318
(800) 492-1751 (in Maryland)

Taxpayer Service Section

(410) 767-1300
(800) 492-1751 (in Maryland)

- ❑ Date to contact: ____________
- ❑ Questions to Ask:
____
____
____
____
- ❑ Who you spoke with:
____
____
____
____
- ❑ Date Replied: ____________

MARYLAND STATE DEPARTMENT OF ASSESSMENTS AND TAXATION *http://www.dat.state.md.us* (Web site)	**Purpose: Registers sole proprietorships, LLPs, LLCs, corporations, and business trade names; collects property taxes.**
Corporate Charter Division 301 West Preston Street, #809 Baltimore, MD 21201 (410) 767-1350 (410) 333-7097 (FAX) **Trade Name Search and Registration** (410) 767-1330 **Corporate Name Availability Search** (410) 767-1330	❑ Date to contact: ______ ❑ Questions to Ask: ______ ______ ❑ Forms/Publications Requested: ______ ______ ❑ Who you spoke with: ______ ______ ❑ Date Replied: ______

MARYLAND DEPARTMENT OF LABOR, LICENSING, AND REGULATION *http://www.dllr.state.md.us* (Web site)	**Purpose: Provides information on state wage laws, employment standards, child labor, and safety and health programs.**
Labor and Industry Division 1100 North Eutaw Street, Room 607 Baltimore, MD 21201 (410) 767-2357 (Employment standards) (410) 333-7303 (FAX) **Maryland Occupational Safety and Health (MOSH) Training and Education Unit** 312 Marshall Avenue Laurel, MD 20707 (301) 483-8406 (301) 483-8332 (FAX) **Office of Unemployment Insurance** Employer Assistance 1100 North Eutaw Street, Room 411 Baltimore, MD 21201 (410) 767-2649	❑ Date to contact: ______ ❑ Questions to Ask: ______ ______ ❑ Forms/Publications Requested: ______ ______ ______ ❑ Who you spoke with: ______ ______ ______ ❑ Date Replied: ______

MARYLAND DEPARTMENT OF BUSINESS AND ECONOMIC DEVELOPMENT *http://www.dbed.state.md.us/dbed* (Web site)	**Purpose: Provides information, services, and publications to support economic growth.**
Division of Regional Development 217 East Redwood Street, 10th Floor Baltimore, MD 21202 (410) 767-0882 (800) 543-1036 (Nationwide) (410) 333-1836 (FAX)	❑ Date to contact: ____________ ❑ Questions to Ask: ____________ ____________ ❑ Forms/Publications Requested: ____________ ____________ ❑ Who you spoke with: ____________ ____________ ❑ Date Replied: ____________
MARYLAND DEPARTMENT OF ENVIRONMENT *http://www.mde.state.md.us* (Web site)	**Purpose: Monitors environmental issues and provides information for business compliance.**
Small Business Assistance Program 2500 Broening Highway Baltimore, MD 21224 (410) 631-3165 (410) 631-4477 (FAX)	❑ Date to contact: ____________ ❑ Questions to Ask: ____________ ____________ ❑ Forms/Publications Requested: ____________ ____________ ❑ Who you spoke with: ____________ ____________ ❑ Date Replied: ____________

MARYLAND STATE DEPARTMENT OF NATURAL RESOURCES *http://www.dnr.state.md.us* (Web site)	Purpose: Regulates air and water quality, noise pollution, sewage and solid waste disposal, and mining.
580 Taylor Avenue Annapolis, MD 21401 (410) 260-8200 (410) 260-8024 (FAX)	❑ Date to contact: ________ ❑ Questions to Ask: ________ ________ ❑ Forms/Publications Requested: ________ ________ ❑ Who you spoke with: ________ ________ ❑ Date Replied: ________

MARYLAND STATE LICENSING BUREAU	Purpose: Provides licensing requirements for your occupation and registration information; will direct you to appropriate licensing agency specific to your occupation.
500 North Calvert Street Baltimore, MD 21202 (410) 333-6200 (410) 333-1229 (FAX)	❑ Date to contact: ________ ❑ Questions to Ask: ________ ________ ❑ Forms/Publications Requested: ________ ________ ❑ Who you spoke with: ________ ________ ❑ Date Replied: ________

WORKERS' COMPENSATION COMMISSION
http://www.charm.net/~wcc/ (Web site)

Purpose: Provides state workers' compensation information and requirements.

6 North Liberty Street
Baltimore, MD 21201-3785
(410) 767-0900
(800) 492-0479 (in Maryland)
(410) 333-8122 (FAX)

- ❑ Date to contact: ____________
- ❑ Questions to Ask:
  ____
  ____
- ❑ Forms/Publications Requested:
  ____
  ____
- ❑ Who you spoke with:
  ____
  ____
- ❑ Date Replied: ____________

INJURED WORKERS' INSURANCE FUND
http://www.iwif.com (Web site)

Purpose: The state fund that offers workers' compensation insurance.

Underwriting Department
8722 Loch Raven Boulevard
Towson, MD 21286-2235
(410) 494-2000
(800) 264-IWIF (Nationwide)
(410) 494-2001 (FAX)

- ❑ Date to contact: ____________
- ❑ Questions to Ask:
  ____
  ____
- ❑ Forms/Publications Requested:
  ____
  ____
- ❑ Who you spoke with:
  ____
  ____
- ❑ Date Replied: ____________

SMALL BUSINESS DEVELOPMENT CENTER (SBDC)
http://www.mbs.umd.edu/sbdc (Web site)

Purpose: This lead center will direct you to nearest SBDC counselor for free training and start-up assistance.

Maryland SBDC Network
7100 Baltimore Avenue, Suite 401
College Park, MD 20740-3627
(301) 403-8300
(301) 403-8303 (FAX)

❑ Date to contact: ____________

❑ Questions to Ask:

____

____

____

❑ Forms/Publications Requested:

____

____

❑ Who you spoke with:

____

____

❑ Date Replied: ____________

MARYLAND STATE DATA CENTER
http://www.inform.umd.edu/UMS+State/MD_Resources/MSDC (Web site)

Purpose: To provide the most updated census data for the state.

Maryland Office of Planning
301 West Preston Street
Baltimore, MD 21201
(410) 767-4450
(410) 767-4480 (FAX)

❑ Date to contact: ____________

❑ Questions to Ask:

____

____

____

❑ Forms/Publications Requested:

____

____

❑ Who you spoke with:

____

____

❑ Date Replied: ____________

MARYLAND CHAMBER OF COMMERCE
http://www.mdchamber.org (Web site)

Purpose: To promote member growth through an alliance of businesses and their employees.

60 West Street, Suite 100
Annapolis, MD 21401
(410) 269-0642
(410) 269-5247 (FAX)

- ❑ **Date to contact:** ________________
- ❑ **Questions to Ask:**

  ____

  ____

  ____
- ❑ **Forms/Publications Requested:**

  ____

  ____
- ❑ **Who you spoke with:**

  ____

  ____
- ❑ **Date Replied:** ________________

BALTIMORE AREA VISITORS CENTER

Purpose: For information on area attractions and events.

Constellation Pier
301 East Pratt Street
Baltimore, MD 21202
(410) 837-4636
(800) 282-6632 (Nationwide)
(410) 837-INFO (Recorded information)
(410) 837-7150 (International assistance)
(410) 576-0022 (International Visitors Center)

- ❑ **Date to contact:** ________________
- ❑ **Questions to Ask:**

  ____

  ____

  ____
- ❑ **Forms/Publications Requested:**

  ____

  ____
- ❑ **Who you spoke with:**

  ____

  ____

  ____
- ❑ **Date Replied:** ________________

STATE BUSINESS PUBLICATIONS

Baltimore Business Journal
111 Market Place, #720
Baltimore, MD 21202-1044
(410) 576-1161
(410) 752-3112 (FAX)

Metropolitan Business News
A.C.E. Communications, Inc.
5 Wood Valley Court, Suite One
Registers Town, MD 21136
(410) 433-0020
(410) 517-0011 (FAX)

Maryland Contract Weekly
P.O. Box 2249
Annapolis, MD 21404-2249
(410) 974-2486

The Daily Record
11 East Saratoga Street
Baltimore, MD 21202
(410) 752-1717

The Maryland Entrepreneur
The Dingman Center for Entrepreneurship
Maryland Business School
Van Munching Hall
College Park, MD 28742-1815
(301) 405-2144
(301) 314-9152 (FAX)

NATIONAL FEDERATION OF INDEPENDENT BUSINESSES (NFIB)

http://www.nfibonline.com (Web site)

Purpose: A nonprofit small business advocacy group that lobbies at both the state and federal level.

Membership Services Office – NFIB
P.O. Box 305043
Nashville, TN 37230-9900
(800) NFIB-NOW
(615) 872-5314 (FAX)

- ❑ Date to contact: ____________
- ❑ Questions to Ask:
  ____
  ____
  ____
- ❑ Forms/Publications Requested:
  ____
  ____
- ❑ Who you spoke with:
  ____
  ____
  ____
- ❑ Date Replied: ____________

NATIONAL ASSOCIATION FOR THE SELF-EMPLOYED® (NASE)

http://www.nase.org (Web site)

Purpose: A membership organization for small business owners; gives advice and valuable competitive information.

NASE Headquarters
P.O. Box 612067
Dallas, TX 75261-2067
(800) 232-NASE
(800) 551-4446 (FAX)

- ❑ Date to contact: ____________
- ❑ Questions to Ask:
  ____
  ____
  ____
- ❑ Forms/Publications Requested:
  ____
  ____
- ❑ Who you spoke with:
  ____
  ____
- ❑ Date Replied: ____________

SOCIETY OF RISK MANAGEMENT CONSULTANTS (SRMC)

Purpose: An organization that can assist in finding a professional and ethical insurance consultant.

SRMC Headquarters
300 Park Avenue, 17th Floor
New York, NY 10022
(800) 765-SRMC
(212) 572-6499 (FAX)

- ❑ Date to contact: ____________
- ❑ Questions to Ask:
  ____
  ____
  ____
- ❑ Forms/Publications Requested:
  ____
  ____
- ❑ Who you spoke with:
  ____
  ____
- ❑ Date Replied: ____________

NATIONAL VENTURE CAPITAL ASSOCIATION (NVCA)

http://www.nvca.org (Web site)

Purpose: To find sources of venture capital.

NVCA Headquarters
1655 North Fort Myer Drive, Suite 850
Arlington, VA 22209
(703) 524-2549
(703) 524-3940 (FAX)

- ❑ Date to contact: ____________
- ❑ Questions to Ask:
  ____
  ____
  ____
- ❑ Forms/Publications Requested:
  ____
  ____
- ❑ Who you spoke with:
  ____
  ____
- ❑ Date Replied: ____________

NATIONAL ASSOCIATION OF SMALL BUSINESS INVESTMENT COMPANIES (NASBIC)

http://www.nasbic.org (Web site)

Purpose: Central contact agency to find SBICs throughout the nation.

NASBIC Headquarters
666 11th Street NW, Suite 750
Washington, D.C. 20001

(202) 628-5055
(202) 628-5080 (FAX)

- ❑ **Date to contact:** ________________
- ❑ **Questions to Ask:**

  ____

  ____
- ❑ **Forms/Publications Requested:**

  ____

  ____
- ❑ **Who you spoke with:**

  ____

  ____
- ❑ **Date Replied:** ________________

APPENDIX D

State Loan Programs

PROGRAMS THROUGH MARYLAND DEPARTMENT OF BUSINESS AND ECONOMIC DEVELOPMENT

The following programs are administered by various state agencies and offices, as noted in each description. However, specific details of all the finance programs under this heading are available from the Marketing Division of the Maryland Department of Business and Economic Development (DBED). This should be the first agency you contact, as it might be able to direct you to newer or more specifically targeted financing programs than are presented here.

Maryland Department of Business and Economic Development
Division of Marketing
217 East Redwood Street
Baltimore, MD 21202
(410) 767-6870
(800) 811-0051
http://www.dbed.state.md.us/dbed (Web site)

ENTERPRISE INVESTMENT PROGRAM

This program makes direct equity investments or offers limited partnership interests up to $500,000 in technology-driven businesses whose principal business activity is located in Maryland. Investment is limited to a 15-year term and may not exceed 25% of total equity of the enterprise. This program is administered by the DBED's Financing Division.

CHALLENGE INVESTMENT PROGRAM

Also administered through the Financing Division, this program makes $50,000 to $100,000 royalty-bearing investments in startups with annual sales of less than $1 million and whose focus is development as opposed to research. To be eligible, a business must be technology driven, must have its principal place of activity located in Maryland, and must have completed its business plan. There is a coinvestor match of 1:1.

MARYLAND INDUSTRIAL DEVELOPMENT FINANCING AUTHORITY (MIDFA)

CONVENTIONAL PROGRAM

This loan program is open to industrial and most commercial businesses with the exception of certain retail establishments. The loans range from $35,000 to $5 million, and the MIDFA typically insures from 20% to 50% of the loan. Funds can be used to finance land, buildings, and machinery and equipment, government contracts, revolving credit lines, and certain costs, as well as provide working capital. Normal terms are 15 to 20 years on real estate, 7 to 10 years on equipment, and 2 to 5 years for term loans. For working capital, the period is usually 1 year or less. The MIDFA may insure up to 80% or $1 million of a loan or other obligation financed by traditional lenders.

MIDFA TAX-EXEMPT REVENUE BOND PROGRAM

Manufacturers and certain nonprofit organizations can apply for loans in the $1 to $10 million range through this tax-exempt, floating or fixed rate revenue bond program to finance land, new and existing buildings, new and used machinery and equipment, eligible costs, and working capital of up to 25% of total project cost. Normally, financing will not exceed 90% of real estate value or 75% of equipment cost. The bonds are issued by political subdivisions or MIDFA. The maximum loan term is 30 years, but normal terms are 15 to 20 years on real estate and 7 to 10 years on equipment.

MIDFA TAXABLE BOND PROGRAM

This $1-million-plus bond program is open to most industrial or commercial businesses and can be used to finance the same items listed for the tax-exempt revenue bond program, with the same terms. The interest is the conventional taxable floating rate. MIDFA may insure up to 100% of bond amount, but bonds may also be issued without MIDFA insurance.

SEAFOOD AND AQUACULTURE LOAN FUND

This secured, below-market-rate loan is available to individuals or businesses involved in seafood processing or aquaculture. Loans range from $20,000 to $800,000, and the maximum loan term is 20 years. The funds may be used to finance acquisition, construction, renovation and excavation of real property or the acquisition of equipment and fixtures. Interest is fixed at 2% below the prime rate.

TRADE FINANCING PROGRAM

If you own an industrial or commercial business that is engaged in the export and import of goods through Maryland ports and airports to the overseas market, this program may help you with pre- and post-shipment working capital needs, standby letters of credit required by foreign buyers, import letters of credit, and revolving credit lines (loan advances against export orders or contracts, and foreign accounts receivables). The program does not offer direct loans, only insurance of commercial loans and other obligations, normally in the $50,000 to $5 million range.

MARYLAND ENERGY FINANCING ADMINISTRATION (MEFA)

ENERGY FINANCING PROGRAM

This $800,000 to $160 million revenue bond program (both tax-exempt and taxable) is available to your business to help you conserve energy, cogenerate energy, produce fuels and other energy sources, or recycle materials. Funds may be used for the purchase of land, machinery, or equipment; acquisition, construction, or rehabilitation of a building or hydroelectric facilities; or working capital of up to 25% of total costs. Maximum participation is 80% to 90% of value, not to exceed 100% of cost. Interest rates can be floating or fixed, as determined by the lender. Normal terms are 15 to 20 years on real estate and 5 to 10 years on equipment.

MARYLAND SMALL BUSINESS DEVELOPMENT FINANCING AUTHORITY (MSBDFA)

CONTRACT FINANCING PROGRAM

If your business is at least 70% owned by socially and economically disadvantaged persons and holds government or public utility contracts, this loan program may be for you. Funds may be used to provide working capital required to begin, continue, and complete government or public utility contracts or to acquire machinery or equipment to perform these contracts. Direct loans of up to $500,000, or loan guarantees of up to 90% of project costs (not to exceed a maximum participation of $500,000), may be made for projects up to $2 million. The maximum interest rate is prime plus 2% for guaranteed loans, and 15% for direct loans.

MSBDFA LONG-TERM GUARANTY PROGRAM

Businesses that are owned 70% or more by socially and economically disadvantaged persons with 18 successive months of experience in the trade or business can apply for loan guarantees not to exceed the lesser of 80% of a loan or $600,000. These funds can be used to provide working capital; to acquire machinery, equipment, or real property to be used in the business; or to make improvements to real property owned by the business. Interest is variable, but no more than 2% over prime, and the loan term can extend up to ten years.

MSBDFA SURETY BOND PROGRAM

This program is available in two forms to independently owned small businesses. The guaranty program guarantees up to 90% of the face value of the bond (not to exceed a total exposure of $900,000) and guarantees reimbursement of losses on a bid, payment, or performance bond required in connection with projects where the majority of funds are from government or a regulated public utility. The direct bond program can directly issue bonds (not to exceed $750,000) on projects where the majority of funds are from government or a regulated public utility.

MSBDFA EQUITY PARTICIPATION INVESTMENT PROGRAM – TECHNOLOGY AND BUSINESS ACQUISITION COMPONENTS

Technology-based businesses and business acquisitions (the latter must be at least five years old and profitable two of the last three years) which will be owned 70% or more by disabled or socially or economically disadvantaged persons are eligible for this program. Funds from $100,000 to $3 million may be used to purchase machinery and equipment, real estate, inventory, sign packages and supplies, or furniture and fixtures; to finance leasehold improvements, construction, major renovation, or stock purchases; or to provide working capital. Maximum loan and investment term is seven years.

MSBDFA EQUITY PARTICIPATION INVESTMENT PROGRAM – FRANCHISE COMPONENT

To be eligible for this program, your business must be a franchise that is, or will be, at least 70% owned by disabled or socially or economically disadvantaged persons, and the owner's equity must equal at least 10% of the total project cost. Funds from $50,000 to $1.5 million may be used to purchase machinery and equipment, real estate, inventory, or furniture and fixtures; to finance leasehold improvements, construction, major renovation, or stock purchases; to pay franchise fees, or to provide working capital. Maximum loan and investment term is seven years for business acquisition and up to ten years for technology-based businesses.

MARYLAND DEPARTMENT OF HOUSING AND COMMUNITY DEVELOPMENT PROGRAMS

The Maryland Department of Housing and Community Development oversees a number of programs, mostly aimed at community assistance rather than business development although, some of these programs may empower communities to assist your business as well. A notable exception is the Neighborhood Business Development Program, described below, which directly assists businesses. For more information on this program, contact:

Maryland Department of Housing and Community Development
Neighborhood Business Development Program
Office of Neighborhood Revitalization
100 Community Place
Crownsville, MD 21032
(410) 514-7288
(410) 987-4660 (FAX)

NEIGHBORHOOD BUSINESS DEVELOPMENT PROGRAM (NBDP)

This program will provide flexible, gap financing of up to 50% of total project cost for your small business if you are starting up or expanding in an urban, suburban, or rural revitalization area in Maryland. To be eligible, your business' activities must contribute to a broader revitalization effort; for example, reuse of a vacant building or providing a needed service to area residents in a revitalization area. Personal guarantees and collateral are required for NBDP loans. The funds may be used for real estate acquisition and rehabilitation, construction, or expansion; for development of mixed-use projects (defined as up to twelve residential units with street-level commercial use); for leasehold improvements; for machinery and equipment purchases in tandem with renovation; and for working capital, again, in tandem with renovation.

Financing ranges from $25,000 to $500,000, not to exceed 50% of total project cost; the term is 5 to 20 years; and interest is at below-market fixed rates, currently ranging from 2% to 6%. A pre-lease of at least 51% of the structure is required. Speculative developments will not be considered.

Index

E

F

G

H

I

J

L

M

The Oasis Press® Order Form

SS03/98

Call, Mail, Email, or Fax Your Order to: PSI Research, P.O. Box 3727, Central Point, OR 97502
Email: sales@psi-research.com Website: http://www.psi-research.com
Order Phone USA & Canada: +1 800 228-2275 Inquiries & International Orders: +1 541 479-9464 Fax: +1 541 476-1479

TITLE	✔ BINDER	✔ PAPERBACK	QUANTITY	COST
Advertising Without An Agency		❏ $19.95		
Bottom Line Basics	❏ $39.95	❏ $19.95		
BusinessBasics: A Mircrobusiness Startup Guide		❏ $17.95		
The Business Environmental Handbook	❏ $39.95	❏ $19.95		
Business Owner's Guide to Accounting & Bookkeeping		❏ $19.95		
Buyer's Guide to Business Insurance	❏ $39.95	❏ $19.95		
California Corporation Formation Package	❏ $39.95	❏ $29.95		
Collection Techniques for a Small Business	❏ $39.95	❏ $19.95		
A Company Policy and Personnel Workbook	❏ $49.95	❏ $29.95		
Company Relocation Handbook	❏ $39.95	❏ $19.95		
CompControl: The Secrets of Reducing Worker's Compensation Costs	❏ $39.95	❏ $19.95		
Complete Book of Business Forms		❏ $19.95		
Connecting Online: Creating a Successful Image on the Internet		❏ $21.95		
Customer Engineering: Cutting Edge Selling Strategies	❏ $39.95	❏ $19.95		
Develop & Market Your Creative Ideas		❏ $15.95		
Developing International Markets		❏ $19.95		
Doing Business in Russia		❏ $19.95		
Draw The Line: A Sexual Harassment Free Workplace		❏ $17.95		
Entrepreneurial Decisionmaking		❏ $19.95		
The Essential Corporation Handbook		❏ $21.95		
the Essential Limited Liability Company Handbook	❏ $39.95	❏ $21.95		
Export Now: A Guide for Small Business	❏ $39.95	❏ $24.95		
Financial Decisionmaking: A Guide for the Non-Accountant		❏ $19.95		
Financial Management Techniques for Small Business	❏ $39.95	❏ $19.95		
Financing Your Small Business		❏ $19.95		
Franchise Bible: How to Buy a Franchise or Franchise Your Own Business	❏ $39.95	❏ $24.95		
Friendship Marketing: Growing Your Business by Cultivating Strategic Relationships		❏ $18.95		
Funding High-Tech Ventures		❏ $21.95		
Home Business Made Easy		❏ $19.95		
Information Breakthrough		❏ $22.95		
The Insider's Guide to Small Business Loans	❏ $29.95	❏ $19.95		
InstaCorp – Incorporate In Any State (Book & Software)		❏ $29.95		
Joysticks, Blinking Lights and Thrills		❏ $18.95		
Keeping Score: An Inside Look at Sports Marketing		❏ $18.95		
Know Your Market: How to Do Low-Cost Market Research	❏ $39.95	❏ $19.95		
The Leader's Guide		❏ $19.95		
Legal Expense Defense: How to Control Your Business' Legal Costs and Problems	❏ $39.95	❏ $19.95		
Location, Location, Location: How to Select the Best Site for Your Business		❏ $19.95		
Mail Order Legal Guide	❏ $45.00	❏ $29.95		
Managing People: A Practical Guide		❏ $21.95		
Marketing for the New Millennium: Applying New Techniques		❏ $19.95		
Marketing Mastery: Your Seven Step Guide to Success	❏ $39.95	❏ $19.95		
The Money Connection: Where and How to Apply for Business Loans and Venture Capital	❏ $39.95	❏ $24.95		
Moonlighting: Earn a Second Income at Home		❏ $15.95		
People Investment	❏ $39.95	❏ $19.95		
Power Marketing for Small Business	❏ $39.95	❏ $19.95		
Profit Power: 101 Pointers to Give Your Business a Competitive Edge		❏ $19.95		
Proposal Development: How to Respond and Win the Bid	❏ $39.95	❏ $21.95		
Raising Capital		❏ $19.95		
Renaissance 2000: Liberal Arts Essentials for Tomorrow's Leaders		❏ $22.95		
Retail in Detail: How to Start and Manage a Small Retail Business		❏ $15.95		
Secrets to High Ticket Selling		❏ $19.95		
Secrets to Buying and Selling a Business		❏ $24.95		
Secure Your Future: Financial Planning at Any Age	❏ $39.95	❏ $19.95		
The Small Business Insider's Guide to Bankers		❏ $18.95		
SmartStart Your (State) Business... series		❏ $19.95		
PLEASE SPECIFY WHICH STATE(S) YOU WANT:				
Smile Training Isn't Enough: The Three Secrets to Excellent Customer Service		❏ $19.95		
Start Your Business *(Available as a book and disk package)*		❏ $ 9.95 (without disk)		
BOOK SUB-TOTAL (Additional titles on other side)				

TITLE	✔ BINDER	✔ PAPERBACK	QUANTITY	COST
Starting and Operating a Business in...series *Includes FEDERAL section PLUS ONE STATE section*	❑ $34.95	❑ $27.95		
PLEASE SPECIFY WHICH STATE(S) YOU WANT:				
STATE SECTION ONLY (BINDER NOT INCLUDED) SPECIFY STATE(S):	❑ $8.95			
FEDERAL SECTION ONLY (BINDER NOT INCLUDED)	❑ $12.95			
U.S. EDITION (FEDERAL SECTION – 50 STATES AND WASHINGTON DC IN 11-BINDER SET)	❑ $295.95			
Successful Business Plan: Secrets & Strategies	❑ $49.95	❑ $27.95		
Successful Network Marketing for The 21st Century		❑ $15.95		
Surviving Success		❑ $19.95		
TargetSmart! Database Marketing for the Small Business		❑ $19.95		
Top Tax Saving Ideas for Today's Small Business		❑ $16.95		
Twenty-One Sales in a Sale: What Sales Are You Missing?		❑ $19.95		
Which Business? Help in Selecting Your New Venture		❑ $18.95		
Write Your Own Business Contracts	❑ $39.95	❑ $24.95		
BOOK SUB-TOTAL (Be sure to figure your amount from the previous side)				

OASIS SOFTWARE **Please specify which computer operating system you use (DOS, MacOS, or Windows)**

TITLE	✔ Windows	✔ MacOS	Price	QUANTITY	COST
California Corporation Formation Package ASCII Software	❑	❑	$ 39.95		
Company Policy & Personnel Software Text Files	❑	❑	$ 49.95		
Financial Management Techniques (Full Standalone)	❑		$ 99.95		
Financial Templates	❑	❑	$ 69.95		
The Insurance Assistant Software (Full Standalone)	❑		$ 29.95		
Start Your Business (Software for Windows™)	❑		$ 19.95		
Successful Business Plan (Software for Windows™)	❑		$ 99.95		
Successful Business Plan Templates	❑	❑	$ 69.95		
The Survey Genie - Customer Edition (Full Standalone)	❑ $199.95 (WIN)	❑ $149.95 (DOS)			
The Survey Genie - Employee Edition (Full Standalone)	❑ $199.95 (WIN)	❑ $149.95 (DOS)			
SOFTWARE SUB-TOTAL					

BOOK & DISK PACKAGES **Please specify which computer operating system you use (DOS, MacOS, or Windows)**

TITLE	✔ Windows	✔ MacOS	✔ Binder	✔ Paperback	QUANTITY	COST
The Buyer's Guide to Business Insurance w/ Insurance Assistant	❑		❑ $ 59.95	❑ $ 39.95		
California Corporation Formation Binder Book & ASCII Software	❑	❑	❑ $ 69.95	❑ $ 59.95		
Company Policy & Personnel Book & Software Text Files	❑	❑	❑ $ 89.95	❑ $ 69.95		
Financial Management Techniques Book & Software	❑		❑ $129.95	❑ $ 119.95		
Start Your Business Paperback & Software (Software for Windows™)	❑			❑ $ 24.95		
Successful Business Plan Book & Software for Windows™	❑		❑ $125.95	❑ $109.95		
Successful Business Plan Book & Software Templates	❑	❑	❑ $109.95	❑ $ 89.95		
BOOK & DISK PACKAGE SUB-TOTAL						

AUDIO CASSETTES

TITLE	Price	QUANTITY	COST
Power Marketing Tools For Small Business	❑ $ 49.95		
The Secrets To Buying & Selling A Business	❑ $ 49.95		
AUDIO CASSETTES SUB-TOTAL			

Sold To: **Please give street address**

NAME:

Title:

Company:

Street Address:

City/State/Zip:

Daytime Phone: Email:

Ship To: **If different than above, please give alternate street address**

NAME:

Title:

Company:

Street Address:

City/State/Zip:

Daytime Phone:

Your Grand Total

SUB-TOTALS (from other side)	$
SUB-TOTALS (from this side)	$
SHIPPING (see chart below)	$
TOTAL ORDER	$

If your purchase is:	Shipping costs within the USA:
$0 - $25	$5.00
$25.01 - $50	$6.00
$50.01 - $100	$7.00
$100.01 - $175	$9.00
$175.01 - $250	$13.00
$250.01 - $500	$18.00
$500.01+	4% of total merchandise

Payment Information: **Rush service is available, call for details.**
International and Canadian Orders: Please call for quote on shipping.

☐ CHECK Enclosed payable to PSI Research — Charge: ☐ VISA ☐ MASTERCARD ☐ AMEX ☐ DISCOVER

Card Number: — Expires:

Signature: — Name On Card:

Use this form to register for an advance notification of updates, new books and software releases, plus special customer discounts!

Please answer these questions to let us know how our products are working for you, and what we could do to serve you better.

SmartStart Your Maryland Business

Rate this product's overall quality of information:
☐ Excellent
☐ Good
☐ Fair
☐ Poor

Rate the quality of printed materials:
☐ Excellent
☐ Good
☐ Fair
☐ Poor

Rate the format:
☐ Excellent
☐ Good
☐ Fair
☐ Poor

Did the product provide what you needed?
☐ Yes ☐ No

If not, what should be added?

____
____
____
____
____
____
____
____
____
____
____
____

This product is:
☐ Clear and easy to follow
☐ Too complicated
☐ Too elementary

Were the worksheets easy to use?
☐ Yes ☐ No ☐ N/A

Should we include?
☐ More worksheets
☐ Fewer worksheets
☐ No worksheets

How do you feel about the price?
☐ Lower than expected
☐ About right
☐ Too expensive

How many employees are in your company?
☐ Under 10 employees
☐ 10 - 50 employees
☐ 51 - 99 employees
☐ 100 - 250 employees
☐ Over 250 employees

How many people in the city your company is in?
☐ 50,000 - 100,000
☐ 100,000 - 500,000
☐ 500,000 - 1,000,000
☐ Over 1,000,000
☐ Rural (Under 50,000)

What is your type of business?
☐ Retail
☐ Service
☐ Government
☐ Manufacturing
☐ Distributor
☐ Education

What types of products or services do you sell?

____
____
____

What is your position in the company?
(please check one)
☐ Owner
☐ Administrative
☐ Sales/Marketing
☐ Finance
☐ Human Resources
☐ Production
☐ Operations
☐ Computer/MIS

How did you learn about this product?
☐ Recommended by a friend
☐ Used in a seminar or class
☐ Have used other PSI products
☐ Received a mailing
☐ Saw in bookstore
☐ Saw in library
☐ Saw review in:
  ☐ Newspaper
  ☐ Magazine
  ☐ Radio/TV

Where did you buy this product?
☐ Catalog
☐ Bookstore
☐ Office supply
☐ Consultant

Would you purchase other business tools from us?
☐ Yes ☐ No

If so, which products interest you?
☐ EXECARDS® Communications Cards
☐ Books for business
☐ Software

Would you recommend this product to a friend?
☐ Yes ☐ No

Do you use a personal computer?
☐ Yes ☐ No

If yes, which?
☐ Macintosh
☐ PC Compatible
☐ Other

Check all the ways you use computers?
☐ Word processing
☐ Accounting
☐ Spreadsheet
☐ Inventory
☐ Order processing
☐ Design/Graphics
☐ General Data Base
☐ Customer Information
☐ Scheduling
☐ Internet

May we call you to follow up on your comments?
☐ Yes ☐ No

May we add your name to our mailing list? ☐ Yes ☐ No

If you'd like us to send associates or friends a catalog, just list names and addresses on back.

Is there anything we should do to improve our products?

____

Just fill in your name and address here, fold (see back) and mail.

Name ______________________________________
Title ______________________________________
Company ____________________________________
Phone ______________________________________
Address _____________________________________
City/State/Zip _______________________________
Email Address (Home) _______________ (Business) _____________

PSI Research creates this family of fine products to help you more easily and effectively manage your business activities:

The Oasis Press®
PSI Successful Business Library
PSI Successful Business Software
EXECARDS® Communication Tools

If you have friends or associates who might appreciate receiving our catalogs, please list here. Thanks!

Name__________	Name__________
Title__________	Title__________
Company__________	Company__________
Phone__________	Phone__________
Address__________	Address__________
Address__________	Address__________

FOLD HERE FIRST

NO POSTAGE
NECESSARY
IF MAILED
IN THE
UNITED STATES

BUSINESS REPLY MAIL

FIRST CLASS MAIL PERMIT NO. 002 MERLIN, OREGON

POSTAGE WILL BE PAID BY ADDRESSEE

PSI Research
PO BOX 1414
Merlin OR 97532-9900

FOLD HERE SECOND, THEN TAPE TOGETHER

Please cut along this vertical line, fold twice, tape together and mail.